The Kirby House

Cookbook

A compendium of fascinating facts about the Kirby Family, their home and social customs of the times. Also contained within are the recipes from the kitchens of the Kirby House Restaurant.

written and compiled by

Meta Newell West

The Kirby House Cookbook
Published by
KH Publishing
Author: Meta Newell West
E-mail: bwest@access-one.com
% The Kirby House
205 N.E. 3rd
Abilene, Kansas 67410

For additional copies contact:
Vangie Henry @ The Kirby House
E-Mail: grtfood@kirby-house.com
Website: http://www.kirby-house.com
Phone: 785-263-7336
Fax: 785 263-1885

Library of Congress control number 2001097489
ISBN 0-9713195-0-2

First Edition
First Printing--5,000 copies; November, 2001

Original Illustrations by Barry L. West
Copyright© 2001

Text Layout and Design by Judy Burgess Leyerzapf

Thank You

❖to Vangie Henry, owner and operator of The Kirby House. She has given me complete access to the restaurant's recipes in addition to providing both moral and financial support throughout this project. Vangie has provided me with an unforgettable experience and I have gained a friend in the process.

❖to Barry L. West for his support though the 33 years of our marriage. He has endured my many obsessions and allowed me the freedom to pursue my passions. And, in the process of accompanying me as I've attended cooking classes, culinary institutes, etc., he, too, has developed a passion for cooking. He also helped me put into words many of those unwritten recipes developed by the great cooks at The Kirby House.

❖to my mother, Phyllis Newell, for her help and support during this project.

❖to John (Jack) Alexander, great grandson of Thomas and Anna Kirby for his assistance and help with family history. The "Kirby Family Tree" was provided by Jack and I have thoroughly enjoyed corresponding with him via e-mail.

❖to Terry Tietjens for sharing the information about the renovation and creation of the original Kirby House Restaurant. He allowed me free use of the files and materials at The Seelye Mansion.

❖to the staff at the Abilene Public Library for access to their files and the inter library loan system.

❖to Jeff Sheets at the Dickinson Country Historical Society for his willingness to track down information and to check the historical accuracy of this text relating to Abilene history.

❖to Edwina Anderson for use of her many books and papers related to the Victorian era. Eddie discovered the copy of *"Recipes, My Friends' and My Own."* Two recipes, submitted by Gertrude Kirby, from that book appear in this publication.

❖to Nancy Baird at the Department of Library Special Collections, The Kentucky Building, Western Kentucky University, Bowling Green, KY., 42101-3576 for providing information on the Victorian era.

❖to Larkin Mayo and Gary Yuschalk, owners of the historic Lebold mansion in Abilene, for their expertise on all things Victorian and their willingness to provide feedback on Part I of this text. Their ideas on formatting helped me to finally piece all the parts together and they also provided the idea for the book cover.

❖to Elinor Haas, I owe a debt of gratitude. Elinor, a former English teacher at Abilene High School, edited the historical sections of the text. She provided advice and also helped me with the focus of the book. Elinor, was a dedicated and respected teacher and continues to share her knowledge with others.

❖to Jane Medina, a good friend, for editing the recipe section of this book. She also provided feedback on whether or not directions were easy to follow and made sense.

❖to Judy Leyerzapf, for preparing the text for publication. Her expertise and vast computer skills never cease to amaze me and this book would never have come together without those skills.

Notes from Meta and Vangie . . .

I grew up in a family where "good" food was the standard. Dinners at Grandma Richardson's were always unforgettable events complete with linens and china. I remember trips with her to Hutchinson where we dined in tea rooms and elegant restaurants. We baked pies, made homemade applesauce, harvested and cooked fresh vegetables, and even dug garlic. Fried chicken, mashed potatoes, fresh snap beans, homemade rolls, and cobblers were the type of meals my mother, Phyllis Newell, prepared for the harvest fields. So my passion for food developed at an early age.

Later I majored in Home Economics at Kansas State University and for the past 33 years have taught at Abilene High School. Over the years Home Economics was renamed Family and Consumer Science, and the subject matter evolved to include an occupational emphasis. Consequently, I implemented a Catering class which gained a reputation throughout the state for its quality food production, good service, and presentation. In my attempt to learn more about the restaurant and food production business, I applied to the State Department of Education for a summer internship and worked and observed in area businesses. I also had the opportunity to attend several summer workshops at the School of Culinary Arts of The Colorado Institute of Art.

I pursued a career based, in part, around food, but it has also been the basis of my social life. Most gatherings are centered around food, and many of my friends share my interest in entertaining. These friends have been an inspiration and another reason to expand my culinary knowledge. My husband always makes reference to the fact that I never seemed to outgrow the "tea party stage." And speaking of tea parties--I began doing a series of tea parties for the Kirby House a couple of years ago. Then, one day, Vangie Henry (owner of the Kirby House) suggested that I put together a cookbook, and that's how this project started. I had experience assimilating recipe collections for each year's Catering class, knew the process for recipe standardization, and the methods for recipe quantity adjustment. Also, I had years of practice rewriting recipes into user-friendly formats. So, how difficult could this be? Well, I've learned lots . . . mainly I discovered how much I didn't know!

The historical sections in this book were researched and developed, for the most part, in the summer and early fall of 2000. Recipe writing and adjustment has been an on-going process since then with editing, recipe testing, and revisions continuing throughout. This has been an interesting experience and an opportunity to incorporate my knowledge and experience as well as an avenue to expand my learning.

I also discovered that writing a book is not an individual job but involves a community of people, and I feel privileged to have had help from "the best." However, I must acknowledge any errors, that might have been overlooked must be blamed on only my oversight. It should also be noted that all quotes, in the pages that follow are printed as they originally occurred, and some include errors in spelling and grammar reminiscent of an earlier era.

It is my hope that you will expand your knowledge of local history and of the Victorian era as well as enjoy preparing the many recipes provided in the pages that follow.

Meta Newell West

Like many people of my day, I started cooking before I was tall enough to reach the stove. I would pull a chair to the stove and stir gravy, stew or whatever mom was preparing. I'm sure, more times than not, I was a hindrance to her. With our large family, however, we were all expected to help at a very early age. I dare say my three brothers "may" be better cooks than any of the five sisters.

A number of people laid the groundwork for the wonderful food we serve at the Kirby House. With the collaboration of Debbie Correll Tasker and Cheryl Correll Zumbrunn, the first menu was set up when we opened in November of 1998. Many of the recipes we used, including the famous "Miss Ellie's Carrot Cake," came from their mother, Eleanor Correll.

Our present kitchen manager, Chris LaPorte, has contributed greatly to the savory recipes we now enjoy, especially the "Country Fried Steak." Chris is also a master on the grill and has built quite a reputation for "great steaks." Other cooks, bakers, and friends have shared a delectable collection, including the "Melt in Your Mouth Roast Beef" of Von Flora.

A big thank you to the wait staff, hostesses, and cashiers at The Kirby House. Their professional service and willingness to "go the extra mile" is certainty an asset to the restaurant.

The most wonderful experience for me has been my association with Meta Newell West. She is a dynamite cook! I have learned so much from her. In the process of working with her as she wrote this book and as we kicked off a catering business, we have also built a treasured friendship.

I hope you enjoy this work of art and love Meta has put together for us.

Vangie Henry

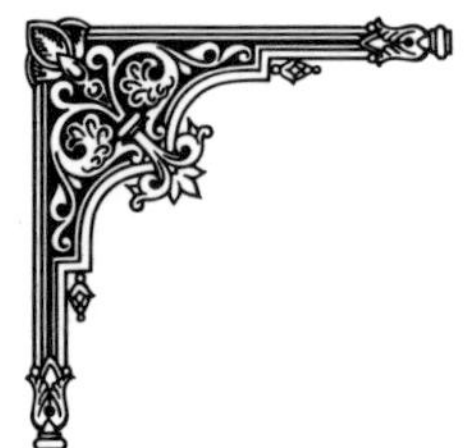
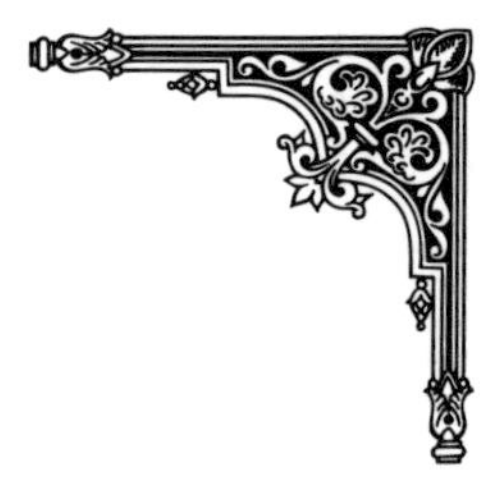

Contents

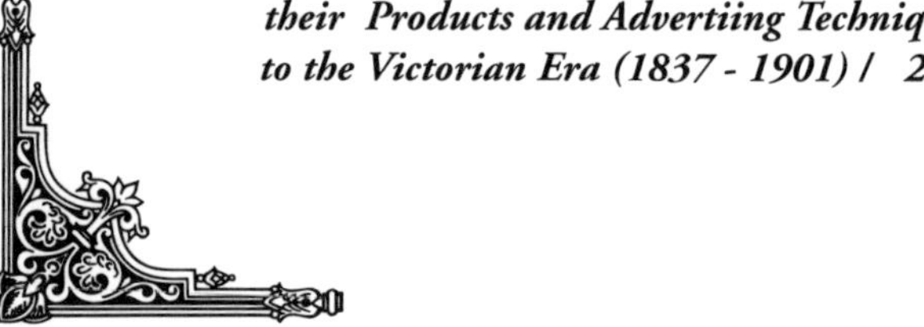

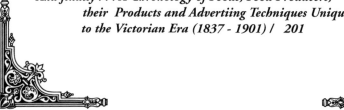

PART I:

The Kirby House History

This sketch first appeared in a promotional booklet, *A Gem, "The City of the Plains,"*[1] The purpose of this booklet was to promote Abilene as a "good place to live and do business" as well as to further the campaign for removal of the state capitol to a central location. The Kirby House was one of ten prized houses to be included in this 1887 booklet.

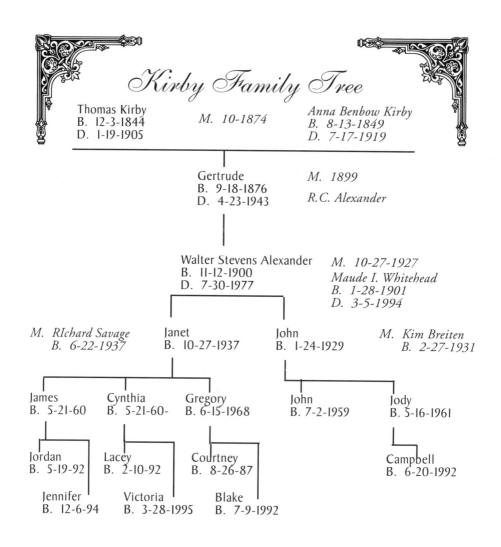

Kirby Family Tree

Thomas Kirby
B. 12-3-1844
D. 1-19-1905

M. 10-1874

Anna Benbow Kirby
B. 8-13-1849
D. 7-17-1919

Gertrude
B. 9-18-1876
D. 4-23-1943

M. 1899

R.C. Alexander

Walter Stevens Alexander
B. 11-12-1900
D. 7-30-1977

M. 10-27-1927
Maude I. Whitehead
B. 1-28-1901
D. 3-5-1994

M. RIchard Savage
B. 6-22-1937

Janet
B. 10-27-1937

John
B. 1-24-1929

M. Kim Breiten
B. 2-27-1931

James
B. 5-21-60

Cynthia
B. 5-21-60-

Gregory
B. 6-15-1968

John
B. 7-2-1959

Jody
B. 5-16-1961

Jordan
B. 5-19-92

Jennifer
B. 12-6-94

Lacey
B. 2-10-92

Victoria
B. 3-28-1995

Courtney
B. 8-26-87

Blake
B. 7-9-1992

Campbell
B. 6-20-1992

Thomas, Anna and Gertrude were all laid to rest
in Lot 13, Abilene City Cemetery.

Kirby Family Tree provided to author by
John Alexander, great grandson of
Thomas and Anna Kirby.

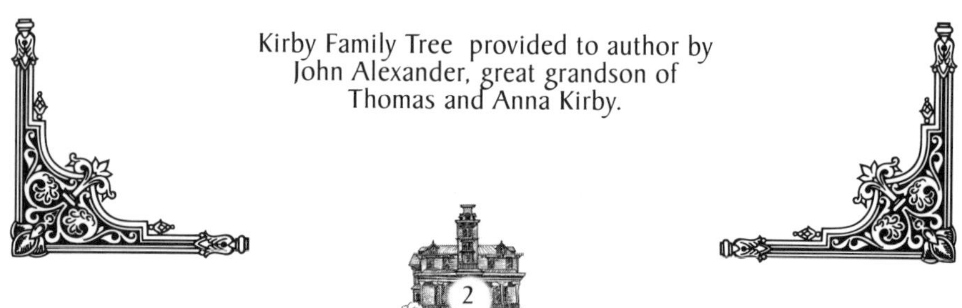

I. THE KIRBY FAMILY AND THEIR HOUSE

"Home became a banner, something to be held aloft and pressed forward. It showed where a man had got to, and he clung to it and waved it until the day came when he could exchange it for a bigger and better one." [2]

his quote seems to capture the importance of the Victorian home. And for the Thomas Kirby family, formerly of Pennsylvania, the Kirby House represented that "bigger and better one" reflecting their position and status in the community. The March 13, 1885 edition of *The Abilene Gazette* reported, "County treasurer Kirby has let the contract for a $6,000 residence, to be erected on his beautiful grounds on East 3d street. Abilene will boom the coming season."

The Kirby House Exterior

The Italianate influence is evidenced in the architectural style chosen by the Kirby family. "This 2 1/2-story example is symmetrically composed and features a four-story tower and a full-width porch. Typically Italianate details include the paired eave brackets, arched windows, a square tower with mansard roof, and an emphasis on verticality. This is expressed in the tower, the tall and narrow windows, and the chamfered square porch supports." [3]

Exteriors were typically painted multi-colored shades. According to records discovered by Terry Tietjens (who purchased and renovated the house in 1986), the Kirbys painted their new home two tones of green trimmed in dark red.[4] As depicted in a sketch of the original Kirby House, Victorians seemed content to leave their house foundations unplanted. This practice was thought to improve drainage and ventilation and to prevent infestation. Outdoor areas were generally well separated from the rest of the world by a fence, often made of cast iron as the one shown in the Kirby House sketch on page 1. Fences protected cultivated areas from intruders of all kinds, helped distinguish between public and private property, and helped to deter the spread of weeds.

Stone hitching posts in front of the fence gate sport the carved initials "GK." This is where Gertrude, daughter of Thomas, actually tied her horses.

Abilene -- A City on the Move!

The 1887 promotional book, *"A Gem, "The City of the Plains,"* portrays Abilene as a thrifty but progressive town with superior offerings. It describes a healthy and beautiful city having some of the finest residences in Kansas.

> Abilene has clean macadamized streets, broad and beautifully graded avenues, along which are builded the largest number, proportionately, of modern city residences that grace any city east or west . . . The citizens of Abilene have won an enviable reputation far and wide, for their liberal, hospitable and social qualities. Her capitalists, and we have a large number of very wealthy citizens, are her best and most philanthropic friend.

Singing the praises of Abilene, *A Gem* goes on to extol the virtues of the

commercial district which consisted of nearly three miles of business blocks most of which were new three-story brick buildings five streets long and wide. The city included a beautiful park, spacious court house, a superior grammar and high school, a flourishing commercial and mathematical school, fourteen churches, a finely equipped opera house, four banking houses, six hotels, carriage and wagon manufacturers, a canning factory, three extensive flouring mills, four large elevators, a foundry and machine shop, two planing mills, lock works, a water works system, a telephone exchange plus many public buildings and private dwellings boasted Edison's electric light. It also supported three weekly and two daily newspapers which received the Associated press dispatches and railroads provided through connection from New York to San Francisco.[5] Abilene in 1885 was definitely a city on the move and Thomas Kirby, a prominent citizen, was one of those keeping it in motion.

The Thomas Kirby Family and the building of The Kirby House

Thomas Kirby came to Abilene, in 1872, as a bank cashier and by 1878 he founded the Kirby Bank. In prosperous, respectable Victorian families gender roles were clearly defined. So in 1885, as head of the household, Mr. Kirby, went off to his bank each day leaving Mrs. Kirby in charge of the household supervision and their only daughter, Gertrude. The wife of an affluent Victorian gentleman was expected to be "useless" since this was an indication of her husband's prosperity and his ability to support his family in style. Yet it is interesting to note that in order to create a tidy and orderly Victorian household (with its array of endless objects, knickknacks and tasks to be completed) it must have meant that the lady of the household was anything but "useless".

Thomas amassed a fortune with which he purchased several city blocks and large tracts of land in the county. This money was also used in the building of the Kirby House, to keep his bank up-to-date and for philanthropic causes. He donated both time and money to projects such as the building of Mount Saint Joseph's Academy [an orphanage] and the establishment of the "Kirby Park." Also, as a civic minded man, Thomas Kirby served as county treasurer for two terms.

The Kirby House Interior

The homes of the Victorian affluent were meant to be showplaces reflecting the prosperity and status of the resident. Literature of that period also confirms the home as a retreat from the demands of the workplace and as a moral haven for the proper nurturing of children and the transmission of traditional cultural values. Thus it became a woman's charge to create a home which welcomed the family, yet molded its moral character, and, at the same time, was impressive enough to dazzle guests.

<u>The Kirby House Floor Plan and Layout</u>

Characteristic of many mansions during this era, the public spaces were located in the front of the house with utilitarian rooms at the rear. Also, following the prescription of the day, private quarters were clearly segregated from the social zone

of the house and relegated to the upper stories. Specialized rooms abounded which some critics of the time period refer to as a series of "decorated boxes."

The Foyer

A uniformed servant would probably have greeted "callers" at the double front doors in 1885. The foyer was used to screen visitors, and this would have been especially important since the Kirby home was located close to the commercial-residential area of downtown. As guests were conducted through the foyer, they must surely have noticed the beautiful parquet floor of walnut, mahogany, oak, and maple inlaid in a geometric design. The leaded glass and hardware were also sure to make an impression as they continue to do today.

The Entryway and Staircase

As guests entered the mansion in 1885, a sense of awe must have been created as their eyes swept upward to the 12-foot ceilings and the elaborate walnut staircase. A landing at the bend in the staircase housed a casket niche . . . a handy addition in a period when wakes and funerals were often held in the home. The main hall both separated and connected visitors to a series of three parlors and the dining room.

The Parlors

During the "gilded age of decoration," parlors contained an eclectic assortment of ornamentation including ceiling fans, moulding, medallions, borders, stenciling, friezes, wallpapers that were flocked, embossed, or highly patterned (the Victorians frequently used more than one pattern of paper in the same area), Oriental carpets, and elaborately festooned and trimmed curtains. A profusion of furniture, some of it very specialized such as fainting couches for ladies, often crowded the room and included a large number of chairs. There were many chairs in Victorian rooms because a gentleman would always stand when a lady entered the room. Furthermore, he wouldn't think of allowing a lady to sit in his warmed chair, and so there always had to be a cool one available. This multitude of furniture was generally organized into conversational groupings. In addition, collections of bric-a-brac adorned the walls, "whatnot" shelves, table tops, or any available space. Collections might include paintings, art prints, hanging tapestries, family photographs, busts of historical figures, maps, globes, travel souvenirs, musical instruments, games for family and visitors entertainment, objects and trinkets depicting cultural interests, leather books, animal specimens, minerals, house plants, and displays of needlework often with a religious theme. This optical clutter seemed to be dictated by the time period and allowed families to show their cultural refinement, their intellectual curiosity, their moral sensibility, their economic prowess, and their fashion consciousness.

To further understand this decorating style, it is important to realize that America was moving toward a consumer-oriented society with the economy revolving around acquisition rather than production. Unlike the Puritan attitude of self-denial, Victorians were concerned with self-fulfillment and materialism. And, due to improved printing technology, ladies magazines and literature abounded and linked success to the accumulation of consumer goods. It is also interesting to note that pocket doors (still in use today) separated one room from another, allowing for privacy and solving the practical need to contain the heat.

The two rooms on the left side (west) of the entrance are believed to have originally been used as front and rear parlors. These parlors were probably used to entertain distinguished guests and would have served as public spaces in which rites of passage (weddings, funerals, christenings) could have been conducted. Gertrude Kirby, who would have been nine in 1885, was an accomplished pianist and perhaps her piano was housed in the bay window area.

The front parlor, located to the right (east) of the entryway, still features the original birdseye maple fireplace. This parlor was probably a reception area or family sitting room. Perhaps it provided the family with a retreat from the noise and cares of the household and outside world. Parlor games were quite popular through the 19th century; perhaps the Kirby family gathered around a central table enjoying games of chess, checkers, backgammon, a variety of card games, or even the new board game, "Game of Banking" which was introduced in 1883. Adjoining this parlor was the Kirby family's dining room.

The Dining Room

The dining room was a late 19th century addition to the family home when dining became an "event" during the Victorian era. With a wide array of foods, a well appointed table, and servants to cater to every whim, dining in those days was anything but "fast," a meal often lasting one to two and sometimes three or more hours.

Even after the introduction of electricity, candles were still widely used as they provided an atmospheric lighting which the Victorians considered the most suitable for dining. It was expected that an elaborate floral arrangement would adorn the table. Isabella Beeton in *The Book of Household Management,* 1861, asserted ". . . there should always be flowers on the (dining room) table, and as they form no item of expense, there is no reason why they should not be employed every day."[6]

Other than the table and chairs, the most important piece of furniture was the sideboard. It was often fitted with a mirror, shelves, drawers and cabinets. Sideboards often groaned under the weight of a family's display of silver, china and crystal.

The Kitchen

The kitchen of 1885 is no longer in existence; it would have been located in what is now used as "Mrs. Kirby's Coffee Shop" at the back of the house. Originally it was connected to the dining room by a butler's pantry.

A butler's pantry served as a place to make final preparation to the display of the food prior to serving it. The pantry also served as storage space for tableware and kept the odors of the kitchen from penetrating into the social quarters.

The main kitchen area in most Victorian households contained a large, centrally

positioned table with shallow drawers for utensils underneath, rather than the built-in counters in most kitchens today. Glass-fronted cabinets in the Kirby kitchen held all manner of utensils, dishes, pots, and equipment. The Victorians seemed to like the convenience of everything being visible, and in some ways the home kitchen of 1885 might look similar to a commercial kitchen of today. It is even likely that the floors might have been covered in linoleum which was being used extensively toward the end of the 19th century.

Scientific research and invention had provided the Kirby's cook with a gas stove (in addition to a wood burning one), an insulated icebox, and a porcelain sink with both hot and cold running water. However, one can assume kitchen work was still complex and back-breaking. Most foods had to be prepared from "scratch," and those who could afford it seemed to prefer any and every embellishment that was available. Without servants, it is unlikely that the Victorians would have been able to participate in the formal and elaborate style of eating which was prevalent among the wealthy.

The Second Story

Mr. and Mrs. Kirby's bedroom and sitting room (separated by pocket doors) were located on the left or west side of the house; Gertrude's room, a guest room, and the open porch were on the east with the servants' rooms located at the back of the house.

In an era when built-in closets were still a novelty, there were two in the Kirby's private quarters. But these were quite small by today's standards, and one wonders, considering all the huge dresses and bustles, why there were so few closets in a Victorian bedroom, and why they were so small. Zingman-Leith explores this question in the text of *The Secret Life of Victorian Houses,*

> There is a widespread myth that homeowners were charged property tax based on the number of closets in the house. This was never true. The real explanation for the scarcity of closets is the abundance of servants. The lady of the house would leave a card on her vanity describing the evening's outfit, and her maid would retrieve the clothes from an upstairs room where they were packed in chests of drawers, armoires, and boxes. The maid would steam or iron the clothes and lay them out on the bed ready to be put on. There was no incentive for making clothes storage convenient as long as someone else fetched them. Anyone with enough money for a substantial wardrobe also had servants and extra rooms for storage.[7]

Victorian deportment seemed to require first-floor rooms to follow acceptable "codes of standard" for that time period, but the private rooms gave individuals a chance to exercise their personal preferences within limits. Even then, it was expected that children's rooms utilize gender themes: shipping and baseball bats for young men and ruffles and frills for the young ladies.

Bedrooms of the 19th century were often furnished with manufactured suites of furniture that included storage pieces and dressing tables or vanities. Dust ruffles were used on beds to control dust and dressing table tops were covered with both grooming and personal knickknacks. Dresserware (referred to an "toiletware") for the lady's boudoir might have included "toilet sets" containing bottles and jars for cologne, toilet water or perhaps Seelye's Crab-apple perfume, and puffs; hairpin boxes; curling sets; hair-brushes, combs and hair receivers; mirrors; cloth brushes; hat brushes; hat-pin stands; button hooks, handkerchief and glove boxes; watch stands, and jewel "caskets" (boxes) to mention a few. Gentlemen's accessories, fewer in number, might have included shaving cups, soap boxes, shoe horns, shaving brushes, whisk brooms, collar-button boxes, horse-hide razor strops.

The convenience of "indoor plumbing" was not a luxury afforded by most Victorians. Yet, the Kirby's original bathroom boasted a water-closet (toilet), plus a footed bathtub and a lavatory (sink), both equipped with hot and cold running water. Patent medicines were part of the late 19th century search for a healthy life so surely some of Dr. A.B. Seelye's medicines, produced in Abilene, lined the shelves of this room. Dr. Seelye's famous Wasa-Tusa, Ner-Vena or Seelye's Magic Cough Cure would have been considered necessities for the prevention and cure of all sorts of maladies. The original bathroom is the site of the present-day "Ladies" room.

Weather permitting, many Victorians took to sleeping on porches at night, and, perhaps, the Kirby's upstairs porch was used for this very thing. Nineteenth century Victorians reasoned that breathing "used" air was unhealthy, and so " fresh" air became a prescription for good health. This porch is now enclosed and houses a solarium.

<u>The Tower</u>

The mansard-roofed tower rises four stories above the street and was entirely reconstructed during the 1986 renovation. According to local history, Mrs. Kirby, weather permitting, enjoyed the tower's cool breezes and natural lighting as she did her handiwork. Mrs. Kirby did not need to worry about insects because by the 1800's machine-made wire window screens (known as "bug bars" by the Victorians) were being manufactured. Today the tower is available for private dining by reservation.

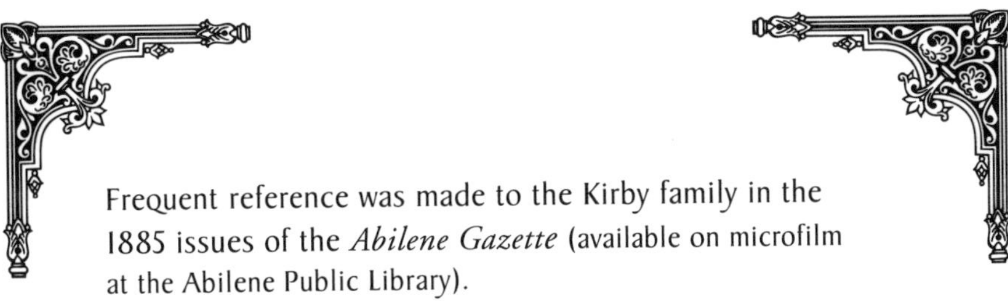

Frequent reference was made to the Kirby family in the 1885 issues of the *Abilene Gazette* (available on microfilm at the Abilene Public Library).

April 10, 1885 -- "Thomas Kirby, has papered and refitted his bank room in elegant shape, and now has one of the handsomest rooms in the city."

June 12, 1885 -- "Mrs. Thomas Kirby and daughter Miss Gertie, returned home last evening from their visit to the old home in Pennsylvania. Tommy has a smile on his face to-day similar to the one he carried the day Cleveland's election was officially announced."

July 10, 1885 -- "Thomas Kirby made his semi-annual settlement with the State Treasurer promptly on July 1st."

July 17, 1885 -- Thomas Kirby has departed for the east, on the Saratoga Springs excursion. He will be gone for some weeks."

Photo of Gertrude and Anna Kirby from family photo album (undated). They are standing next to the porch of the Kirby family home with Fido, the family dog.

Time Line for Thomas Kirby

1844 -- born in Ireland.
1848 -- immigrated, with his parents, to Johnstown, Pa.
1868 - 1872 -- ran a bank in Johnstown, Pa.
1872 -- moved to Abilene, Ks. to take a position as cashier of the Lebold-Fisher bank, a job he held for 6 years.
1874 -- wed Miss Anna Benbow in Johnstown, Pa.
1876 -- wife Anna gave birth to Gertrude on September 18th.
1878 -- went into the banking business for himself. The Thomas Kirby Bank began in the Gleissner building, a framed structure, located at 205 North Broadway. He conducted the bank as a private institution being its sole proprietor.
1882 -- elected county treasurer on the Democratic ticket even though the county had a large Republican majority.
After fire destroyed the previous bank structure, he relocated at 306 N.W. 2nd. By now the bank is considered "one of the most influential in this part of the state," according to an article in a local paper, that ran following his death.
1884 -- reelected to second term as county treasurer.
1885 -- built the Kirby House on what was then known as Grand Avenue. According to evidence found during the 1986-87 renovation, it is believed the construction was completed on August 19th.
1888 -- honored with the Democratic nomination for state treasurer, but it was not to be a Democratic year.
1893 to 1896 -- severe financial depression and panic swept the country. Throughout this period he was generous and kind hearted. According to another obituary article in the Abilene Weekly Reflector, "No one ever went to 'Tom' Kirby for assistance and failed to get it if it was within his power to grant the request." Against advice of the state bank commissioner, he paid 6 and 7 cents on time deposits when other banks paid only 3 and 4 cents.
1898 April 5 -- published a statement showing that bank resources and liabilities were equal.
June 28 -- Bank Commissioner Breidenthal arrived about 4:00 p.m.; Thomas was with him until the wee hours of the morning trying to save the bank. Although Mr. Kirby owned a great deal of real estate, he was not allowed to turn it in as an asset. Also ignored is the fact he had kept a large cash reserve, and he had always held more gold than any bank in this part of the State.
June 29 -- Bank Commissioner Breidenthal posted a notice stating the bank was closed. Customers and employees alike were completely surprised. Later that day, bank depositors held a mass meeting and voted unanimously to select a committee to meet with the proper authorities in order to convince them to allow Mr. Kirby to resume business. Despite the efforts of Thomas, his depositors, other local banks, and overwhelming support, the bank commission, on the advice of Mr. Breidenthal, did indeed shut down the bank. According to local news coverage of the time, the general

opinion was that Mr. Kirby's bank would never have closed if he had been left alone and been allowed to manage it himself. It was also believed that Breidenthal had been "out to get" the progressive Kirby and finally did just that. After the bank closing, he retired.

1899 -- marriage of daughter Gertrude to R.C. Alexander.
1900 -- birth of grandson Walter Stevens Alexander on November 12th.
1905 -- death of Thomas Kirby, age 60, at his home on East Third street after a period of poor health.

(Time line constructed from information and miscellaneous newspaper clippings from the Tietjens' files located at The Seelye Mansion and The Abilene Public Library.)

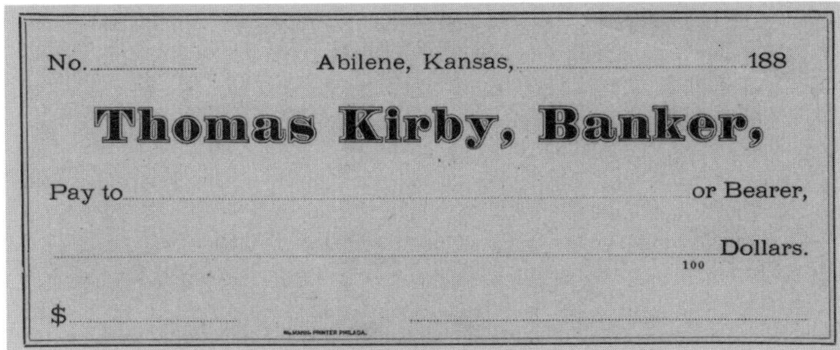

No. .... Abilene, Kansas, ... 188

Thomas Kirby, Banker,

Pay to .... or Bearer,

.... Dollars.
100

$ ....

An original Kirby Bank check.

What was referred to as "The Kirby Park" consisted of a public fountain on the corner of Second street (in what is now the Civic Center parking lot). This fountain provided "Sand Springs Water" to those desiring a cool, refreshing drink. The purity of this water as stated in the 1904-05 Abilene Directory, was 99.98%, and it was piped to Abilene from nearby Sand Springs.[8]

Long before plastic ketchup squeeze bottles . . .

The Victorians put their catsup in a glass bottle (often cut or crystal) and placed it in a revolving caster with other slots for things such as vinegar, oil, pepper, salt and perhaps mustard. People today often refer to these as "cruet sets," but catalogs of the day listed them as "dinner casters" and they were in heavy demand.

Caster Set [9]

Spoons of all sizes, shapes, and uses were standard fare in the Victorian era. Consequently spoon holders, like the one shown here, were often found on the tea tray or added to the table for the dessert course.

Spoon Holder [10]

A Practical Novelty

Silverplated spoons, knives featuring serrated back blades, special bowls, and even a special peeler -- all to aid in the serving of oranges "at table." A silverplated orange peeler was patented in August, 1879, by the Holes, Booth & Haydens Company; their advertisement stated, . . ."it will fill a want the Orange-loving public have long felt. Who has not experienced the necessity for something of the kind, when compelled to peel this luscious fruit (for want of a better means) with thumb and fingers?" These peelers sold for $12.00 a dozen; their competitors, Rogers & Bros., had their own version which sold for $6.00 a dozen. [11]

II. DINING DURING THE VICTORIAN ERA

Dinner parties, a primary form of entertainment during the Victorian era, allowed the lady of the house to show off the dining room and the family's vast collection of silver, delicate china, and crystal serving pieces. In order to accommodate the bevy of sauces and condiments plus the large quantities of food on the menu, special dinnerware was necessary. These included such things as silver dinner casters fitted with cut glass sauce bottles, pickle casters, crystal salt cellars, preserve dishes, porcelain sauce and gravy boats, special dishes for sardines, soup tureens, butter dishes, nut bowls, tiered dishes for fruit, and bonbon dishes. Special collections of vases and epergnes were used for the ever-present centerpieces that crowned the table top.

Victorian Table Setting

An abundance of ornately encrusted flatware graced a proper table, providing diners with task-specific tools: spoons for salt, coffee, soup, and eggs; specialized forks for berries, pickles, lettuce, terrapin, oysters, sardines, beef and ice cream; tongs specifically for asparagus; jelly and cheese knives; macaroni servers and butter picks. In a period known for its excesses, some silver companies were offering more than 150 different flatware pieces for each place setting; an upper middle-class family's set might include 300 to 500 pieces of flatware. These bulging silver chests were due, at least in part, to the mass machine production of silver in the 1850's. The Industrial Revolution also created the technology for silver electroplating; quadruple silver plating was a sign of quality and gained a place alongside sterling silver. [12]

Dining Etiquette or "The Art of Victorian Dining

As a new class of people (white-collar workers as a result of the Industrial Revolution in the 1850's) developed, the desire was to copy the life and manners of the gentry. Detailed rules (both written and unwritten) became the vehicle to achieving this goal. Nothing seemed to indicate social standing so much as manners at the dining table; table manners separated those with "good" breeding from those considered vulgar and coarse. Rules applied to the host and hostess as well as to the guests. A knowing hostess understood that married couples were never to be seated together (there being time enough "at home" for husband and wife to enjoy one another's company). Of course, a dinner party must consist of even rather than odd numbers so that all ladies could be escorted by a gentleman. And all educated Victorians knew that the senior lady, either by age or social standing, should be led in first by the host of the party. The hostess arrived last on the arm of the senior male. The following selected quotes from *The Gentlemen's Book of Etiquette* emphasize how strongly manners gripped the sophisticated Victorian:

- Before taking your place at table, wait until your place is pointed out to you, unless there are cards bearing the names of the guest upon the plates; in the latter case, take the place thus marked for you.
- Watch that the lady whom you escorted to the table is well helped. Lift and change her plate for her, pass her bread, salt, and butter, . . . and

pay her every attention in your power.

- ❖ Put your napkin upon your lap, covering your knees. It is out of date and now looked upon as a vulgar habit to put your napkin up over your breast.
- ❖ Always wipe your mouth before drinking, as nothing is more ill-bred than to grease your glass with your lips.
- ❖ Never blow your soup if it is too hot, but wait until it cools. Never raise your plate to your lips, but eat with your spoon.
- ❖ Never touch either your knife or your fork until after you have finished eating your soup. Leave your spoon in your soup plate, that the servant may remove them both. Never take soup twice.
- ❖ Use always the salt-spoon, sugar-tongs, and butter knife; to use your own knife, spoon, or fingers, evinces a shocking want of good-breeding.
- ❖ Do not bite your bread from the roll or slice, nor cut it with your knife; break off small pieces and put these in your mouth with your fingers.
- ❖ Never criticize any dish before you. If a dish is distasteful to you, decline it, but make no remarks about it.
- ❖ Never put bones, or the seeds of fruit upon the tablecloth. Put them upon the edge of your plate. [Special bone dishes were provided with some china sets.]
- ❖ Never use your knife for any purpose but to cut your food. It is not meant to be put in your mouth. Your fork is intended to carry the food from your plate to your mouth.
- ❖ Never pile the food on your plate as if you were starving, but take a little at a time; the dishes will not run away.
- ❖ Do not cut fruit with a steel knife. Use a silver one. [This is because the acid in fruit corrodes steel.]
- ❖ Never put fruit or bon-bons in your pocket to carry them from the table.
- ❖ When the finger-glasses are passed, dip your fingers into them and then wipe them upon your napkin.
- ❖ It is excessively rude to leave the house as soon as dinner is over. Respect to your hostess obliges you to stay in the drawing-room at least an hour.[13]

No longer did you have to be "born with a silver spoon" in order to use one. Books and articles on civility abounded for those desiring to learn the strict social codes of the era.

Victorian Cuisine

Gingerbread detailing decorated their housing exteriors; ruffles and lace adorned their clothes; their walls were ablaze with a multitude of wall coverings. Is it any wonder that vegetables, too, must be "dressed"? Why serve plain vegetables when they could be scalloped, creamed, pickled, or curried?

Condiments such as mushroom and walnut catsup, flavored mustards, and spicy chutney were generally found on the Victorian table. "Without these [condiments], soups, sauces, meats and all dishes would be insipid," stated *The New Cyclopedia of Domestic Economy*.[14] Many of these additions were homemade. However, during this period commercially bottled sauces and condiments, such as Worcestershire

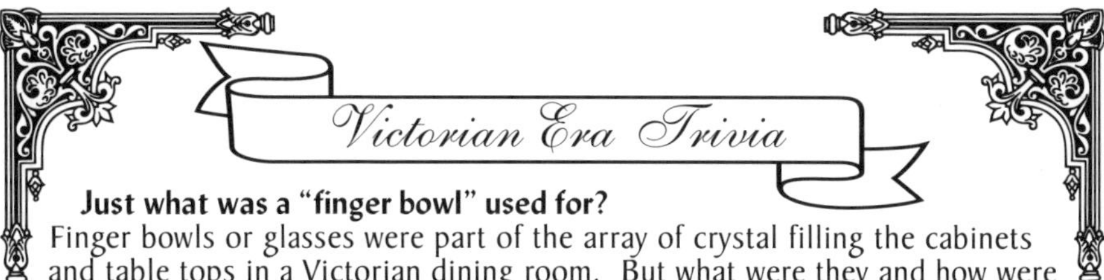

Just what was a "finger bowl" used for?
Finger bowls or glasses were part of the array of crystal filling the cabinets and table tops in a Victorian dining room. But what were they and how were they used? According to an 1860 etiquette book, "Finger glasses . . . come on with the dessert, and are filled with warm water. Wet a corner of your napkin and wipe your mouth, then rinse your fingers; but do not practice the filthy custom of gargling your mouth at table, albeit the usage prevails among a few, who think that because it is a foreign habit it cannot be disgusting."[15]

Why were there so many rules?
Special utensils and rules for tableware were not always just pretentious, pompous dictates. There were often underlying reasons for these customs as in the use of specialized flatware for eating fish and instructions for its consumption. "Fish is always helped with a silver or plated fish-slice, and when you have it on your plate you should use your fork only in eating it. The application of a knife to fish is likely to destroy the delicacy of its flavor; besides which, fish sauces are often acidulated; acids corrode steel, and draws from it a disagreeable taste." Some silver sets also provided fish-knives for individual use but actually the above guideline refers to an earlier time when knifes were generally made of steel. [16]

Which method would "Miss Manners" recommend?
What did the Victorians do with soiled silverware? Knife rests, consisting of metal bars supported by side pieces, might have been one solution as they showed up frequently in silver catalogs of the day. However, in *Etiquette and The Usages of Society*, Mr. Henry P. Willis describes two other quite different suggestions, both in use in 1860: "In sending your plate for anything you should leave your knife and fork upon it. There seems also to be a reason for the custom in the fact that to hold them in your hand would be awkward, and to lay them on the table-cloth might soil it." [17] However, he then goes on to explain that another respected authority suggests that it is still quite proper to retain the silver in hand or rest it upon your bread which had been placed directly on the tablecloth. Furthermore, "If furnished with potatoes in small dishes, you will put the skins back into the dish again . . . otherwise potato-skins will be placed upon the table-cloth." [18] Obviously with the number of etiquette books on the market, it seems only natural that there would have been conflicting advice.

KNIFE REST[19]

Knife, Fork or SPOON?
On the use of spoons at the table . . . "Peas, tomatoes, tarts, puddings, &c. should always be eaten with a spoon. As a general rule, when helping any one at table, never use a knife when you can use a spoon."[20]

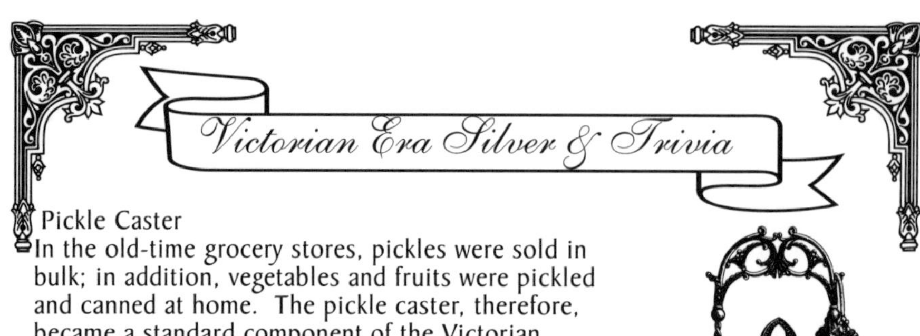

Pickle Caster

In the old-time grocery stores, pickles were sold in bulk; in addition, vegetables and fruits were pickled and canned at home. The pickle caster, therefore, became a standard component of the Victorian table. The pickle stand usually included a hook for the serving fork or tongs.

PICKLE CASTER [21]

BUTTER DISH [23]

The "Good Old Days"

In the "good old days" before butter came in quarter pound sticks, people made their own. And, butter dishes (such as the one shown here) became very popular in the the 1880's and '90's. An ice receptacle under a glass plate, in some styles, kept the butter cool. [22]

Pease Porridge Hot

"Serving oatmeal as a first course enables the cook to prepare many dishes, such as steaks, omelets, etc., just as the family sit down to breakfast; and when the porridge is eaten, she is ready with the other dishes 'smoking hot.'" Quote from Mary Henderson, *Practical Cooking and Dinner Giving, 1876.*[24]

Bon Bon Tray

Bon Bon trays were used to present confections to Victorian guests.

BON BON TRAY [25]

and Tabasco sauce, were also available. Many a Victorian lunch or dinner was complemented with a serving of pickles whether it be pickled fruits, cucumbers or other vegetables. Flower- and herb-flavored vinegars were used to add tang to sauces or gravies or mixed with olive oil for a salad dressing or a marinade. Preserves, fruit butters, jams and jellies were spread on breads but could also be used as delicious additions to roast meats and fowl. Herbs and spices were used abundantly, when available, and it is said that the Victorians were eager for the "shockingly strong" taste of ginger in all forms.

Garnishes could be quite impressive. "Foods lending themselves to shaping (such as pates, fish loaves, etc.) were often formed into fanciful shapes--a cooked fish mixture, for example, would be baked in a fish-shaped mold, resulting in a piscine culinary creation. An ice sculpture might even glorify the table of the quite wealthy."[26]

Urbanization changed the American food supply. Eggs, fowl and produce were provided to city folk by area farms while the railroads brought an abundance of other food-stuffs to local grocery stores. However, with the beginning of this separation of food production from the consumer, unscrupulous producers began to abound. Tea was often stretched with iron filings, chalk dust was added to flour as a filler, and unsanitary conditions often abounded. To counter strong reactions in the declining quality of food and to aid in sanitation, reputable food producers began to package their foods adding logos and graphic labels. When consumers could now be assured of quality and purity, they began to develop brand name loyalties. This, in turn, was the beginning of the advertising industry as we know it today.

Victorian Menus and Special Events

The occasion, the social standing and tastes of the master and mistress of the house, the availability of servants, the trends of the day including which author of etiquette the family chose to follow--these all helped formulate Victorian menus and the way they were served.

The Victorians loved to entertain as is evidenced by the party menus and details that follow.

Breakfast Parties

The breakfast party, stated Mary Henderson in her 1876 *Practical Cooking and Dinner Giving* text, was . . ."less expensive than dinners, and just as satisfactory to guests."[27] Later in the era (1896), Maud C. Cooke, in *Social Etiquette,* observed, "Breakfast parties are a very convenient mode of social entertainment for those whose limited means will not admit of a more extensive display of hospitality." Menus for breakfast parties abounded and Cooke went on to explain, "A breakfast should invariably begin with fruit, followed by a course of eggs. The entree' and the meat may form one course, if a slice of duck with olives, fried chicken or some such dish be selected." Hot breads and breakfast cakes and perhaps even oatmeal served with thick cream and powdered sugar could be added to the menu. "The closing course should be hot cakes served with honey or maple syrup,"[28] according to Maud C. Cooke and she went on to offer the menu that follows on page 19.

Victorian Era Silver

SILVER TEA SET[29]

Set of Six Pieces
$68.00.

Tea, SIx Half Pints
$13.25.

Sugar
$8.50.

Slop, Gold Lined
$8.25.

Coffee
$16.50.

Tea, FIve Half Pints
$12.25.

Cream, Gold LIned
$9.25.

26 inch Waiter, Chased to match the set, $60.00

The goal of every housewife . . .
"Quantities of silverplate appeared on Victorian tables. It became the true status symbol of the period. A complete tea and coffee service was the goal of every housewife. Most sets included three pots, sugar bowl, creamer, and waste bowl [often referred to as a slop bowl]. The largest of these pots was the coffeepot . . . stamped '7.' The teapot was stamped '6,' and the third pot, for hot water, stamped '5.' This [the numbers] denoted the capacity in half-pints."[30] To this basic set was added a spoon holder, syrup pitcher, butter dish, and coffee urn for a total of ten pieces for an affluent housewife. Trays, referred to as "waiters," were sold separately and were expensive in comparison to the other pieces in the set.[31]

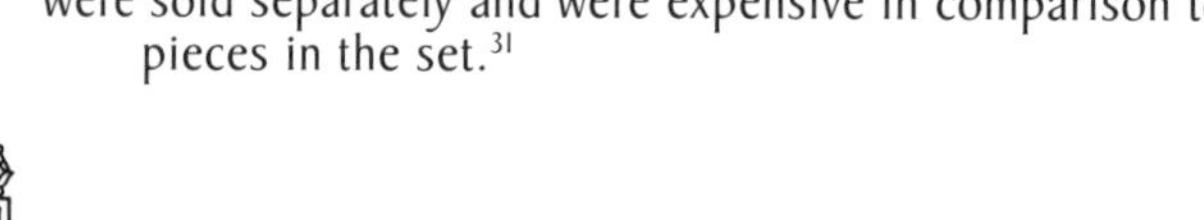

Bill of Fare for Breakfast

Melons. Grapes. Oranges. Fried Perch with Sauce Tartare.
Young Chickens with Cream Gravy. Saratoga Potatoes.
Poached Eggs on Toast. Broiled Quails. Baked Mushrooms.
Tomatoes or Celery. Bread and Butter.
Crackers. Hot Cakes. Coffee. Tea. Chocolate.
(Note: menu is printed in a similar manner to its appearance in original text.)

A limited number of servants would be needed to serve this meal with perhaps the hostess dispensing beverages and other dishes served from the side-table.

Luncheon Parties

In Victorian times, a "luncheon" signified an entertainment given by a woman generally for other women in contrast to a "lunch" which was merely a midday meal informally eaten by members of the household.

Whether the invitation was informal or more formal, it was expected that the hostess pay attention to every detail. "The repast may be elaborately made up of salads, oysters, small game, chocolate, ices, and a variety of dishes which will destroy the appetite for dinner, or it may simply consist of a cup of tea or chocolate, thin sliced bread and butter, chip beef or cold tongue, but there is the same opportunity to display good taste and a well-appointed table as at a grander entertainment." It was customary to provide favors and/or name cards as souvenirs, and it was even suggested that . . . "bon-bons, salted almonds and olives be disposed here and there in small dishes of cut glass or silver." [32] Mottos or "Motto kisses,"--candies wrapped in fancy paper and inscribed with a sentimental meaning, might even be provided for guests.

Tea Parties

Once upon a time, morning and afternoon "tea" was a way of life among affluent city ladies. The party choices were many and ranged from the very simple (tea, thin bread and "good" butter) to quite elegant. Tea types were varied: "elevensies," cream teas, wedding teas, tea dances, bridge teas, tennis teas, nursery teas for children, family teas, "ham teas" for post-funeral get-togethers, "strawberry teas" to introduce a new season, and even teas to present a debutante or honor a special guest . "High tea" could be substituted for supper although it was most frequently partaken of by the country folk. Afternoon teas could be served at several different times, but elaborate "five-o'clocks" were quite popular. "Pink and blue teas" were the rage for a time and simply meant the hostess used a monochromatic theme when selecting tableware, centerpieces, linens, and, to some extent, even food.

Ladies made it a point to be "at home" on a certain day at a given hour. They served tea from their drawing-room while offering accompaniments such as wafers, "biscuits" (what we now would call cookies), fancy cakes, or small delicate sandwiches to "drop-in" lady friends and, perhaps, even a gentleman who might stop by for a few minutes. With the popularity of Queen Victoria, Americans once again

Another Product of the Victorian Age -- Napkin Rings

Napkin rings are considered a product of the Victorian age and made their first appearance in literature in "*Work-Woman's Guide*," a magazine devoted to needlework. This 1838 article included directions for knitting your own. By 1860, silverplating companies were beginning to offer several styles of rings which eventually ranged from the simple to the extremely fancy. One distinctive style had a small glass bud vase attached, but animals and "children at play" were common decorative attachments to the rings.

NAPKIN RING[33]

CALL BELL [34]

Yes Madam!
In the days when domestic help was both plentiful and cheap, call bells were used by the lady of the house to let the maid know it was time for the next course.

embraced all things English, and this was evidenced by the addition of such foods as scones, crumpets, lemon curd, and clotted cream to the tea table.

The word *tea* was something of a misnomer, for at these entertainments guests were generally offered coffee and chocolate, or both; tea was usually included, but sometimes it was missing altogether. Of course, a well-bred lady could not conduct a proper tea without the correct equipment, and so a proliferation of tea pots, coffee pots, and chocolate sets flooded the market during this era.

Dinner Parties

Although Mrs. Beeton, in her 1861 book of household management, touted dinner menus for 6, 8, 10, 12, and 18 diners, she also mentioned this adage which appeared repeatedly in etiquette books of the era, "For a very pleasant social affair the rule is not to have the company when seated exceed twelve in number. With a party of that size the conversation can be general, and all are likely to feel more at ease than if the number be larger, provided a selection of guests is made that are congenial to each other. None of them should be conspicuously superior to the others, and all should be from the same circle of society."[35] In accordance with the ideal dinner for 12, Mrs. Beeton offered this menu:[36]

DINNER FOR 12 PERSONS (January).
First Course.
Carrot Soup `a la Crecy. Oxtail Soup.
Turbot and Lobster Sauce. Fried Smelts, with Dutch Sauce.

———

Entrees.
Mutton Cutlets, with Soubise Sauce. Sweetbreads.
Oyster Patties. Fillets of Rabbits.

———

Second Course.
Roast Turkey. Stewed Rump of Beef `a la Jardiniere.
Boiled Ham, garnished with Brussels Sprouts.
Boiled Chickens and Celery Sauce.

———

Third Course.
Roast Hare. Teal.
Eggs `a la Neige. Vol-au-Vent of Preserved Fruit. 1 Jelly. 1 Cream.
Potatoes `a las Maitre d'Hotel. Grilled Mushrooms.

———

Desserts and Ices.
(Note: menu is printed in a similar manner to its appearance in original text.)

It was reported by Mrs. E.B. Duffey in *The Ladies' And Gentlemen's Etiquette*, 1877, that the dinner hour could be five, six, or even seven o'clock. Although styles of service might vary from house to house, Mrs. Duffey went on to explain, "The

latest and most satisfactory plan for serving dinners is the dinner a la Russe, in which all the food is placed upon a side table and servants do the carving."[37] This style also allowed for more profuse ornamentation of the table as it was free of serving dishes. "Russian service" consisted of courses being served by gloved servants who presented food to each person. Servants set and removed a plate for every course without guests having to pass food as in an earlier era. A dinner might include ten or more courses, and it was often the custom to place small menus on the table describing the food the guests would be served.[38]

Concerning wine at dinner, Henry P. Willis observed, "If either a lady or gentleman be invited to take wine at table, they should not refuse; it is very gauche to do so. They need not drink half a glass with each person, but merely taste it, or touch their lips to the glass." [39] A proper Victorian would never ask for claret and champagne! They would have requested claret wine or champagne wine. [40]

Following a dinner party, it was often the custom for the ladies to retire to the parlor, leaving the men to their cigars and port.

Everyday Menus

For everyday dining, Isabella Beeton in her book on household management, 1861, offered weekly menu planning guides for the "mistress" of the house such as the one that follows. [41]

PLAIN FAMILY DINNERS FOR DECEMBER

Sunday. --- 1. Carrot soup. 2. Roast beef, horseradish sauce, vegetables. 3. Plum-pudding, mince pies.

Monday. --- 1. Fried whitings, melted butter. 2. Rabbit pie, cold beef, mashed potatoes. 3. Plum-pudding cut in slices and warmed; apple tart.

Tuesday. --- 1. Hashed beef and broiled bones, pork cutlets and tomato sauce; vegetables. 2. Baked lemon pudding.

Wednesday. --- 1. Boiled neck of mutton and vegetables; the broth served first with a little pearl barley or rice boiled in it. 2. Bakewell pudding.

Thursday. --- 1. Roast leg of pork, apple sauce, vegetables. 2. Rice snowballs.

Friday. --- 1. Soles `a la Crême. 2. Cold pork and mashed potatoes, broiled rump-steaks and oyster sauce. 3. Rolled jam pudding.

Saturday. --- 1. The remains of cold pork curried, dish of rice, mutton cutlets, and mashed potatoes. 2. Baked apple dumplings

(Note: menu is printed in a similar manner to its appearance in original text.)

An Outdoor Outing

In a quest for good health, the Victorians took to the out-of-doors. Bicycling, tennis, croquet and badminton were just a few of the activities enjoyed by men, women and children of the day.

Nature themes were often used as motifs in the dining room on wallpaper, dinnerware and silver. But better yet, a picnic was a chance to enjoy the real scenic beauty of the out-of-doors as well as to breathe "fresh air." However, in case one

should think this might have been an impromptu event where a few sandwiches were thrown in a hamper, think again. Isabella Beeton in *The Book of Household Management*, 1861, provided very specific instructions on how to prepare for a picnic:

BILL OF FARE FOR A PICNIC FOR 40 PERSONS.

"A joint of cold roast beef, a joint of cold boiled beef, 2 ribs of lamb, 2 shoulders of lamb, 4 roast fowls, 2 roast ducks, 1 ham, 1 tongue, 2 veal-and-ham pies, 2 pigeon pies, 6 medium-sized lobsters, 1 piece of collared calf's head, 18 lettuces, 6 baskets of salad, 6 cucumbers.

Stewed fruit well sweetened, and put into glass bottles well corked; 3 or 4 dozen plain pastry biscuits to eat with the stewed fruit, 2 dozen fruit turnovers, 4 dozen cheesecakes, 2 cold cabinet puddings in molds, 2 blanc-manges in moulds, a few jam puffs, 1 large cold plum-pudding (this must be good), a few baskets of fresh fruit, 3 dozen plain biscuits, a piece of cheese, 6 lbs. of butter (this, of course, includes the butter for tea), 4 quarterern loaves of household bread, 3 dozen rolls, 6 loaves of tin bread (for tea), 2 plain plum cakes, 2 pound cakes, 2 sponge cakes, a tin of mixed biscuits, 1/2 lb. of tea. Coffee is not suitable for a picnic, being difficult to make."

As to . . . "Things not to be forgotten at a Picnic. A stick of horseradish, a bottle of mint-sauce well corked, a bottle of salad dressing, a bottle of vinegar, made mustard, pepper, salt, good oil, and pounded sugar. If it can be managed, take a little ice. It is scarcely necessary to say that plates, tumblers, wine-glasses, knives, forks, and spoons, must not be forgotten; as also teacups and saucers, 3 or 4 teapots, some lump sugar, and milk, if this last-name article cannot be obtained in the neighbourhood. Take 3 corkscrews. 3 dozen quart bottles of ale, packed in hampers; ginger-beer, soda-water, and lemonade, of each 2 dozen bottles; 6 bottles of sherry, 6 bottles of claret, champagne `a discretion, and any other light wine that may be preferred, and 2 bottles of brandy. Water can usually be obtained so it is useless to take it." [42]

(NOTE: attempt was made to recreate a similar print set, size and scripting as used in the original text.

Ginger Beer

Often referred to as "small beer," ginger beer was actually a carbonated soda made by a process related to the production of beer and wine dating back at least to the 1600's. However, unlike its alcoholic cousins, these carbonated beverages were drunk before the yeast had a chance to completely consume all of the sugars. These beverages were brewed from molasses, vinegar and ginger. Although referred to as "non alcoholic," in truth, most "small beers" contained low amounts of alcohol (probably 2 to 4 per cent) and were quite popular according to Victorian literature.[43]

Local Restaurant Dining

Most small towns or cities contained some type of eating establishments, many of which were found in boarding houses. Abilene was unique in that hotels with dining rooms had sprung up to accommodate the eastern cattle buyers flocking to the city. Reported to be some of the finest and best equipped hotels between Kansas City and Denver, these establishments lived on after the cattle trade had left. The Henry House, built in 1875 by T. C. Henry, later housed the Stanton House Restaurant and eventually became the Union Pacific House. The Pacific House contained a large dining room and an experienced chef; it stood where the parking lot of the Abilene Convention and Visitors Bureau (201 N.W. 2nd) is now located. Another well known eatery was the Drovers Cottage, built in 1867 by Joseph G. McCoy, the individual credited with masterminding the plan to extend the Chisholm Trail to Abilene. The Drovers Cottage would have been located in the gravel parking lot east of the Dickinson County Courthouse (where the Belle Springs Creamery later stood).

The one restaurant menu available from the files at The Dickinson County Historical Society appears on the facing page. It was originally printed by "Chronicle Print" and the menu style approximates the original. Should the terms Irish "do" and Mashed "do" seem unfamiliar, this was a common way of referring to "ditto". Both terms are listed under Sweet Potatoes, thus, Irish and Mashed "do" simply refer to "ditto" for potatoes.

DROVERS COTTAGE
ABILENE, KANSAS,
WEDNESDAY, APRIL 26, 1871

================================

BILL OF FARE.

SOUP.

Oyster.

ROAST.

Beef. Turkey and-Cranberry Sauce.

BOILED.

English Leg of Mutton and Caper Sauce.
Turkey and Oyster Sauce,
Ham.
Tongue.

ENTREES.

Chicken Salad. Escalloped Oysters.
Pigeon Pie. Oyster Pies.

GAME.

Woodcook. Quail Larded. Partridge Larded.

RELISHES.

Lettuce, Pickles. London Club Sauce,
Cranberry Sauce. Beets, Cucumbers.
Worcestershire Sauce, Horse Radish.

VEGETABLES.

Sweet Potatoes. Green Peas.
Irish do Tomatoes. Turnips.
Mashed do Corn. Squash.

PASTRY.

Plum Pudding. Apple Pie.
Blanc Mange. Raspberry Pie.
Squash Pie. Peach Tarts.
Raspberry Tarts. Lady Fingers.
Charlotte Russe. Cranberry Sauce.
Fancy Cake.

DESSERT

Oranges. Apples.
Filberts. Walnuts.
Raisins. Almonds.
Strawberry and Vanilla Ice Cream.
Chocolate, Tea, Coffee.

This menu was served in honor of the fifty-second anniversary of the I.O.O.F. Lodge.

The Remoldeled Kirby House
(circa 1914)

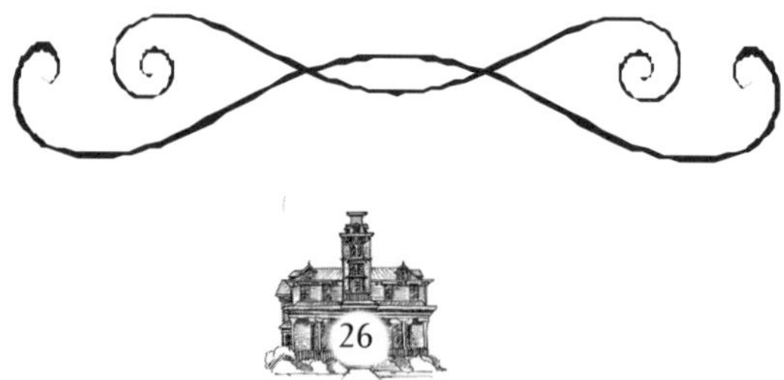

III. A NEW ERA FOR THE HOUSE

The Kirby House is Sold

Although Thomas died in 1905, Anna lived on in their beautiful home until 1914. At that time she sold it to the Abilene Commercial Club, the forerunner of the Abilene Chamber of Commerce. A one-story dining hall was added to the north side, and the front tower and dormer windows were removed; a new front porch with four large two-story pillars replaced the original Italianate style porch. In the 1930's the home met the fate of many other grand houses and was divided into six apartments.

Creation of The Kirby House Restaurant

In 1986, Terry and Jerry Tietjens purchased the structure with the intention of using the home for a fine dining establishment. After much research, an eleven-month restoration began, and the home was returned to its 1885 grandeur. The restaurant opened for business in 1987, serving an American Traditional Midwestern fare of steak, seafood, chicken, and pork.

The house has passed through several hands since Mr. Tietjens sold it in 1996. The present owner, Vangie Henry, purchased the house in January, 2000.

"It is easy to forget the social realities of the 19th century. Victorian homes document a way of life which has largely disappeared."[44] Yet even today Mrs. Henry and her staff help keep the past alive as they provide daily lunch or dinner menus in the elegant, but casual, atmosphere of the Victorian Kirby House.

As evidenced in the previous section, food had an important influence in the social and family lives of the Victorians. And, now more than a century later, food continues to play a prominent role in our lives. Family members often reminisce about time spent around the dinner table and it is almost impossible to imagine a social event without food. The Kirby House provides a gathering place for the enjoyment of good food and so, in the spirit of true hospitality, in Part 2 offers recipes for your home dining pleasure.

Recipes are traditions, not just random wads of ingredients.

Anonymous

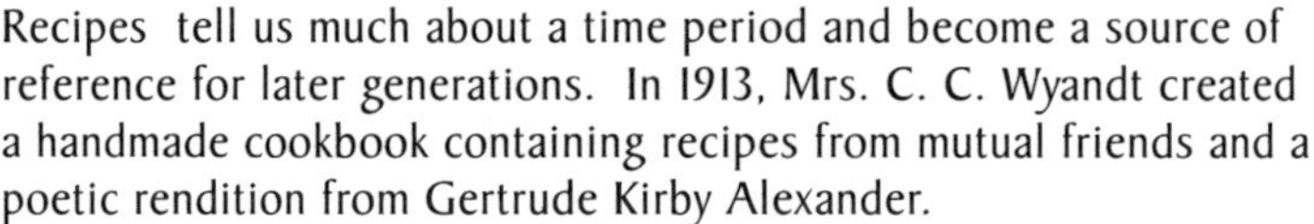

Recipes tell us much about a time period and become a source of reference for later generations. In 1913, Mrs. C. C. Wyandt created a handmade cookbook containing recipes from mutual friends and a poetic rendition from Gertrude Kirby Alexander.

Apricot Ice

If this decoction you would know
Just note directions found below
For this unique, refreshing ice
Is quickly made, and very nice.
Of apricots, a can you'll need,
The contents cut quite fine indeed.
A pint of sugar add, no more;
On this a quart of water pour,
And when the sugar doth dissolve
Tis time the freezer to revolve!
Now turn the crank a time or two
To freeze the mixture half way through.
A pint of cream whipped light as snow
Must then into the freezer go
And soon your troubles will be o'er,
For when the crank will turn no more,
Just look into the can again,
And find a food for "Gods and Men."[45]

Gertrude (Kirby) Alexander

Gertrude's recipe appeared in a handmade cookbook, *"Recipes, My Friends' and My Own,"* which was compiled by Mrs. C. C. Wyandt as a gift to Mrs. M. H. Malott at Christmas, 1913. According to a notation added to the original cookbook by Deane W. Malott in 1989, the Wyandts, the Malotts, the Homer Ellsions (living on Broadway), and Mrs. Gertrude Kirby Alexander enjoyed socializing. Among other things, they frequently dined together, and the men cooked dinner for the ladies once a year. The original recipe book was presented to The Dickinson Country Historical Society of Abilene, Kansas, in honor of the 100th anniversary of the birth of Dwight David Eisenhower.

Part 2:

The Kirby House Restaurant Recipes

"A restaurant is a fantasy, a kind of living theater in which diners are the most important members of the cast."

Quote from restaurant owner Warner LeRoy (1936-2001) in a 1976 interview. LeRoy is credited with being a founder of the Off-Broadway movement in New York but is best known for bringing glamour and pizzaz to renowned eateries such as Tavern on the Green, The Russian Tea Room and Maxwell's Plum.

Waldorf Salad, Eggs Benedict, Thousand Island Dressing -- What do they have in common?

The year was 1893 and an ambitious and enterprising Swiss had left his job as head waiter at the fashionable Delmonico's Restaurant in New York to join the staff of a new hotel being built by William Waldorf Astor on ground he inherited from his father, John Jacob Astor, Jr., at the corner of 5th Avenue and 34th Street. The new job would lead to a career more successful than he dreamed, and he would be credited for the invention / introduction of at least three foods Americans would enjoy in centuries to come. Oscar Tschirky presenting to the world Waldorf Salad, Eggs Benedict, and Thousand Island Dressing. He was also the man who defined for Americans the job of "maitre d'," the one in charge of a grand restaurant catering to the great and near-great among fashionable diners; he never was, and never claimed to be, a chef.

Waldorf Salad: In 1893 New Yorkers began enjoying an unusual salad on the menu, consisting of just three ingredients: cubed apples, chopped celery and mayonnaise. It was called the Waldorf salad, reputed to be the brain child of Oscar Tschirky, and it was an instant hit. Later, chopped walnuts were added, then grapes or raisins.

Eggs Benedict: According to an interview in "The New Yorker" magazine, a young wall street broker wandered into the Waldorf Hotel in 1894, hoping to cure his morning hangover. Lemuel Benedict ordered buttered toast, poached eggs, crisp bacon and a hooker of hollandaise. His order prompted Oscar to put the unusual combination on the menu substituting ham and a recently-introduced delicacy from England, the English muffin.

Thousand Island Dressing: Thousand Island dressing was created in Clayton, N.Y. by Mrs. Sophia LaLonde. She passed the recipe on to May Irwin, a prominent N.Y. actress, a renowned cook and cookbook authoress. Miss. Irwin named the dressing "Thousand Island," and passed it to others. Eventually maitre d' Tschirky put the dressing on the menu at the Waldorf and in so doing earned credit for introducing the dressing to the "world."[46]

THE KIRBY HOUSE RESTAURANT RECIPES

Excessive, flamboyant, ostentatious, pretentious, over-indulgent are all words that have been used to describe the Victorian era. But let's also add "*elegant.*" Above all, this period in history added a new elegance to the lives of the Kirby family and to many others, as well. Today The Kirby House Restaurant allows guests to enjoy that same elegance as they dine in a Victorian setting. Mrs. Henry and her staff would like to share the recipes they use to create the foods enjoyed by the guests at The Kirby House. These include . . .

- recipes regularly featured on the menu.
- "specials" offered either weekly or upon occasion.
- pastries offered in Mrs. Kirby's coffee shop.
- a few special event items including some of the recipes and menus used at the teas offered at the restaurant.
- also, a collection of both menus and recipes for custom-planned events. Specialized catering and individualized menu planning are services offered by The Kirby House.

Note: Most of recipes in this book come from the notebooks at The Kirby House restaurant. Many of those recipes are from the staff and some are original recipes created by those staff members. In the preparation of this cookbook, every attempt was made to closely replicate the ingredients and preparation procedures as recipe sizes were adjusted and procedures adapted for home use. Furthermore, all recipe adjustments were tested and/or checked for accuracy.
However, it should be noted . . . the staff at the restaurant (like all good cooks) use their senses as they prepare food. For them a recipe is a guide, not something that has to be followed without question. Please use the recipes that follow in a similar manner and enjoy the results.

It should also be noted that the staff is continuously testing and creating new recipes. Every attempt was made to include the majority of recipes available prior to the publication of this book.

And finally, every attempt was made to correctly credit other individuals who have allowed the restaurant to use their recipes. We thank them for allowing us to publish those recipes and regret any omission of names that might be due to oversight.

Salad from the Victorian era . . .

Oysters appear somewhat frequently in Victorian menus and this Oyster Salad dates back to the 1880's. According to local history, fresh oysters and other delicacies were actually delivered by rail to Abilene.

Oyster Salad

Drain the liquor from a quart of fresh oysters. Put them in hot vinegar enough to cover them placed over the fire. Let them remain until plump, but not cooked, then drop them immediately in cold water. Drain off and mix them with two pickled cucumbers cut fine, also a quart of celery cut in dice pieces, some seasoning of pepper and salt. Mix all well together, tossing up with a silver fork. Pour over the whole a mayonnaise dressing. Garnish with celery tips and slices of hard-boiled eggs arranged tastefully.[47]

Gertrude Kirby's Recipe for Salad Dressing . . . 1913

Oil Dressing

Mix 1/2 teas. of salt
1 teas. of sugar
2 teas. of dry mustard
and a pinch of paprika & red pepper
add a tablespoon of water
stir until the salt & sugar dissolve
put in a tablespoon of lemon juice or vinegar
Break in one egg Beat vigorously few seconds.
pour in about a tablespoon of oil Beat vigorously until the dressing starts to thicken; add two cupfuls oil in larger amounts.
Beat well after each addition.

G. H. K. [Gertrude Kirby]

This recipe appeared in a handmade cookbook "*Recipes, My Friends' and My Own*"[48] dated 1913. The recipe appears in a format similar to the original and was contributed by Gertrude Kirby, daughter of Thomas and Anna.

Kirby House
Salads and Salad Dressings

Bacon Dressing *Yield: about 1 1/2 cups*

This dressing can be made in advance and stored in the refrigerator. It is especially good on spinach greens.

4 slices bacon
1/4 cup + 2 tablespoons bacon grease (add butter if necessary to equal measure)
1/4 cup + 2 tablespoons white distilled vinegar
1/4 cup + 2 tablespoons water
1/4 cup + 2 tablespoons granulated sugar
2 large eggs, beaten

Cook and crumble bacon; set aside.
Combine bacon grease, vinegar, water and sugar in a medium saucepan and heat to boiling. Cool slightly.
Beat eggs in a mixing bowl and temper by slowly drizzling up to half of the hot mixture into the egg yolks while whisking constantly. Then blend the tempered egg mixture into the hot ingredients in saucepan. (To insure safety, this egg mixture should be cooked until a thermometer registers 180°.) Strain mixture to remove any bits of cooked egg that might form.
Store in refrigerator. Let dressing return to room temperature or heat to warm before dressing the salad.

Blue Cheese Dressing *Yield: about 2 1/2 cups*

1 cup mayonnaise
1 cup buttermilk
1/3 cup sour cream
1 1/2 tablespoon lemon juice
1 teaspoon Worcestershire sauce
1/8 teaspoon each of garlic salt & Tex Joy® Steak seasoning
1/4 pound (4-ounces) blue cheese, crumbled

Thoroughly combine in the work bowl of a food processor or in a mixing bowl: mayonnaise, buttermilk, sour cream, lemon juice, Worcestershire sauce, salt and seasoning. Process or whisk until smooth. Add crumbled blue cheese and process or whisk until blended. Taste and adjust seasonings. Use immediately or cover and refrigerate.

Salad Dressing Storage
Most homemade dressings can be stored, tightly covered, in the refrigerator for up to 2 weeks. Always whisk or shake just before adding them to salad greens to mix the ingredients.

Caesar Salad Dressing *Yield: about 2 1/2 cups*

1/4 cup + 2 tablespoons lemon juice
1 teaspoon Worcestershire sauce
1 teaspoon garlic salt
1 1/2 teaspoon dry mustard
1/2 teaspoon pepper
2/3 cup grated Parmesan cheese
1 1/2 cups olive oil

Combine the first six ingredients in a mixing bowl, jar or blender (depending on which of the mixing methods will be used. Slowly add the olive oil using one of the three methods listed on p. 36.
Refrigerate until ready to use.

Celery Seed Dressing *Yield: about 2 3/4 cups*
The "House Dressing"--a favorite of guests at the restaurant!

2/3 cup granulated sugar
2 teaspoons salt
1 teaspoon celery seed
Scant teaspoon onion powder
2 teaspoons dry mustard
2/3 cup white distilled vinegar
2 cups vegetable oil

Mix sugar, salt, celery seed, and onion powder in a mixing bowl. Using an electric mixer, slowly add half of the vinegar mixing at a low speed until blended. Slowly add the remaining vinegar and then the oil. Blend on medium speed until creamy. Store at room temperature.

Dijon Vinaigrette *Yield: about 2/3 cup*

1/3 cup white wine vinegar
1 teaspoon Dijon mustard
1 tablespoon granulated sugar
1/2 teaspoon coarse black pepper
1/4 teaspoon salt
2 garlic cloves, finely minced
1/3 cup olive oil

Combine the first six ingredients in a mixing bowl, jar or blender (depending on which of the mixing methods will be used. Slowly add the olive oil using one of the three methods listed on p. 36. Refrigerate until ready to use.

How Much Dressing To Use?
Dress the greens with only enough dressing to lightly coat them right before serving. The normal ratio is one-third ounce (about 2 teaspoons) of dressing per ounce of greens (about 1 handful). Of course, the salad dressing can be served from a small pitcher allowing each guest to add the amount desired.

Lemon-Oregano Vinaigrette *Yield: about 1 3/4 cups*

- 1/2 cup + scant tablespoon red wine vinegar
- 1/4 cup + 2 tablespoons lemon juice
- 1 1/2 teaspoons ground oregano
- 1 tablespoon granulated sugar
- 1/4 teaspoon garlic powder
- 3/4 teaspoon pepper
- 1 cup olive oil

Combine the first six ingredients in a mixing bowl, jar or blender (depending on which of the mixing methods will be used). Slowly add the olive oil using one of the three methods listed below. Refrigerate until ready to use.

Poppy Seed Dressing *Yield: about 2 to 2 1/4 cups*
This is good with greens but also delicious with a blend of fruit.

- 1/2 cup red wine vinegar
- 1/2 cup granulated sugar
- 2 tablespoons orange juice
- 1 3/4 teaspoons poppy seeds
- 1 1/2 teaspoons orange zest
- 1/4 teaspoon salt
- 1/4 teaspoon white pepper
- 1 1/2 cups olive oil

Combine the first seven ingredients in a mixing bowl, jar or blender (depending on which of the mixing methods will be used). Slowly add the olive oil using one of the three methods listed below. Refrigerate until ready to use.

About Dressing Ingredients & How To Combine:
The essential ingredients in vinaigrette type dressings are oil and vinegar. However, without special treatment, these two liquids are immiscible with oil floating on the surface and the vinegar sinking to the bottom. To create a smooth dressing with the ingredients dispersed, it is necessary to reduce the surface tension between the oil and vinegar. This can be achieved in various ways:

1. Whisk together the vinegar and/or lemon juice and the seasonings in a small to medium mixing bowl. Then slowly add the oil, drop by drop, whisking as you go, until the dressing begins to thicken. Note: as the dressing thickens, speed up the addition of the oil.
2. Place the vinegar and/or lemon juice and seasonings in a small jar with a tight-fitting lid and shake to blend. Then add the oil in 3 to 4 additions shaking thoroughly between additions.
3. Mix the vinegar and/or lemon juice and seasonings in a blender and then add the oil in a slow, steady stream (through the top lid opening) as the blender is running.

Lemon Juice--fresh squeezed juice will give the most desirable flavor especially in a recipe that is uncooked. For maximum juice yield, use lemons at room temperature and roll them between the palms of your hands before cutting and squeezing.

Kirby House Salad *Serves 6*

This is the dinner salad featured at The Kirby House.

Romaine Lettuce and Spring Mix lettuce blend--approximately 6 handfuls (equal combination or use all Spring Mix, etc.)
I to 2 tomatoes, cut into thin wedges
1/4 to 1/2 cucumber, thinly sliced
1/4 to 1/2 cup Celery Seed Dressing, p. 35

Sort and wash lettuce. Cut Romaine lettuce into bite-size pieces. In a large bowl, toss lettuce with the vegetables. Place about I handful of greens on salad plate and dress with Celery Seed Dressing.

Apple Salad *Serves 6*

Crisp red apples, celery and walnuts add a taste and texture treat to this green salad.

Spring Mix lettuce blend or your choice of lettuce blends--approximately 6 handfuls
2 to 3 crisp red apples, cored & chopped into small pieces
1/2 to 3/4 cup diced celery
1/3 to 1/2 cup coarsely chopped walnut pieces
1/4 to 1/2 cup Poppy Seed Dressing, p. 36

Sort and wash lettuce; cut or tear into bite-size pieces; place about I handful of greens on each salad plate. In a small bowl, toss apples, celery, and nuts. Sprinkle divided apple mixture on salad greens and drizzle with Poppy Seed Dressing.

Tip: Add lemon juice or orange juice to a small spray bottle and mist cut apples lightly, but thoroughly (the ascorbic acid in the citrus juice will help prevent browning). If preparing salad in advance, wait until the last minute to add the apples.

Hints For Preparing Salad Greens

- ❖ Clean greens by plunging in and out of cold water (prolonged soaking causes soggy greens).
- ❖ Separate core from leaves; rinse and dry. Remove bad spots.
- ❖ To store clean greens, layer in a plastic container with paper towels.
- ❖ Cut sturdy greens (Romaine) and tear delicate greens (Bib, Boston or Leaf) into bite-size pieces.
- ❖ A general guide . . . allow about I handful of greens for each side salad. Using that guideline the yield for Romaine lettuce is usually 6 to 7 servings and loose-leaf lettuce generally yields 5 to 6 servings.

Cranberry-Pecan Salad with Orange Vinaigrette *Yield: 8 servings*

<u>Honeyed Pecans</u>
3/4 cup pecan halves
2/3 cup honey
1/4 cup butter, melted
1/2 cup granulated sugar

Stir together the pecans, honey and butter; spread in a shallow roasting or baking pan. Bake at 325° for 12 to 15 minutes; stir often and watch carefully to prevent over-browning. Remove and toss with sugar.

<u>Salad</u>
1 - 2 bunches lettuce--green and red Leaf lettuce or fancy mixed salad greens (equivalent to 8 handfuls cleaned greens)
2 - 3 oranges or tangerines, peeled and sectioned with seeds removed
1/4 - 1/2 cup dried, sweetened cranberries

In a large bowl, toss all ingredients together.

<u>Orange Vinaigrette</u>
2/3 cup orange juice
1/3 cup white wine or rice vinegar
2 tablespoons Dijon mustard
2 green onions, minced (use white and light green parts)
1/2 teaspoon salt
1 1/2 teaspoons pepper
1/2 cup olive oil

Process all ingredients, except oil, in a blender or food processor. Slowly add oil and blend to create an emulsion.

<u>To Assemble</u>: Place a handful of salad greens & fruit on each plate. Sprinkle with honeyed pecans and drizzle with vinaigrette.

 **A SPECIAL TOUCH!** 

Chilled Salad Plates

Place salads on cold plates for a refreshing effect. To do this--simply stack salad plates in the refrigerator prior to salad assembly.

A SPECIAL TOUCH!

Salad Accompaniment --- Crouton Toasts

Another special touch for a special event--crouton toasts are easy to make yet will impress guests. You'll need white bread, olive oil, your choice of herbs, a cookie sheet lined with parchment paper, a rolling pin, cookie cutters of your choice and a pastry brush. To prepare: On a cutting board or work surface, lay out bread slices. Lightly flatten the bread with the rolling pin. Cut out shapes (flowers for summer, stars at Christmas, etc.). Place bread shapes on the lined cookie sheet; brush lightly with olive oil and sprinkle with herbs that will compliment the other flavors in the salad. Place cookie sheet in a preheated oven set at 350° and bake about 10 minutes (checking frequently) or until croutons are golden brown and crisp. Cool and store in an air-tight container until ready to use. Arrange about 3 of these on top or on the side of a tossed salad.

A SPECIAL TOUCH!

Salad Baskets and Toppers

Crisp Parmesan Baskets *Yield: 8 baskets*

8 teaspoons butter
3 cups coarsely grated Parmesan cheese (about 9 -ounces)

Invert one 1 1/4 -cup capacity custard cup on a work surface. Cover with paper towel. Melt 1 teaspoon butter in large non-stick skillet over medium-low heat. Sprinkle about 1/3 of the cheese into center of skillet, forming a 6" round. Cook until cheese melts and bottom is golden, about 4 minutes, pressing on cheese with spatula to help flatten during cooking. Turn cheese over and cook until second side is golden, about 3 minutes. Place cheese round atop paper towel covered cup. Top with 2 folded paper towels and immediately press down on cheese to form a cup shape--about 30 seconds. Remove paper towel. Turn cheese basket right side up; cool. Repeat with remaining cheese and butter, using clean paper towels for each basket. Basket can be made about 6 hours ahead. Store at room temperature in a covered container. Fill baskets with assorted salad greens for an interesting and tasty presentation.

Parmesan Toppers

Non-stick cooking spray
Coarsely grated Parmesan cheese

Preheat oven to 350°.

Line a cookie sheet with aluminum foil and lightly spray with the non-stick coating. Arrange about 1 tablespoon of cheese to form a 2" round circle, rectangle, etc., on the prepared cookie sheet. Continue making as many as desired, leaving around 1" between toppers. Bake for 8 minutes of until lightly browned. Using a spatula, quickly remove cheese from the cookie sheet to a cooling rack. Cool completely and store in air-tight container. To serve: Mound salad greens on a plate and add a topper for an interesting presentation.

Cinnamon Apples *Yield: about 16 servings (allowing 3 quarters per person)*
This recipe, from Lucille West, can be made several days in advance. Serve on a lettuce leaf, as a fruit salad, or as a brunch accompaniment.

9 -ounce package Cinnamon Imperials® (or "red hots")
1 cup granulated sugar
1 1/2 cups water
3 pounds Jonathan apples (about 12 medium), peeled, cored and quartered

Place Cinnamon Imperials® in bottom of a saucepan; cover with sugar and water. Let mixture come to a boil and stir until candies are dissolved. Add apples and cook only until tender but not mushy. Turn apples often so they will absorb the red color evenly. Chill.
Note: For a thicker syrup, add only 1 cup water.

Macedonia di Frutta *Yield: about ten 4 -ounce (1/2 cup) servings*
This Italian fruit salad is a wonderful accompaniment to brunch. Choose from an Amaretto or Fruit Juice dressing.

Combine 5 cups fruit (such as honeydew; cantaloupe; seedless red grapes, halved; bing cherries, fresh peaches or other fruits of choice)

<u>Amaretto Dressing</u>
1 cup granulated sugar
1 cup Amaretto liqueur
Or
<u>Fruit Juice Dressing</u>
1/2 cup orange juice
1/4 cup fresh lemon juice
3 tablespoons granulated sugar

Prepare fruit; combine in a large bowl. In another bowl, whisk the dressing ingredients until combined and pour over fruit. Chill, allowing mixture to set about an hour to distribute flavor.

Orange Ambrosia *Yield: about 6 servings*

4 medium oranges, peeled and thinly sliced (across the grain)
1/2 cup orange juice
2 - 3 tablespoons honey
1/4 - 1/2 cup flaked coconut

Place sliced oranges in a mixing bowl. In another smaller bowl, whisk together the orange juice and honey. Pour over the orange slices and chill. Just before serving, transfer orange slices to a serving bowl and sprinkle with coconut.

How to **professionally cut fruit** . . . oranges, grapefruit, pineapple, any melon, etc. This technique is safe, efficient and removes the pith (the bitter white part) from citrus fruit.

1. Using a sharp knife, cut a 1/2" slice off the top and bottom ends of fruit.

2. Stand the fruit on one end. Using a knife (small paring knife for small fruit; larger for melons, pineapple, etc.), follow the outline of the fruit as closely as possible to slice off the rind or outer cover. For citrus . . . be sure to remove all the white pith.

Pickled Peaches *Yield: 12 to 16 servings (depending on actual number of peach halves per can); allow at least 1 peach per serving.*
This recipe from Phyllis Newell can be made several days in advance; the peaches make a nice addition to a relish dish. Serve on a bed of lettuce for a fruit salad or with a brunch menu.

2 -1 lb. 13 oz. cans peach halves, in heavy or light syrup
3 whole cloves for each peach half (about 36 to 48)
1 cup granulated sugar
1/2 cup Cinnamon Imperials® (also referred to as "red hots")
1 cup reserved peach syrup
1 cup water
1/2 cup white distilled vinegar

Drain peaches, reserving the juice. Place cloves in peach halves and set aside. In a saucepan, mix together the sugar, Cinnamon Imperials®, peach syrup, water and vinegar; stir and simmer until candies are dissolved. Add peaches and simmer for 10 minutes. May be prepared several days in advance and refrigerated. If desired, remove cloves before serving.

Getting Organized in the Kitchen:
mise en place: [MEEZ ahn plahs] A French term referring to having all the ingredients necessary for a dish prepared and ready to combine up to the point of cooking. Mise en place is a concept used to prep ingredients for line cooking in restaurants; the home cook can also employ this technique to aid in organization.

Other tips for efficiency:
Read through the recipe carefully before you start and speculate what can be done in advance; do any pre-preparation (or prep work) that could aid in smooth assembly of the recipe . . .
For example:
- Wash and peel fruits and vegetables
- Cut or chop apple, nuts, celery, etc.
- Brown meat or onions
- Cook noodles or macaroni
- Measure out ingredients in advance for quick combining later on

Gather all equipment and grease baking pans, preheat ovens, etc. so they will be ready as needed.

Waldorf Slaw *Yield: about 10 to 12 servings*

- 1/2 cup *apples, chopped and tossed in lemon juice (to prevent browning)
- 1/3 cup chopped celery
- 2 - 3 tablespoons coarsely chopped walnuts
- 1 - 2 tablespoons raisins
- 4 cups chopped cabbage (about 1 pound)
- 2/3 cup Waldorf Slaw Dressing

Drain lemon juice from apples. Mix all ingredients together. Chill until ready to serve.

Waldorf Slaw Dressing; *Yields: about 2 1/4 cups total*

This can be made up and held in the refrigerator for a couple of weeks. Add to above salad ingredients as needed.

- 2 cups mayonnaise
- 2/3 cup granulated sugar
- 1/4 cup white distilled vinegar

Mix all ingredients and let stand to allow sugar to dissolve. Stir again before adding to salad.

***Eating Apples** -- *these varieties will yield a crisp texture and refreshing taste when eaten fresh:*

Jonathan A mildly tart, crisp apple. Tends to be small to medium-sized and is deep shiny red.

Golden Delicious Crisp, fine-grained. It has a somewhat sweet taste with a mild-flavor.

Red Delicious Is mild-flavored, firm in the early season but be sure these are fresh as they tend to be mealy after long storage.

Winesap Bright deep red apple. The flesh is very juicy, crisp, and slightly acid.

German Potato Salad *Yield: about 8 to 10 servings*

- 10 medium baked potatoes, peeled and diced (about 10 cups) OR use red potatoes (unpeeled), cooked, and diced
- 5 slices bacon, fried and crumbled (reserve 1/4 cup + 2 tablespoons bacon grease; add butter if needed to equal measure)
- 1/2 cup chopped yellow onions
- 1/4 cup all-purpose flour
- 1 1/2 teaspoons salt
- 1/4 teaspoon pepper
- 3 tablespoons granulated sugar
- 1/2 cup white distilled vinegar
- 1 cup water

Place cooked, diced potatoes and cooked, crumbled bacon in a bowl; set aside.
Heat bacon grease in a medium skillet and sauté the chopped onions just until they turn translucent.
Add flour, salt, pepper, and sugar. Blend with onions and bacon grease to make a smooth roux (French term for a flour-fat "paste"). Add vinegar and water slowly, stirring with a whisk, until mixture is thickened and smooth.
Pour just enough sauce over potatoes and bacon to coat; toss lightly to mix. Serve warm.
Refrigerate any unused sauce for later use.

Red Potato Salad *Yield: about 8 to 10 servings*

12 medium red potatoes
Cook potatoes in their jackets (unpeeled) until just done but still firm. Cool slightly, peel and slice into a bowl and set aside.

Dressing:
- 2 cups mayonnaise
- 1/2 cup granulated sugar
- 1/2 cup minced onion
- 1/4 cup minced fresh parsley
- 1 tablespoon lemon juice
- 1 tablespoon dry mustard
- 3/4 teaspoon pepper
- 1 cup sour cream
- 1/2 cup minced celery
- 1/4 cup cider vinegar
- 1 tablespoon Worcestershire sauce
- 1 tablespoon salt

Dressing: Combine ingredients in a bowl and whisk or mix thoroughly. Taste and adjust for seasoning as desired. Pour enough sauce over potatoes to coat; toss lightly to mix. Refrigerate and allow potatoes to marinate in the dressing.

FYI: Small red waxy potatoes are best for potato salad as they hold their shape and don't crumble when sliced or diced.

Celebration Salad *directions for 1 salad*

Fresh mixed greens--allow about 1 handful per person
1/2 - 1 cup deep-fat fried chicken nuggets per salad
1/4 to 1/3 cup fresh fruit such as: strawberry slices, pineapple chunks or seedless grape halves
Celery Seed dressing (p. 35)
Almond slices, toasted (see p. 176)

Arrange a bed of mixed greens on salad plate and top with chicken nuggets and the fruit (select according to seasonal availability). Drizzle with dressing and garnish with a sprinkling of toasted almonds.

Chicken Salad / Sandwich Filling *Yield: about 3 1/2 cups*

This is a versatile chicken salad recipe that can be scooped onto a bed of lettuce for a luncheon or spread on bread for a substantial sandwich. This recipe is also suitable as a filling for tea sandwiches.

1/2 cup + 2 tablespoons mayonnaise
1 tablespoon vegetable oil
3 cups cooked chicken breast, finely chopped or about 24 -ounces canned chicken, drained
3 green onions, (mince white & green parts to yield approximately 1/4 cup)
salt and pepper to taste

In a mixing bowl, combine mayonnaise and oil. Add finely chopped chicken and thoroughly combine. Add green onions plus salt and pepper to taste. Refrigerate, covered, until ready to use.

Grilled Steak Salad *directions for 1 salad*

Marinated sirloin (Steak Marinade on p. 186), grilled. Allow approximately 2 - 3 ounces of steak per person
Fresh mixed greens--allow about 1 handful per person
3 - 4 slices of fresh tomato (1/4" thick)
3 slices of cucumber (1/4" thick)
4 (1/4" thick) avocado wedges
2 - 3 mushrooms sliced thin (about 6 slices)
Choice of dressing

Advance Preparation: Marinate steak briefly for added flavor.

Grill steak and then slice into 1/4" diagonal slices. Arrange a bed of mixed greens on salad plate and place steak strips in the center. Cut tomato and cucumber slices in half. Arrange the tomatoes, cucumbers, avocado and mushroom so they radiate around the steak. Serve with choice of dressing.

Tijuana Tom Salad *directions for 1 salad*

Fresh mixed greens--about 1 handful per person
Smoked turkey, cut into long 1/4" thick strips--allow about 2 -ounces per person
Fresh mango--allow 3 to 4 slices per person
Fresh pineapple, cut into small wedges or chunks--allow about 1/4 to 1/2 cup per person
Garnish with:
Fried tortilla strips, dipped in cinnamon-sugar
Green onions , sliced diagonally
Pistachios, chopped
Honey-Lime Vinaigrette

Arrange a bed of mixed greens on salad plate and top with turkey and fruit.
Garnish with fried tortilla strips, green onions and pistachios; drizzle with dressing.

To prepare fried tortilla strips:
Cut flour tortillas in 1/2" strips; lightly fry in vegetable oil; drain and then dip in cinnamon-sugar (see suggested proportions on p. 134)

Honey-Lime Vinaigrette *Yield: about 2 cups*

1/3 cup lime juice
1/3 cup honey
2 tablespoons Dijon mustard
1/4 cup chopped fresh cilantro
3/4 cup vegetable oil

Add first 4 ingredients to a mixing bowl and blend with electric mixer. Then slowly add oil while continuing to blend with mixer. Store in refrigerator.

Tropical Chicken Salad *Yield: about 5 1/2 cups total; eleven 1/2 cup servings or five generous 1 cup servings*

2 cups baked chicken breasts, chopped (see note below)
2 cups *mesquite-grilled chicken strips, chopped into bite-size pieces
1/2 cup mayonnaise
1/2 cup seedless red grapes, halved
1/4 cup raisins
1/4 cup celery, chopped
1/2 teaspoon ground ginger
1/4 teaspoon onion salt
Dash curry powder or to taste

Mix together all ingredients in a large bowl. Store in refrigerator to blend flavors until ready to serve.
Serve on a bed of leaf lettuce.

Note: 1 cooked chicken breast will generally yield about 1 cup of diced or chopped chicken meat.
*Mesquite-flavored pre-cooked chicken may be purchased in the frozen food section of many grocery stores.

A SPECIAL TOUCH!

Tips for Arranging Salads

- Select the right plate or bowl for the portion size allowing enough room to keep the salad off the rim of the dish. Picture the serving plate as a frame for the salad.
- Build salad appeal by balancing colors . . . green lettuce, red grapes, creamy white dressing. However, avoid the mistake of too many colors which can be unappetizing.
- Height adds eye appeal. Ingredients that are mounded on a plate are more interesting and appealing than if they are just spread out flat. Place tomato or fruit wedges so they overlap or lean on each other. Arrange fried tortilla strips so they create a spiral effect. On the other hand, keep the arrangement simple enough so that the salad appears edible.
- Be sure every ingredient is cut large enough so it can be easily identified. Bite-size pieces are preferable, unless the food item can be cut with a fork, such as tomato slices or cucumber. Items used as seasonings, such as onions, can be finely chopped.

Santa Fe Sizzler *directions for 1 salad*
This salad is a favorite luncheon entree at the restaurant.

- 1/2 teaspoon each of chili powder and cumin
- 4 -ounces boneless, skinless chicken breast per person
- Fried tortilla bowl, drained--The Kirby House uses chipotle tortillas to create their tasty bowls!
- Fresh mixed greens with a little chopped red cabbage added to mix--allow about 1 handful per person
- Black Beans, drained--1/3 to 1/2 cup per salad
- Chopped tomatoes--about 1/4 cup per salad
- Cheddar Cheese, grated--2 to 3 tablespoons per salad
- Pico de Gallo
- Sour cream--about 1 tablespoon per salad
- Small bowl of salsa to be served on the side

Mix together the chili powder and cumin in a low, flat bowl.
Pound chicken breast with a meat cleaver to uniform thickness. Coat the chicken breast in the chili powder/ cumin mixture and place on a preheated grill (if a grill unit is not available at home, use a grill pan on top of a heating unit). Turn after chicken is browned and contains the characteristic grill markings; grill on remaining side until chicken is well done throughout or until an internal temperature of 170° is reached. Remove from grill and slice diagonally into 1/2" slices.
Fill fried tortilla bowl with mixed greens and then layer with black beans, chopped tomatoes and cheddar cheese. Arrange the grilled, sliced chicken breast on top and garnish with Pico de Gallo and sour cream. Serve with salsa on the side.

<u>Pico de Gallo</u> *Yield: about 3 1/2 cups*
Similar to salsa but chunkier!

- 1 cup chopped onion
- 1/4 - 1/2 teaspoon minced garlic
- 1 - 2 jalapeno peppers (depending on level of heat desired); remove seeds and mince
- 2 1/2 cups chopped tomatoes, drained
- 1 tablespoon lime juice
- 1 teaspoon each salt and pepper, or more to taste, as desired

In a mixing bowl, combine the chopped onions, minced garlic, and jalapeno peppers. Add the chopped tomatoes, lime juice, salt and pepper. Blend until the tomatoes are partly liquefied but still lumpy. Chill in the refrigerator for 2 to 3 hours before serving to blend flavors.

Wild Rice Chicken Salad *Yield: 6 to 8 servings*

A great salad luncheon or try it for a covered dish dinner. This salad is so versatile--see ideas for variations or be creative and make your own substitutions or additions.

Salad:

1 package (6 -ounces) long grain and wild rice (such as Uncle Ben's® brand with flavor packet)
2 1/2 - 3 cups cooked, diced chicken
2 cups finely chopped celery
1 1/2 - 2 cups thinly sliced mushrooms
1/2 cup sliced green onions
1/4 cup diced tomatoes (or substitute red bell pepper)
1/2 cup sliced almonds, toasted (see p. 176)

Prepare rice according to package directions and set aside to cool. In a serving bowl, toss prepared chicken, celery, mushrooms, onions, and tomatoes; add rice and almonds. Whisk dressing ingredients until well blended and stir into salad. Serve this salad chilled, surrounded by lettuce.

Note: If making salad ahead--combine all ingredients except almonds and dressing, refrigerate and toss with missing ingredients just prior to serving.

Dressing:

1/2 cup vegetable oil
1/4 cup red wine vinegar
2 tablespoons Dijon mustard
1/2 teaspoon black pepper

Variations: Add water chestnuts and/or Rice Noodles (such as China Boy®) for added crunch and flavor. Substitute other cooked meats (pork, turkey, etc.). Experiment with other flavored vinegars in place of the red wine vinegar.

This salad may also be served warm.

"The kitchen is generally the least interesting place in a fine house, unless you expect to make it your home. Then it suddenly acquires a personal interest to the good housewife not to be exceeded by any room in the house."

-Marcus p. Hatfield, 1887.

Soups from the Victorian era . . .

Clear soups and thick ones were offered as a first, or even second course during the Victorian era. Special spoons for each were deemed essential and soup tureens were a part of china sets.

Bouillon Blanc--white broth.

"Place in a large stock-urn on a moderate fire a good heavy knuckle of a fine white veal with all the scraps of meat, including bones, remaining in the kitchen (but not of game); cover fully with cold water, adding a handful of salt; and as it comes to a boil, be very careful to skim all the scum off--no particle of scum should be left on--and then put in two large, sound, well-scraped carrots (whole), one whole, cleaned, sound turnip, one whole, peeled, large, sound onion, one well-cleaned parsley root, three thoroughly washed leeks, and a few leaves of cleaned celery. Boil very slowly for six hours on the corner of the range; keenly skim the grease off; then strain well through a wet cloth into a china bowl or a stone jar, and put it away in a cool place for general use. *TheTable,* (Soups) by Delmonico's Chef, Alessandro Filippini, 1889."[49]

To flavor their soups, Victorian cooks might have prepared a "bouquet" of herbs and spices made from the recipe that follows . . .

A Bouquet.-how to prepare.

"Take four branches of well-washed parsley-stalks--if the branches be small, take six; one branch of soup-celery, well washed; one blade of bay-leaf, one sprig of thyme, and two cloves, placed in the centre of the parsley, so as to prevent cloves, thyme, and bay-leaf from dropping out of the bouquet while cooking; fold it well, and tightly tie with a string, and use when required in various recipes. *The Table,* by Delmonico's Chef, Alessandro, Filippini, 1889."[50]

Kirby House Soups

Blueberry Soup *Yield: about 4 cups*

1 10 -ounce bag frozen blueberries
3/4 cup + 2 tablespoons water
1/4 cup granulated sugar
1/4 teaspoon ground cinnamon
Rind from 1/4 of a large lemon cut into wide strips (when removing rind, cut only the yellow surface; avoid the white pith)
1/2 cup sour cream

Place all ingredients, except the sour cream, into medium saucepan and bring to boil. Simmer for several minutes until blueberries are soft. Pour into a large stainless steel, ceramic, plastic or glass mixing bowl and set in the refrigerator until cooled (20 to 30 minutes).
Pour cooled mixture into blender. Cover blender lid with a towel to prevent soup spraying out when blended. Blend for several minutes or until completely pureed. Add sour cream, blending until smooth. Thoroughly chill prior to serving.

Peach Soup *Yield: about 2 1/2 cups*

1 10 -ounce bag frozen peaches
1/4 cup orange juice
1/4 cup pineapple juice OR, substitute 1/2 cup pineapple-orange juice in place of the orange and pineapple juices
1 tablespoon Amaretto (an almond based liqueur)
3/4 teaspoon lemon juice
1 tablespoon + 1 1/2 teaspoons granulated sugar or to taste
1/2 cup sour cream

Place all ingredients, except the sour cream, into medium saucepan and bring to boil. Simmer for several minutes until peaches are soft. Pour into a large stainless steel, ceramic, plastic or glass mixing bowl and set in the refrigerator until cooled (20 to 30 minutes).
Pour cooled mixture into blender. Cover blender lid with a towel to prevent soup spraying out when blended. Blend for several minutes or until completely pureed. Add sour cream, blending until smooth. Thoroughly chill prior to serving.

Strawberry Soup *Yield: about 3 cups*
A delicious but oh-so-easy fruit soup!

2 cups frozen, sweetened strawberries--partially thawed
1 cup sour cream

Add strawberries and sour cream to a blender. Cover blender lid with a towel to prevent soup spraying out when blended. Blend for several minutes or until completely pureed. Thoroughly chill prior to serving.

Clam Chowder *Yield: about 7 to 8 cups*

2 1/2 cups diced red potatoes, unpeeled
Approximately 1 teaspoon salt
4 slices of bacon
2 - 3 medium yellow onions, diced
3/4 cup all-purpose flour
3 - 4 cups whole milk
2 6.5 -ounce cans minced clams, undrained

Heat only until hot.
DO NOT BOIL!

Place potatoes in a medium to large saucepan; add water to barely cover; season with salt. Cook just until tender (about 10 minutes). Do not drain.
Sauté bacon (in a large skillet or sauce pot) until cooked but not crispy. Remove bacon from pan and add the diced onion. Sauté onions until tender and translucent. Add flour (a little bit at a time) to the sautéed onions, stirring constantly until blended. Slowly stir in 3 cups milk, stirring constantly until smooth and thickened. If too thick, thin with the remaining cup of milk, as needed. Stir in minced clams and clam juice; add thickened cream sauce to the potatoes and potato water. Mix in cooked bacon and taste for salt.

Lobster Bisque *Yield: about 10 cups*

2/3 cup butter (divided)
1 pound small frozen lobster tails, defrosted & each cut into 2-3 pieces, (with shells on)
2 carrots, diced
2 cups onions, diced
3 sprigs fresh parsley, minced;
1 bay leaf
Dash ground thyme
1/2 cup white wine
1/4 cup brandy (divided)
14.5 -ounces chicken broth (1 can)
1/4 cup tomato paste
3/4 cup all-purpose flour
2 cups heavy whipping cream
4 cups milk (1 quart)
1 teaspoon salt
1/4 teaspoon pepper

Melt 3 tablespoons of the butter in a heavy, large saucepan on low to medium heat. Add lobster and sauté 5 minutes until shells turn red. Add carrots, onions and herbs; cook until tender. Add wine and half the brandy. Cook 1 minute. Add broth and tomato paste. Bring to boiling, then simmer 8 to 10 minutes. Remove lobster with slotted spoon. Cool and remove meat from shells. Dice meat and reserve. Return shells to pan for added flavor. (Remove shells before serving.)
Melt remaining butter in another (smaller) saucepan over medium heat. Stir in flour and cook 1 minute. Add cream, milk, salt and pepper. Simmer 5 minutes. Mix with above broth mixture and simmer 30 minutes. Strain vegetables & bay leaf from the cream sauce (discard vegetables and bay leaf). Add lobster and remaining brandy to the cream sauce.

Chili *Yield: about 11 cups*

2 pounds lean ground beef
1/4 teaspoon *minced garlic
1/2 cup chopped onion
1/4 cup chopped green pepper
2 1 -ounce packages chili seasoning
1 tablespoon all-purpose flour
1 tablespoon granulated sugar
24 -ounces tomato juice
1 14 1/2 -ounce can crushed tomatoes
1 15 -ounce can red beans, undrained
1 15 -ounce can pinto beans, undrained
1 15 -ounce can chili beans, undrained

Brown ground beef in a skillet on medium high; add next 3 ingredients (garlic, onion and green pepper) and cook until the onion becomes soft and translucent. Drain off grease. Place hamburger mixture in a crock pot; add remaining ingredients stirring to combine. Simmer on low for several hours to allow flavors to blend.
Or, simmer hamburger mixture on top of the range in a covered soup pot until flavors are blended and well developed.

* Mince: To cut food into very small pieces. The terms "finely chopped" and "minced" are interchangeable.

Pork Chili *Yield: about 7 cups*

2 - 3 tablespoons vegetable oil
2 pounds pork loin, cubed
2 tablespoons all-purpose flour
3/4 teaspoon crushed red pepper
1 1/2 teaspoons minced garlic
1 1/2 teaspoons onion powder
1/4 teaspoon ground cumin
1 1/2 teaspoons black pepper
2 tablespoons chili powder
2 cups tomato paste
1 cup water
15 -ounce can chili beans, undrained
Salt to taste

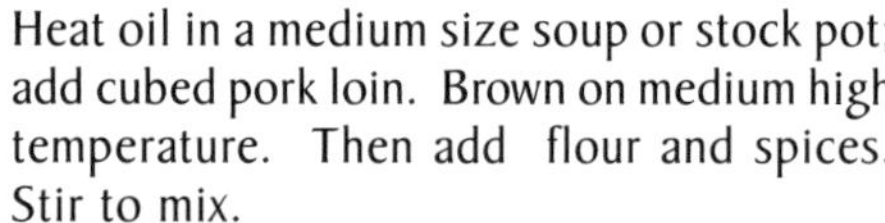

Heat oil in a medium size soup or stock pot; add cubed pork loin. Brown on medium high temperature. Then add flour and spices. Stir to mix.
Add the remaining ingredients and heat to bubbling. Reduce temperature and simmer until meat is tender to the fork and flavors have blended (about 30 minutes to 1 hour).

With or without beans?
Chili is a blend of cubed or ground meat with spicy seasonings. It originated in Texas and is often made without the addition of beans. However, recipes vary and in many parts of the country beans are requisite.

Broccoli and Cheese Soup *Yield: about 8 cups*

1 large head broccoli, steamed
1/4 cup butter
2 tablespoons chopped onion (yellow or white)
3 celery ribs, minced
1/4 cup all-purpose flour
4 cups chicken stock (can be prepared from a concentrate such as Minor's® Chicken Base)
2 cups whole milk
Salt and pepper to taste
2 cups Cheddar cheese, grated

Drain steamed broccoli and finely chop (by hand or pulse in the food processor).
Melt butter in a medium size saucepan or stock pot over medium heat. Add chopped onion and minced celery and sauté until tender and the onion is translucent. Stir in flour. Slowly stir in the chicken stock and bring to the boiling point. Add the chopped broccoli and heat. Reduce the temperature and add the milk and grated cheese; heat but do not boil.

French Onion Soup *Yield: about 6 cups*

3 cups thinly sliced white onions
3 tablespoons butter
4 cups beef broth (can be prepared from a concentrate such as Minor's® Beef Base)
2 cups chicken broths (can be prepared from a concentrate such as Minor's® Chicken Base)
1/4 teaspoon ground black pepper
Additional butter for coating serving dishes
6 slices French bread (about 1/2" thick)
6 thin slices Provolone cheese
Chili powder

In a medium saucepan or stock pot using medium heat, sauté the onions in the butter until well browned, but not scorched. Add beef and chicken broth plus the pepper. Cover and cook over low heat, about 30 minutes. The soup is now ready to add to individual heat-proof casserole dishes or souffle dishes. Prepare these dishes by coating lightly with butter. Place a slice of French bread (trim or tear to size if needed) in the bottom of the bowl; ladle in soup and add a slice of Provolone cheese. Sprinkle liberally with chili powder.
Heat in 275° oven about 5 minutes or until the cheese is melted. Or, individual bowls may be microwaved for a few minutes.

Minnesota Wild Rice Soup *Yield: 7 to 8 cups soup*

1 6 -ounce box of Long Grain & Wild Rice (such as Uncle Ben's® brand) with flavor packet
1/2 cup chopped onion
1/2 cup butter (1 stick)
3/4 cup all-purpose flour
3 teaspoons chicken base (such as Minor's® Chicken Base) diluted in 3 cups hot water, or use 3 cups chicken broth
1 cup cooked chicken, finely chopped
1/2 cup grated carrots
1 cup heavy whipping cream
Half-and-half, as needed, to thin the soup

Cook or steam rice according to package directions adding the flavor packet during this cooking process.
In a medium to large saucepan or stock pot, sauté the onions in butter over medium heat until they are tender and translucent. Sprinkle in the flour, stirring to create a roux. Add chicken base and water (or the chicken broth) to the roux stirring to thoroughly incorporate. Add cooked chicken and carrots and simmer for at least 30 minutes. Before serving, add heavy cream (using low to medium temperatures) and thin, as needed, with half-and-half.

About Onions
Once considered a breakfast "health" food, onions are used today both as food and flavoring. Onions come in many different sizes, shapes and colors; tastes can vary from mild to strong.

Why do onions cause tears? Chopping or slicing brings the onion's sulfur-containing amino acids into contact with enzymes to form sulfuric acid which is a volatile compound. This is what causes irritation to eyes and nose. Generally the older the onion, the stronger these compounds. A chemical change, which actually diminishes these irritating effect, occurs when cooking onions.

To lessen eye irritation, hold onions under cold running water as you peel. The water carries away some of the sulfur compounds before they can affect your eyes.

What is a scallion? Simply another name for a green or young onion pulled from the ground when the bulb is quite small.

Yield: 1 pound (lb.) mature onions = 4 to 5 medium
1 lb. fresh onions = 2 to 3 cups chopped
1 lb. green onions = 2 cups chopped

Potato Soup *Yield: about 7 cups*

1/2 cup diced onions
1/2 cup butter (1 stick)
1/2 cup + 2 tablespoons all-purpose flour
2 cups hot water
1 heaping tablespoon chicken base (such as Minor's® Chicken Base)
1/2 - 1 teaspoon Tex Joy® Steak Seasoning
4 - 5 cups warm mashed potatoes
1/2 cup + 2 tablespoons half-and-half
1/2 - 1 1/3 cups whole milk
Salt & pepper to taste.
1 1/2 - 2 teaspoons chopped, fresh parsley

In a medium to large saucepan or stock pot, sauté the onions in butter over medium heat until they are tender and translucent. Stir flour into the butter-onion mixture until smooth to create a roux. Mix the hot water, chicken base and Tex Joy® seasoning and slowly add to the roux. Stir until smooth and thickened. Add mashed potatoes to soup, stirring until smooth. Slowly add half-and-half to soup, stirring to thoroughly mix. Then add as much milk as needed until soup is desired consistency--similar to a light cream sauce. Season with salt and pepper to taste. Add parsley and simmer for 10 to 15 minutes, but do not boil.

Tortilla Soup *Yield: about 8 or 9 cups*

1 - 2 tablespoons butter
1/2 cup chopped onions
1 1/2 teaspoon garlic powder
1 tablespoon chili powder
2 1/4 teaspoons ground cumin
1/2 teaspoon ground oregano
6 cups water
1/4 cup chicken base (such as Minor's® Chicken Base)
1 cup tomato sauce (or an 8 -ounce can)
1/2 teaspoon Cajun pepper (or substitute cayenne pepper)
1 pound chicken, bones included (chicken breasts work well)
1 1/4 cup corn (frozen or fresh, cut off cob)
Garnishes: fried tortilla strips, sour cream, chopped cilantro and red onions

In a medium to large saucepan or stock pot, sauté the onions in butter over medium heat until they are tender and translucent. Add seasonings--garlic powder, chili powder, cumin and oregano.

Add water, chicken base, tomato sauce and Cajun pepper to the stock pot. Bring to a boil. Reduce the heat and add the chicken. Simmer until the chicken is cooked through, about 30 to 45 minutes. Remove the chicken from the pot and discard the skin and bones, cool and then chop into bite-size cubes. Meanwhile, add the corn and continue to simmer until it is tender. Return cubed chicken to soup pot.

Prepare garnishes ahead; add to soup after it has been ladled into soup bowls. Or when preparing at home, pass garnishes and let each guest add as desired.

To prepare fried tortilla strips:

Cut flour tortillas in 1/2-inch strips; lightly fry in vegetable oil; drain.

Sandwiches during the Victorian era . . .

Hamburgers and French Fries -- A Victorian Invention !

The Hamburger Sandwich

"It is said that the Hamburgers (folks that lived in Hamburg) got the idea to tenderize beef from the Tartars several centuries back, and they would eat it either raw, the way the Tartars did, or cook it with onions. An English doctor and food enthusiast adapted the dish as part of his beef-three-times-a-day food regimen. His name was Dr. J. H. Salisbury; hence Salisbury Steak. With the wave of German immigrants to the United States in the 1800's the word 'Hamburg Steak' or 'hamburger' began appearing on menus. To serve the 'hamburger' as a sandwich, well, somebody had to think that up, or rather, cook that up. As in most things American, there is a diversity of opinion between the northeast and the southwest, with still another opinion coming from the Midwest. In the northeast, they say that the burger was first grilled by Louis Lassen of New Haven, Connecticut who ground up some scraps of beef and served it as a sandwich to a customer who was in a hurry in 1900. In Athens,Texas, they say a man named Fletcher Davis fried a beef patty and put it between two slices of bread as a sandwich in the late 1880's and took it to the 1904 World's Fair in St. Louis. However, there is some evidence to support the theory that the hamburger got its start at the World's Columbia Exposition in 1893 in Chicago. Other Midwesterners claim that Charlie Nagreen of Seymour, Wisconsin invented it in 1885, introducing it at the Outagamie County Fair."[51]

And, what's a Hamburger without French Fries . . . Saratoga Chips

According to the account in *Panati's Origins of Everyday Things* by Charles Panati (published by Harper and Row, 1987), potato chips were invented in 1853 in Saratoga Springs, New York. "A visitor to that resort city, who is often identified as Cornelius Vanderbilt (called 'The Commodore'), returned a meal to the kitchen, complaining that the fried potatoes were not sliced thin enough to suit his taste." After repeated attempts and rejections, George Crum finally sliced the potatoes so thin they couldn't be eaten with a fork. Crum decided not only to keep on making them that way, but eventually he opened his own restaurant and featured what became known as "Saratoga chips." By 1880, "Saratoga potatoes" were featured in *Buckeye Cookery and Practical Housekeeping,* edited by Estelle Woods Wilcox.[52]

Kirby House Sandwiches

Note: All entree sandwich directions are for individual sandwich assembly. The Kirby House serves these sandwiches with a choice of two sides: Waldorf Salad, p. 43, Cottage Cheese, Fresh Seasonal Fruit, Garden Side Salad, Seasoned Waffle Fries, Mashed Potatoes & Gravy, pp. 108 & 185 Potato Salad, p. 44 or a cup of Soup, pp. 52-57.

Beef Baron Sandwich *Yield: 1 sandwich*

Tomato basil focaccia bread, purchased, 2 pieces (or substitute any other flavor)
Butter for grilling
Russian-Horseradish sauce, enough for spreading
Deli sliced roast beef, 2 to 4 ounces
Sautéed onions (p. 107), 2 to 4 slices
Roasted red bell pepper, purchased (or see directions), several strips

Cut focaccia into size and shape similar to a slice of sandwich bread. Butter insides of focaccia and grill; spread the insides of focaccia with Russian-Horseradish Sauce and add remaining ingredients.

Roast red bell peppers by letting the skin blacken and blister under a broiler or in a very hot oven. Place blistered peppers in a covered plastic container or even a paper sack (which steams the pepper and facilitates peeling) to cool. Then peel, remove seeds and slice peppers.

Russian-Horseradish Sauce *Yield: about 1 cup*

1/2 cup A.1.® steak sauce
1/2 cup purchased Russian dressing
1 teaspoon prepared horseradish

In a small bowl, mix ingredients thoroughly.

Focaccia is a chewy Italian flatbread that is a trendy addition to menus throughout the country. Similar to pizza dough, focaccia is often just brushed with rich olive oil and sprinkled with herbs.

Club Sandwich *Yield: 1 sandwich*

Sourdough bun, split
Honey mustard, enough for spreading
Mayonnaise, enough for spreading
Deli sliced ham, 1 1/2 to 2 slices
Deli turkey, 1 1/2 to 2 slices
3 strips of bacon, crisply fried and drained
1 to 2 leaves of Leaf lettuce
Thinly sliced tomatoes, about 3 slices

Spread one side of the split bun with honey mustard; the other side with mayonnaise.
To assemble: Stack remaining ingredients between the sourdough bun.
The Kirby House cuts this sandwich in half, secures each side with a toothpick, and stands each half on edge for plate presentation.

Continental Reuben *Yield: 1 sandwich*

Deli sliced pastrami, 2 to 4 slices
Sauerkraut, drained, about 1/4 cup
Melted butter for grilling bread
Marbled rye, 2 slices
Thousand Island spread, enough for spreading
Honey mustard, enough for spreading
Swiss cheese, 1 slice

Place pastrami on a microwave safe plate; top with sauerkraut and microwave briefly to heat through.
Brush one side of bread with melted butter. Place on grill (or in skillet), butter side down, to lightly brown. Spread one grilled bread slice with Thousand Island spread; the other with honey mustard and the Swiss cheese.
To assemble: Layer the warm pastrami and sauerkraut between the grilled bread slices. Cut in half for serving.

Kirby Burger *Yield: 1 sandwich*

1/3 pound lean ground beef
Onion Kaiser bun, grilled
Melted butter for grilling bun
1 to 2 leaves of Leaf lettuce
Thinly sliced tomatoes, about 3 slices
Thin slice of red onion
Dill pickle slices, enough for a thin layer

Lightly shape beef into a 1" thick patty. Grill (or fry) each side approximately 5 to 6 minutes or cook hamburgers to an internal temperature of at least 160° or until the center is no longer pink and the juices are clear. Brush inside of bun with melted butter and grill lightly.

To assemble: Place grilled hamburger between bun and plate with the lettuce, tomatoes, onion and pickles on the side.

Kirby Bacon Cheese Burger *Yield: 1 sandwich*

1 Kirby Burger
1 slice American cheese
3 strips bacon, crisply fried and drained

Prepare Kirby Burger, as directed above, adding cheese and bacon to the grilled patty.

Barry Burger *Yield: 1 sandwich*

A recent addition to the menu is this burger created by Barry L. West. Barry, a retired art teacher, is now using his talents in the culinary arts field.

1 Kirby Bacon Cheese Burger
1 slice ham
1 slice turkey
3 - 4 tablespoon sautéed mushrooms, p. 107

Prepare Kirby Bacon Cheese Burger, as directed above, adding ham, turkey and sautéed mushrooms to the grilled patty.

Patty Melt *Yield: 1 sandwich*

Another delicious variation of the typical hamburger.

1/3 pound lean ground beef
1 slice Swiss cheese
3 - 4 tablespoons sautéed onions, p. 107
2 slices marbled rye bread, buttered on one side

Prepare burger as directed above. Add cheese and sautéed onions; serve on grilled bread. (To grill--place bread on grill, or in skillet, butter side down and lightly brown.)

Quesadillas *Yield: 1 quesdadilla*

This recipe is offered at The Kirby House as an appetizer but could also be used for a sandwich entree.

1 tablespoon butter
1/4 of a medium green pepper, thinly sliced
2 green onions, chopped
2 - 4 mushrooms, sliced thin
1 12" chipotle tortillas or substitute plain flour tortillas
1/2 - 3/4 cup shredded Cheddar cheese, or combination of Cheddar & Monterey Jack cheese, divided
Alternative--add cooked and sliced chicken or beef to the filling.

Serve with any of the following: Pico de gallo , p. 48; Guacamole, p. 192; Sliced Avocados; Salsa; Sour Cream

In a skillet, heat the butter over medium temperature; sauté the green pepper slices, the chopped green onions and sliced mushrooms.
Heat another large skillet or grill. Brush surface of tortilla lightly with butter (or spray with non-stick pan coating); place tortilla on heated surface and sprinkle with half of the cheese; add sautéed peppers & onions, sprinkle with remaining cheese. Cook until cheese is set and outside of tortilla is lightly browned. Use a large spatula to flatten the tortilla; carefully flip and brown the other side. Remove from pan and cut into four or more triangular sections.

South Of The Border--Ole! *Yield: 1 sandwich*

1 3 - 4 ounces pork tenderloin, tenderized
Tex Joy® Steak Seasoning
Sourdough bun, grilled or toasted
Mashed Avocado, enough for spreading
Refried beans, enough for spreading
Chili-Mayonnaise, enough for spreading
1 to 2 leaves of Leaf lettuce
Thinly sliced tomatoes, about 3 slices

Coat pork tenderloin liberally with Tex Joy® seasoning and grill 4 to 6 minutes per side or until internal temperature reads 160° and pork is nicely browned.
To assemble: Spread one side of grilled (or toasted) bun with the mashed avocado; the other side with refried beans and chili-mayonnaise. Layer lettuce, grilled pork, and tomato slices between the bun halves.

<u>Chili-Mayonnaise</u> *Yield: about 1 cup of spread*

1 cup mayonnaise
2 tablespoons + 2 teaspoons chili sauce
heaping 1/4 teaspoon chili powder
scant 1/4 teaspoon Tex Joy® Steak Seasoning

In a small bowl, thoroughly combine and mix all ingredients. Refrigerate until ready to use.

Turkey Meltdown *Yield: 1 sandwich*

Melted butter for grilling bread
Marbled rye, 2 slices
Honey mustard, enough for spreading
Deli turkey, 1 1/2 to 2 slices
3 strips of bacon, crisply fried and drained

Brush outside of both slices of bread with melted butter. Place on grill, buttered side down, to lightly brown.
To assemble: Spread insides of bread with honey mustard and add the turkey and bacon. Cut in quarters for serving.

Vegetarian *Yield: 1 sandwich*

Melted butter for grilling bread
Wheat bread, 2 slices
Mashed Avocado, enough for spreading
Tomato Pesto Cream Cheese, enough for spreading
1 to 2 leaves of Leaf lettuce
Cucumber slices, thinly cut--enough for a thin layer
Fresh mushrooms, thinly sliced; use Portobello mushrooms, if available--enough for a thin layer

Brush outside of both slices of bread with melted butter. Place on grill, butter side down, to lightly brown.
To assemble: Spread inside of one slice of bread with the mashed avocado; the other side with the Tomato Pesto Cream Cheese. Place lettuce on bread, layer with cucumber slices and fresh mushrooms. Cut in half and secure with a toothpick. Stand on edge for plate presentation.

<u>Tomato Pesto Cream Cheese</u> *Yield: about 1 cup of spread*

8 -ounces cream cheese, softened
1 Roma tomato, finely chopped
1/2 teaspoon Italian seasoning
1/4 teaspoon garlic powder or salt
1/4 teaspoon pepper

Place all ingredients in the work bowl of a food processor and process until well combined OR place in a mixing bowl and thoroughly combine with an electric mixer. Store unused spread in refrigerator.

These recipes are used frequently for "Teas" held at The Kirby House, for cocktail parties and other special events.

Artichoke Phyllo Triangles *Yield: about 60 triangles*

Note: Phyllo dough is usually sold in the freezer section of the grocery store. Plan ahead when making this recipe as the dough must be thawed.

1 package frozen phyllo dough, thawed according to package directions
2 cups butter, melted
2 cups Artichoke Filling

Preheat over to 400°. Lightly spray a parchment lined cookie sheet with pan coating.

Artichoke Filling *Yield: 2 cups filling*

1 can (14 -ounces) artichokes hearts, drained and diced
1/2 cup sour cream
1 cup (4 -ounces) grated Cheddar cheese
2 cloves garlic, minced
1 teaspoon dried oregano

In a medium bowl, mix all ingredients until well blended.

Unroll phyllo dough and remove 2 sheets. Cover unused dough with plastic wrap and enclose in a damp towel (from which all excess moisture has been squeezed) to keep sheets from drying out; make sure the damp towel does not come in direct contact with the phyllo. Brush each sheet lightly with melted butter and stack one on top of the other. The phyllo sheets are approximately 15 x 11" so cut the 15" length into five -3" strips using a sharp knife. Place a rounded teaspoon of filling at the end of each strip. Fold phyllo corner diagonally over teaspoon of filling to form a triangle. Continue folding flag-fashion to opposite end. Brush bottoms and tops with butter and place on prepared pan. Repeat process until all dough is used. Bake until light golden brown, 10 to 15 minutes.

Buttery Ham Mousse Spread *Yield: about 4 cups*

This filling is delicious spread on bread (plain or toasted), or crackers. Or, cut purchased Puff Pastry dough into small rounds; bake as directed. Split baked rounds in half and fill with Ham Mousse Spread for delicious tea sandwiches or use for hors d'oeuvres.

1 cup butter, softened
8 -ounces cream cheese, softened
10 -ounces cooked ham, ground
2 tablespoons finely chopped green onions
1 tablespoon lemon juice
1/4 teaspoon salt
1/8 teaspoon coarse-grind pepper

Place butter and cream cheese in a mixing bowl; using an electric mixer, beat mixture at medium speed until creamy. Add ham and remaining ingredients, mixing well. Use immediately or cover and chill if making in advance. (Note: If this mixture is made in advance, let stand at room temperature or briefly soften in microwave so it will be spreadable.)

Cucumber Filling *Yield: about 2 cups.*

8 -ounces cream cheese, softened
1/4 - 1/2 cup mayonnaise
1 medium cucumber, peeled, seeded, & finely chopped; press through a colander to remove excess moisture
1/2 teaspoon chopped fresh dill weed or about 1/4 teaspoon dried
1/4 teaspoon garlic salt

Process cream cheese and mayonnaise in a blender or food processor until smooth, stopping once to scrape down sides. Combine cream cheese mixture, cucumber, dill weed and garlic salt.

Chill until ready to use allowing flavors to blend.

Ham & Apricot Tea Sandwiches . . . *A quick and easy sandwich with a succulent blend of flavors that is hard to stop eating! A favorite sandwich at Kirby House teas.* Mix 3 parts cream cheese with 1 part apricot preserves. Blend well. Spread mixture on a slice of bread and top with a very thin slice of ham. Top with second slice of bread. Trim crusts and cut into desired shapes. Or, use small biscuits in place of the bread.

Ham and Asparagus Roll Up's . . . *Sandwiches can be left whole or cut into 2 to 3 sections.*

Fresh asparagus spears
Thin sliced white bread, crusts trimmed
Soft butter or mayonnaise
Thin slices of deli style ham

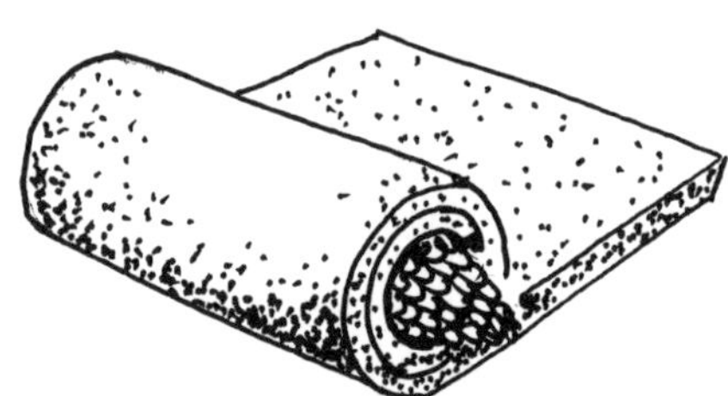

Bring a large pan of water to a full rolling boil, and add the fresh asparagus. Allow to cook only long enough to be tender-crisp -- it is only a matter of a few seconds to a minute or two depending on thickness of the asparagus stalk. Fish a stalk out, run it under cold water, and taste. When it is right (still almost crunchy) quickly pour the water and stalks into a large strainer. Immediately run cold water over the stalks to stop the cooking process. Flatten bread slightly with a rolling pin; spread with a small amount of butter or mayonnaise and place a slice of ham on the bread, trimming it to fit. Place a stalk of asparagus on one end letting the tip stick out, and roll the whole thing up. Place sandwiches on a platter, seam side down, fitting them tightly against one another. Cover with plastic wrap and then a damp (squeezed dry) towel; chill several hours, and serve.

Pimiento Cheese Spread *Yield: about 2 1/2 to 3 cups*

3 -ounces cream cheese, softened
1 cup shredded Cheddar cheese
2 - 3 tablespoons mayonnaise, or more as needed
1/2 - 1 teaspoon Tex Joy® Steak Seasoning
2 - 3 tablespoons diced pimiento, drained
1 teaspoon grated onion
1 teaspoon Worcestershire sauce, optional

Place cream cheese in a mixing bowl and beat with an electric mixer until smooth and fluffy. Add remaining ingredients and beat only until blended. Add additional mayonnaise, if needed, to make a creamy spread. Use immediately or refrigerate.

Pistachio Filling *Yield: about 1 1/2 cups*

8 -ounces cream cheese, softened
3 tablespoon butter
1 tablespoon whole milk or more to thin, as needed
Dash of cayenne pepper
Pinch of salt
1/2 cup pistachios, finely chopped

Place cream cheese and butter in a mixing bowl and beat with an electric mixer until fluffy. Add milk, a little at a time, until a creamy spreading consistency is achieved. Blend in cayenne, salt and pistachios. Use immediately or refrigerate. If refrigerated, it may be necessary to let mixture come to room temperature for spreading.

Tortilla Roll Up's . . . *A simple but delicious recipe. Serve unsliced as an entree sandwich or cut into bite-size wedges for tea sandwiches or hors d'oeuvres.*
Thoroughly mix cream cheese and salsa (1/4 cup salsa to 8 -ounces of cream cheese). Spread a thin layer of this mixture on a chipotle tortilla (or substitute a plain flour tortilla), place a lettuce leaf on top and roll up tightly. Slice into bite-size wedges. Thin slices of deli meats may also be added, if desired. To insure edges seal--make sure cream cheese mixture extends to edge of tortilla.

Salmon Mousse *Yield: about 2 cups*

7 - 8 -ounces canned salmon, drained (about 1 cup)
1 tablespoon grated onion (or more to taste)
1/2 teaspoon lemon juice
8 -ounces cream cheese, softened
Salt & pepper to taste

Place all ingredients in a mixing bowl and beat with an electric mixer until smooth and fluffy. Refrigerate at least 1 hour.

Make Ahead & Storage Tips for Sandwiches:
Most cold sandwiches can be made ahead and layered in an airtight container several hours before serving. Cover each layer with waxed paper and a damp paper towel that has all the excess moisture squeezed out; this will help the sandwiches retain freshness and moisture.

Sandwich shapes--a mixture of shapes adds interest to a sandwich tray:
Triangle Sandwiches--Trim crusts of bread slices and spread 1 slice with about 2 to 3 tablespoons of filling; top with another slice of trimmed bread. Quarter sandwiches diagonally to make triangles.
Finger Sandwiches--Trim crusts of bread. Spread with about 2 to 3 tablespoons of filling. Top with another piece of trimmed bread. Cut sandwich into 3 to 4 equal strips.
Pinwheels--Trim crusts from bread. Using rolling pin, gently flatten each slice to half its original thickness. Spread each slice with about 1 to 2 tablespoons of filling. Starting at one end, roll up tightly, jelly-roll fashion. Cut each roll into 2 to 3 slices.

A SPECIAL TOUCH!

For an interesting and unusual presentation . . . Sesame Crusted Tea Sandwiches: Fill two slices of bread (with crusts trimmed off) with your choice of filling; cut into triangles. Repeat until you have several triangles. Dip one side of each sandwich triangle in melted butter (melt butter in a glass pie plate or other low plate using the microwave) and then into a flat bowl filled with toasted sesame seeds. (Sesame seeds may be purchased toasted or simply add untoasted seeds to a small skillet set on low and stir until they turn a golden brown. Sesame seeds are a natural source of oil, so you do not need to add more to the skillet. Watch closely to avoid burning.) Arrange the sandwiches (on a rectangular platter) in a row to form a horizontal pyramid with sesame seed edges exposed.

Meats/Eggs during the Victorian era . . .

A variety of seafood, beef, pork and wild game added diversity to the Victorian table. In 1885, *Godey's Lady's Book* discussed several methods for the preparation of the Christmas turkey, including boiled turkey with oyster sauce; a galantine of turkey (boned and rolled with pounded veal and chopped tongue, then boiled and served with a jelly glaze) or roasted turkey. [53]

Omelet `a la Vanderbilt

"Take two fine, sound, green peppers, plunge them into hot fat for half a minute then take them up and lay them on a dry cloth; skin them neatly remove all the seeds from the insides, and when emptied cut them into small slices. Put these into a saucepan on the hot stove with two medium-sized fresh, sound, sliced tomatoes, twelve nicely shelled shrimps, and three tablespoonfuls of Madeira wine sauce; then season with half a pinch of salt and a third of a pinch of pepper; cook slowly for fifteen minutes. Break twelve fresh eggs into a bowl, season them with half a pinch of salt and a third of a pinch of pepper, and beat well for five minutes. Put two ounces of good butter in a frying-pan, place it on the hot stove, and when the butter is melted drop in the eggs, and with a spoon or fork mix briskly for two minutes. Fold the opposite side up with a skimmer, lift up the thick part of the prepared sauce, and place it in the centre of the omelet, fold the other side either with a knife or fork, and let it cook for two minutes longer, then turn on a hot dish; pour the rest of the sauce in the saucepan around the omelet, and send to the table very hot. *The Table*, (Eggs) by Delmonico's Chef, Alessandro Filippini, 1889."[54]

Kirby House Entrees

Country Fried Steak

directions are for preparation of 1 steak

This is one of the most frequently ordered entrees at The Kirby House. It is offered on both the lunch and dinner menu.

Eye of the Round beef--The Kirby House allows a 4 -ounce serving for lunch; 6 -ounces for dinner (the restaurant cuts and tenderizes its own beef; tenderized beef purchased at the meat case could also be used)
Seasoned flour, p. 196, for dredging
Buttermilk for dipping
Oil for deep-fat frying (see tips below)

Cooking with Oil

The most important factor influencing the use of oil as a heat medium is the temperature at which it produces smoke--this is called the smoking point.When cooking with any oil, avoid heating it to this smoking point. An oil's smoking point is determined by its fatty-acid content. Oils, such as sunflower, peanut, and canola oil, have high smoking points and are thus suitable for deep fat frying at high heat. These oils (due to the fact they are monounsaturated) are also the most stable and thus hold up best (without as much deterioration) in high heat.

Place the individual portion of steak between two pieces of wax paper and position on a cutting board. Use a meat mallet to pound the beef until it is about 1/4" thick.
To prepare for the dredging of the steak, place enough seasoned flour for dipping in a shallow bowl (large enough in diameter to accommodate the size of steak) and place some buttermilk in another similar size bowl. Dip the tenderized steak lightly into the seasoned flour, turning to coat both sides. Next, dip steak into buttermilk and then again into the flour ... this time pressing flour mixture into the meat using the palm of your hand; turn to coat both sides. Repeat procedure again--dipping steak in buttermilk and ending with flour making sure that the steak is thoroughly coated with the flour mixture.
Meanwhile, fill a deep skillet or deep fat fryer with enough oil to completely cover the steak; heat to approximately 350°. Immerse the prepared steak into the oil and cook until the coating is crisp and golden brown and meat is cooked through.

Frying Safety

Select a heavy-duty skillet or pan for deep-fat frying; it should also have sides high enough to contain the bubbling oil. Hot fat or oil that comes in contact with a heating element can cause a fire. In case of a grease or oil fire, smother it with the lid of the frying pan. Never throw water on it as this can cause the fire to spread. Be sure to dry food thoroughly (or if dipping in liquid and flour, make sure the last dipping is in flour and that the food is completely coated with that flour mixture) before immersing it in hot oil. Water will cause the liquid to splatter and could burn the person who is frying.

Dredge: To thoroughly coat a food with flour or other fine substance.

Meatloaf *Yield: one 9 x 5 x 3 -inch loaf pan; about 8 slices*

1 1/2 pounds lean ground beef
3 slices white bread, cut into small cubes
1/2 cup milk
1/2 cup tomato sauce (4 -ounces)
1 large egg
1/4 cup finely minced onion
1 1/4 teaspoons salt
1/4 teaspoon pepper
1 tablespoon Worcestershire sauce

Preheat oven to 350°. Grease a standard loaf pan.
Lightly combine all ingredients in a large mixing bowl (see tips below). Shape ground beef mixture in prepared loaf pan. Bake at 350° for 1 1/2 hours or until meat thermometer registers 160°.
Meanwhile, prepare meatloaf sauce.
When cooking time (for meat loaf) is up, drain grease; let meat loaf stand for 5 to 10 minutes, turn out of pan, and slice. Top with sauce when plated.

Meatloaf Sauce
1/2 cup catsup
1 tablespoon minced onion
1 tablespoon minced green pepper
2 1/2 tablespoons brown sugar (packed)

Mix all sauce ingredients in a small saucepan and simmer over low heat until vegetables are tender, about 10 to 15 minutes.

Meatloaf Tips:

- ❖Mix ingredients lightly but thoroughly. Over mixing or over working the mixture can result in a heavy and tough product. Meatloaf can be mixed lightly in a mixer, with the tines of a fork or by hand. Of course, be sure to thoroughly wash and sanitize anything that comes in contact with raw meat to avoid cross-contamination.
- ❖For a meatloaf with a crustier surface, hand-shape the meat mixture into a loaf shape and bake in a shallow baking pan. For a more traditional loaf, press meat mixture into a loaf pan.
- ❖Check meatloaf for doneness with a meat thermometer or instant-read thermometer. Meat loaves made with ground beef should be cooked to medium doneness (160°). A meatloaf containing onions, celery and bell peppers may still be slightly pink in the center even at medium doneness. This pink color is due to the natural nitrate content of these ingredients.
- ❖For easier slicing, let meatloaf stand 5 to 10 minutes after removing from pan.
- ❖Bread crumbs give meatloaf its distinctive texture and prevent it from becoming too dense.

"Melt In Your Mouth" Roast & Brown Gravy *allow about 4 to 5 ounces of roast per person. This recipe is a "twist" on the traditional pot roast and is often offered as the Friday "special". It is indicative of the delicious home-style cooking at The Kirby House.*

Eye of the Round Pot Roast
Beef Broth, enough to cover roast (can use concentrated such as Minor's® Beef Base--with water added as needed)
Chopped onion (yellow or white)--about 1/4 onion for every pound of meat
Garlic powder, salt, pepper to taste

Clean and trim excess fat from the roast; place in roaster. Completely cover roast with beef bouillon, add chopped onions and season with garlic powder, salt and pepper. Cover roaster with a lid or aluminum foil and bake at 350° for several hours or until it is "melt in your mouth" tender. Reserve broth & fat drippings for gravy.
When ready to serve, remember--slicing meat against the grain makes it more tender.

General guide for baking:
4 to 5 pound roast: 4 to 5 hours
10 to 12 pound roast : 7 to 8 hours

Brown Gravy with a cornstarch base *Yield: about 2 cups; allow about 1/3 cup per person*

1/4 cup reserved broth & fat drippings
about 2 cups additional beef broth (can use concentrated such as Minor's® Beef Base with water added as needed)
2 tablespoons cornstarch
1/4 cup cold water
Salt and pepper to taste

Measure reserved broth and fat drippings into roasting pan. Stir in additional liquid. Cook over medium heat, stirring to deglaze or to loosen browned particles. Remove from heat. Mix cornstarch and water and slowly stir into roasting pan. Add seasonings. Stirring constantly, bring to a boil over medium heat and boil about 2 minutes or until it achieves desired thickness.

Cornstarch as a Thickener
Cornstarch makes gravy velvety smooth with no floury taste or whitish color. It can be used to thicken gravies, sauces, soups and stews. To use cornstarch when a recipe calls for flour, substitute half as much cornstarch for the flour (1 tablespoon cornstarch = 2 tablespoons flour).

Mushroom-Stuffed Beef Tenderloin

Yield: 6 to 8 servings

3 bacon strips
1 cup chopped fresh mushrooms
2 tablespoons chopped onion
1 garlic clove, minced
3/4 cup dry bread crumbs, divided
2 tablespoons minced fresh parsley
1 beef tenderloin (about 2 pounds), trimmed
1 tablespoon butter
1 tablespoon grated Parmesan cheese

In a skillet, cook bacon until crisp. Remove bacon; crumble and set aside. Drain, reserving 1 tablespoon drippings. In the drippings, sauté the mushrooms, onion and garlic until tender. Remove from the heat; stir in 1/2 cup of bread crumbs, parsley and bacon. Cut a slit lengthwise three-quarters of the way through the tenderloin. Carefully place mushroom stuffing in the pocket and tie with butcher's string or close with toothpicks.

Combine butter and Parmesan cheese; spread over top and sides of meat. Press the remaining bread crumbs onto the surface of the meat and place on a rack in a shallow roasting pan. Bake, uncovered, at 350° for 15 minutes. Cover and bake for 1 hour or until meat reaches desired doneness (Medium rare--145°; Medium--160°; Well-done--170°). Let stand for 10 minutes and remove string or toothpicks before slicing.

When to preheat . . .
Preheating gives the oven time to reach the specified temperature so the food begins to cook right away. Normally, but not always, a recipe will tell you if preheating is needed. The general rule is that preheating is necessary for baked products that have been leavened (addition of baking powder, baking soda, yeast, etc.) and will rise when in the oven. However, meats, vegetables, etc. can also be added to a preheated oven. Note: preheating an oven longer than 10 minutes is usually a waste of energy.

Salisbury Steak *Yield: serves 4*

1 pound lean ground beef
1 large egg
2 tablespoons all-purpose flour
1/4 teaspoon Tex Joy Steak Seasoning
Salt and pepper to taste

In a mixing bowl, combine beef, egg, flour and seasonings. Lightly shape beef mixture into four 1" thick patties. Grill (or fry) each side approximately 5 to 6 minutes or cook hamburgers to an internal temperature of at least 160° or until the center is no longer pink and the juices are clear. Remove meat patties; reserve fat drippings for gravy. Tent meat with foil to keep warm while preparing gravy.

Gravy
1 - 2 tablespoons fat drippings from grilled meat
2 tablespoons all-purpose flour
1 - 1 1/2 cups beef broth (can be prepared from a concentrate such as Minor's Beef Base)
1/2 - 3/4 cup sliced mushrooms
Salt and pepper to taste

Measure reserved fat drippings into a skillet and slowly whisk in the flour. Cook over medium heat until flour is golden brown and has a nut-like flavor (watch carefully to avoid burning this mixture). Slowly whisk in the beef broth and add the sliced mushrooms. Continue to simmer until mushrooms are tender; add salt and pepper as needed. Add patties to gravy and serve immediately or transfer patties and gravy to a covered baking dish and place in a 275° to 300° oven until ready to serve (this mixture could be in oven about 1 to 2 hours prior to serving).

Safety Tips for Ground Beef

- Make ground beef and other perishables your final purchase when shopping. After leaving the store, get perishables home quickly and refrigerate or freeze themimmediately. If the trip home is more than an hour, pack them in an ice chest.
- When handling raw ground beef, don't let raw juices cross-contaminate foods that won't be cooked. Wash your hands with soap and hot water before and after handling ground beef to make sure you don't spread bacteria from one surface to another.
- Use soap and hot water to wash utensils and surfaces which have come into contact with the raw meat. When taking hamburgers off the grill, don't put the cooked hamburgers on the same platter which held the raw patties.
- Bacteria multiply rapidly in the "danger zone," between 40° and 140°. To keep bacterial levels low, store ground beef at 40° and use or freeze it within two days.
- Ground beef kept frozen at 0° will maintain its quality up to four months.
- Defrost ground meats correctly. Never leave ground beef, or any perishable food, out on the counter for more than two hours. Thaw it in the refrigerator.
- To be sure bacteria are destroyed, cook hamburgers to 160° or until the center is no longer pink and the juices are clear.

Stuffed Filet Mignon with Green Peppercorn Butter *Yield: 2 servings*

This original recipe, created by Kirby House chef Chris LaPorte, was featured on the food page of The Salina Journal, February 14, 2001. Chef Chris enjoys experimenting with seasonings to create new flavors.

Stuffing

1/2 cup green onions, diced
1/2 cup fresh mushrooms, diced
Salt and pepper
2 tablespoons extra virgin olive oil

2 beef filets, 6 to 8 -ounces

In a small skillet, over high heat, sauté onions and mushrooms, seasoned with salt and pepper, in olive oil for about three minutes. To prepare and assemble: make a horizontal cut with a sharp knife on one side of each steak (filet) to create a pocket. Stuff each pocket with onions and mushrooms. Grill steaks to desired degree of doneness (refer to grilling guide below. Top each steak with a pat of Green Peppercorn Butter.

Green Peppercorn Butter *Yield: about 1 cup*

1/2 cup unsalted butter (1 stick), softened
1/4 cup chopped fresh parsley leaves
1 tablespoon water-packed green peppercorns, drained
1 teaspoon fresh lemon juice
1/2 teaspoon Dijon mustard, or to taste
Worcestershire sauce, to taste

In a mixing bowl, blend all ingredients until well combined.

Stuffed Peppercorn Mushroom Fillet

directions are for preparation of 1 steak

2 medium mushrooms, washed and chopped
1 teaspoon black peppercorns, coarsely ground
1 - 2 tablespoons butter
1 - 8 -ounce Fillet Mignon (Fillet refers to a boneless piece of meat or fish. Filet is the French spelling.)
1 strip bacon

In a small skillet over medium heat, lightly sauté the mushrooms and black pepper. Make a pocket in the fillet by slicing with a very sharp knife; stuff pocket with the sautéed mushroom mixture. Wrap steak with bacon and grill to desired doneness (see grilling guide that follows).

Guide for Grilling Beef Fillets: To achieve the desired degree of doneness, insert an instant-read thermometer into the thickest part of the meat and follow these guidelines: rare--120° to 125°; medium-rare--130° to 135°; medium-- 140° to 145°. Please note that the temperature will continue to rise 5° after being removed from the grill. If steak to be sliced, tent it in foil and allow it to stand about 5 to 10 minutes before slicing.

Swiss Steak *Yield: about 5 to 5 1/2 cups sauce. Prepare as many steaks as desired; refrigerate or freeze unused sauce for later use.*

Swiss Steak Sauce

12 -ounce can tomato sauce
14 1/2 -ounce can diced tomatoes, undrained
1/2 cup chopped yellow onions
1/2 cup chopped celery
1/2 cup chopped green pepper
2 teaspoons Worcestershire sauce
1/4 to 1/2 teaspoon black pepper
Dash garlic powder (about 1/8 teaspoon or fill 1/4 teaspoon about half full)

Mix all ingredients together and store in refrigerator.

Swiss Steak

Use beef round, sliced, 3/4" thick--allow 5 -ounces per person
All-purpose flour seasoned with salt and pepper (allow about 1 teaspoon salt & pepper per 1/2 cup of flour)
Shortening, about 1 tablespoon per steak

Purchase tenderized beef round or pound with meat mallet to tenderize.
Mix flour, salt, and pepper in a low, flat dish or pan. Dredge (or coat on both sides) steaks with seasoned flour.
Heat shortening in skillet and brown meat (on both sides) in hot shortening--until a crisp crust forms. Place browned steaks in a baking pan and ladle Swiss Steak Sauce liberally over the top. Cover tightly with aluminum foil and bake at 350° for 2 to 2 1/2 hours or until meat is fork tender.

Clam Sauce *Yield: about 2 1/4 cups*

1/4 cup butter
1/2 to 3/4 cup finely minced onions
1 large clove garlic, finely minced
1 1/2 to 2 tablespoons all-purpose flour
2 6.5 -ounce cans minced clams, with liquid
3/4 teaspoon salt
3/4 teaspoon dried basil
Dash black pepper (1/8 teaspoon or half of 1/4 teaspoon)

freshly chopped parsley
<u>Pasta</u>--see pasta tips on p. 97

Melt butter in a skillet and sauté the onions and garlic; slowly whisk in flour to create a smooth *roux. Add undrained clams and remaining seasonings to the skillet and heat to boiling; reduce heat and simmer 5 minutes. Serve over cooked and drained pasta. Garnish with freshly chopped parsley.
*Roux--French term for a flour-fat "paste."

Crab Tostadas *Yield: 6 servings*

Guests ordering this entree receive 4 pie-shaped tortilla wedges, each topped with a scoop of crab salad, that are nestled on a lettuce leaf. Fresh fruit (such as cantaloupe and pineapple chunks plus red grapes) add to the attractiveness and taste of this meal.

<u>Crab Salad</u>
10 -ounce package imitation crab meat, flake style (fully cooked)
3/4 cup mayonnaise
1 1/2 tablespoons sweet pickle relish
1/2 cup finely minced celery
1/4 teaspoon onion salt
1/8 teaspoon Tex Joy® Steak Seasoning
Optional: 1 1/2 tablespoon finely minced green olives

6 10" tortillas, fried and cut into 4 pie-shaped wedges

On a cutting surface, finely mince the crab meat and place in a mixing bowl; add mayonnaise, pickle relish, minced celery, onion salt and Tex Joy® and mix until all ingredients are combined. Spoon a heaping scoop of Crab Salad on each tortilla wedge. Serve on lettuce leaves with fresh fruit as an accompaniment.

A Pinch or a Dash:
Pinch = 1/16 of a teaspoon
Dash = scant 1/8 of a teaspoon

Grilled Smokehouse Salmon with Pineapple-Jack Marinade *Instructions for 2 or 10 steaks*

<u>Salmon steaks</u>

Remove all skin from salmon steaks; marinate (see recipe that follows) at least 2 hours.
Prepare grill surface by spraying with non-stick pan coating.
Add steaks to a hot grill--a prepared outdoor charcoal or gas grill OR a grill pan heated to medium-high on the indoor range top. As a general guideline, allow a total cooking time of 8 to 9 minutes per inch of steak thickness; turn once carefully lifting with a spatula to avoid tearing the flesh. Fish is supposed to reach an internal temperature of 145° so use a meat or instant-read thermometer to double-check doneness. Fish should also flake when poked with a fork.

<u>Pineapple-Jack Marinade for Grilled Smokehouse Salmon</u>

For 2 salmon steaks	For 10 salmon steaks
1/4 cup pineapple juice	1 1/2 cups pineapple juice
2 tablespoons Jack Daniels Barbecue Sauce (see p. 182)	2/3 cup Jack Daniels Barbecue Sauce (see p. 182)
2 tablespoons soy sauce	2/3 cup soy sauce
2 tablespoons brown sugar (packed)	2/3 cup brown sugar (packed)
1 teaspoon bourbon whiskey	2 tablespoons bourbon whiskey
1/4 teaspoon black pepper	1 1/2 teaspoons black pepper
Dash garlic powder (1/8 teaspoon or half of 1/4 teaspoon)	3/4 teaspoon garlic powder

Combine above ingredients in a stainless steel, glass or food-grade plastic bowl, whisking to thoroughly mix.

Shrimp Scampi *Yield: 4 servings*

The Kirby House serves the Shrimp Scampi with rice pilaf but pasta would also be a nice accompaniment.

3/4 cup (1 1/2 sticks) butter
1 pound uncooked large shrimp, peeled, deveined
4 large garlic cloves, minced
2 tablespoons white wine (Chablis)
1 teaspoon powdered or finely crushed rosemary

Preheat oven to 400°. Put butter in 13 x 9" baking dish and place in oven until butter melts. Add shrimp, garlic, wine and rosemary to butter and stir to blend. Return dish to oven and bake shrimp about 5 minutes or until shrimp are just cooked through (shrimp will turn a pink color). Or, this may all be done in the skillet on top of the stove.

Judging Shrimp Size

To judge the size of your shrimp, look for a number on the package that indicates the amount of shrimp per pound. For instance, large shrimp will be labeled 21/30 meaning that it takes twenty-one to thirty shrimp to make a pound.

Deveining Shrimp

The vein of a shrimp is actually it's intestinal tract. This must be removed as it can create a bitter taste. To devein--make a shallow cut along the back of a peeled shrimp and pull out the vein with the tip of a knife.

Cranberry Glazed Pork Loin *Yield: 12 serving*

3 pounds pork loin
Cranberry Glaze, p. 182, made with whole berry jellied cranberry sauce

Place pork loin in a shallow baking pan.
Prepare Cranberry Glaze as instructed on p. 182, except remove 1/4 cup of the glaze before it is thickened. Spoon that 1/4 cup glaze over roast. Place roast in a 375° oven and bake for 1 1/2 hours or until a meat thermometer registers at least 160°. Remove roast from oven and allow to stand 15 minutes before slicing. Heat remaining glaze until thickened (as instructed in recipe) and serve with roast.

Frosted Sausage Ring *Yield: serves 12 to 15*
A recipe from "Beyond Parsley", by the Junior League of Kansas City, Missouri. The Kirby House has made a few slight adjustments and used it for brunch buffets.

2 pounds pork sausage (select a quality brand)
1 1/2 cups cracker crumbs (*"Beyond Parsley"* suggests Ritz; the Kirby House uses wheat and onion flavored crackers)
2 large eggs
1 8 -ounce package cream cheese, room temperature

Preheat oven to 325°.
Place sausage, crumbs and eggs in a mixing bowl. With an electric mixer, combine ingredients just until thoroughly mixed. Press into a tube cake pan, ring mold or springform pan with a tube inset; pack meat mixture tightly. Bake 40 to 50 minutes, occasionally draining off grease. Remove from oven; drain again and cover with a rimmed baking sheet; carefully flip sausage ring so that it now rests on the baking sheet. Turn oven to 350° and return sausage ring (on the baking sheet) to the oven and bake until nicely browned and slightly crisp on outside (about 15 minutes). Remove from oven, let cool about 10 minutes and then frost the top of the sausage with cream cheese that has been whipped (using an electric mixer). Surround ring with fresh herbs (fresh sage is the Kirby House preference but parsley or cilantro is also nice) and serve warm.

Conventional versus Convection Oven

Most residential ovens heat conventionally--the heating unit is at the bottom; hot air flows up and circulates around the food in the oven. Commercial ovens heat by convection--adding a fan that circulates heat thus allowing food to cook faster.

Herb Stuffed Pork Loin with Applesauce *Yield: 16 servings*

Stuffed Pork and Gravy

3 tablespoon butter, room temperature
1 1/4 cups chopped onion
2 1/2 cups fresh white bread crumbs
9 tablespoons mixed chopped fresh herbs (such as parsley, thyme, chives, rosemary), divided
Salt and pepper, to taste
1 4 -pound center-cut boneless pork loin roast, trimmed
Butcher's twine to tie the pork loin
2 tablespoons butter
2 tablespoons all-purpose flour
5 1/4 cups chicken broth (can be prepared from a concentrate such as Minor's® Chicken Base or use three 14.5 -ounce cans)
Salt and pepper, to taste

Preheat oven to 375°.

Applesauce

1 1/2 pounds all purpose apples (such as McIntosh), peeled, cored, cut into 2" pieces
1/3 cup granulated sugar
2 tablespoons water

Combine all ingredients in heavy large saucepan. Cover; cook over medium-low heat until apples begin to break down, stirring often, about 20 minutes. Coarsely mash apples in saucepan to chunky sauce; transfer to medium bowl. Can be made 2 days ahead. Cover and chill. The secret to this fresh-tasting applesauce is to cook the apples until tender in a very small amount of water.

Melt 3 tablespoons butter in heavy large skillet over medium heat. Add onion and sauté until tender and very lightly brown, about 5 minutes. Mix in bread crumbs and 6 tablespoons fresh herbs. Season stuffing to taste with salt and pepper. Set aside.

Butterfly pork loin by cutting horizontally almost in half, leaving 1" of 1 long side intact. Line work surface with large piece of plastic wrap. Arrange butterflied pork on plastic and open like a book. Top with another large sheet of plastic. Using mallet or rolling pin, pound pork until about 1/2" thick, 10" wide and 13 to 14" long. Discard top plastic sheet. Spread bread crumb stuffing evenly over surface of the pork. Starting at 1 long side and using bottom plastic sheet as aid, tightly roll up pork. Discard plastic sheet. Tie pork at 2" intervals to hold log shape. Place rack in large roasting pan. Place stuffed pork on rack and roast until thermometer inserted into thickest part registers 160°, about 1 hour and 15 minutes. Transfer pork to platter; tent with foil to keep warm while preparing gravy. (Do not clean roasting pan.)

Mix 2 tablespoons butter and flour in small bowl until smooth. Set roasting pan over medium-high heat. Gradually whisk in 3 cups chicken broth and bring mixture to boil, scraping up any browned bits. Whisk in butter-flour mixture; add remaining 3 tablespoons fresh herbs and chicken broth. Boil gravy until thickened to sauce consistency, whisking constantly, about 4 minutes. Season gravy to taste with salt and pepper.

Cut pork crosswise into about 1/2" thick slices. Place pork slices on plates and top with gravy. Spoon warmed or cold applesauce next to pork.

Oven Baked Bacon
The Kirby House uses this method to prepare bacon in quantity. Try this at home when preparing a brunch or cooking for a crowd. For an extra special treat, sprinkle bacon lightly with brown sugar before baking.

Strips of bacon
Preheat oven to 350°.
For ease in clean up, line jelly-roll type pan, with parchment paper. If strips are hard to separate, place needed bacon section on the pan; as it heats, slide the strips apart. Bake until crisp, 10 to 15 minutes. No turning is necessary. Drain on paper toweling.

Pistachio Crusted Pork Loin *Yield: about 12 servings*
A delicious explosion of flavor is created in this interesting combination of ingredients.

1/4 cup dried, chopped apricots
1/4 cup dried cranberries
Hot water to cover sweetened dried fruit
About 1/2 cup coarsely chopped pistachios
About 1/2 teaspoon powdered rosemary
About 1 - 1 1/2 tablespoons olive oil
3 pound pork loin, trimmed of excess fat
Butcher's twine to tie the pork loin
About 1/4 - 1/3 cup finely chopped pistachios
About 1 teaspoon ground cumin (add more or less depending on preference)

Sauce
1/2 cup chicken stock
1 tablespoon honey
1 tablespoon fresh lemon juice
Salt and pepper
2 tablespoons minced chives

Bring stock, honey, and lemon juice to a boil; simmer for about 8 to 10 minutes. Season to taste with salt and pepper and sprinkle finished sauce with the minced chives.

Heat oven to 325°
In a small bowl, combine dried apricots and cranberries and barely cover with hot water. Let stand about 10 to 15 minutes or until they have plumped, absorbing most of the water. Drain excess liquid and add the coarsely chopped pistachios to the fruit; mix in the rosemary and moisten with olive oil.
Make a pocket in the pork loin by slicing with a very sharp knife; stuff with the fruit and pistachio mixture. Use butcher's twine to tie the pork loin--tie in 3 to 5 places or as needed to keep the filling in place.
Mix finely chopped pistachios with cumin and spread on the surface of a cutting board. Roll tied pork loin across the board, patting to thoroughly coat and encrust the meat. Place in a roasting pan and bake at 325° about 1 to 1 1/2 hours or until loin crust is nicely browned and an internal temperature of at least 160° is achieved. Let loin set 10 minutes before slicing; cut crosswise into about 1/2" thick slices and drizzle with sauce.

Pork Diane *Yield: 4 servings*

1 pound pork tenderloin, trimmed of excess fat
2 tablespoons Lemon Pepper or more as needed (commercial blend of lemon zest & black pepper)
About 1/4 cup butter

Heat oven to 350°.
Place the pork tenderloin in a low, flat pan, rub liberally with Lemon Pepper on all sides. In large skillet, melt butter and brown the tenderloin on all sides. Transfer pork loin to a roasting pan; reserve pan drippings for the sauce. Place pork in a 350° oven; bake approximately 30 to 45 minutes or until tender and cooked through (should reach an internal temperature of at least 160°). Cut loin crosswise into about 1/2" thick slices; drizzle meat slices with sauce.

Sauce
Reserved pan drippings
2 tablespoons lemon juice
1 tablespoon Worcestershire sauce
1 teaspoon Dijon mustard

Add lemon juice, Worcestershire sauce and mustard to the pan juices, bring to a boil and simmer.

Facts about Pork

What is an average serving?
According to the National Pork Producers Association, the "average" serving size for pork is 3 ounces of cooked meat. Start with 4 ounces of boneless, raw pork to yield 3 ounces of cooked pork.

To what temperature should I cook pork?
The U.S. Department of Agriculture (U.S.D.A.) recommends cooking pork to an internal temperature of 160° F. (medium doneness). Use a meat thermometer to judge doneness. When cooking a roast, remove from the oven when the internal temperature reaches 155° F. and allow the roast to stand for 10 minutes before slicing. The roast's internal temperature will rise about five degrees after removing from the oven. A hint of pink blush in the center is ideal for tender, juicy pork.

But, what about trichinosis?
Because of modern feeding practices, trichinosis is no longer a concern. Although trichina is virtually nonexistent in pork, if it were present, it would be killed at 137° F. That's well below the recommended end cooking temperature for pork, which is 160°.

Pork Piccata with Wine-Caper Sauce

Yield: 4 servings

1 pound pork tenderloin, trimmed of excess fat
1 1/2 tablespoons Lemon Pepper (commercial blend of lemon zest & black pepper)
3 tablespoons all-purpose flour
About 1/4 cup butter

Heat oven to 350°.

Place the pork tenderloin in a low, flat pan, rub with Lemon Pepper and dredge in flour on all sides.

In large skillet, melt butter and brown the loin on all sides. Set skillet with leftover butter aside for later use. Transfer pork tenderloin to a roasting pan and place in a 350° oven; bake approximately 30 to 45 minutes or until tender and cooked through (should reach an internal temperature of at least 160°); reserve meat drippings for the sauce. Let tenderloin stand 10 minutes before slicing. Cut tenderloin crosswise into about 1/2" thick slices. Drizzle sauce over entire tenderloin to serve family style, or serve individual slices garnished with Wine-Caper Sauce.

<u>Wine-Caper Sauce</u>

Leftover butter in skillet from browning tenderloin
1 tablespoon all-purpose flour
1/4 cup white wine (Chablis)
1/4 cup lemon juice
Drippings from roasted loin
1 - 2 tablespoons capers

Heat the leftover butter in the skillet; whisk in 1 tablespoon flour. Stir in wine, lemon juice, drippings from the loin and whisk to obtain a thin sauce. Add capers to the sauce or use as a garnish.

<u>Variation</u>: Cut pork loin into medallions (or purchase in this form). Coat each medallion with Lemon Pepper and dredge in flour. In a skillet, sauté the medallions until cooked through. Remove medallions and tent in foil while preparing sauce in the skillet. Everything is done in the skillet in this version.

Caper [KAY-per]

The flower bud of a bush native to the Mediterranean and parts of Asia. The small buds are picked, sun-dried and then pickled in a vinegar brine. Capers range in size from the petite nonpareil variety from southern France (considered the finest), to those from Italy, which can be as large as the tip of your little finger. There are also the Spanish-imported stemmed caperberries that are about the size of a cocktail olive. Capers are generally packed in brine but can also be found salted and sold in bulk. Capers should be rinsed before using to remove excess salt. The pungent flavor of capers lends piquancy to many sauces and condiments; they're also used as a garnish for meat and vegetable dishes.

Smoked Pork Chops with Apple Rum Sauce *directions are for preparation of 1 chop*

1 smoked pork chop

Grill smoked pork chop to desired doneness (should reach an internal temperature of at least 160°).

Apple Rum Sauce
1 tablespoon butter
1 medium apple, cored & thinly sliced
1 tablespoon brown sugar
1 tablespoon Captain Morgan Original Spiced Rum®

In a skillet, melt butter at medium temperature. Add apple slices and sauté until tender. Add brown sugar and rum; cook briefly to form a thickened sauce. Arrange apple slices on pork chop and drizzle with sauce.

What exactly is a smoked pork chop and how does the smoking affect the cooking process ? In earlier times, smoked meats were thought to be either fully or, at least partially cooked. That may or may not be the case when dealing with smoked pork chops purchased today. According to Elizabeth Boyle, K-State Research & Extension, "USDA regulations for meat require that any product that is NOT considered a ready-to-eat meat must carry a 'safe handling label.' If a consumer purchases a smoked pork chop and the package carries a safe handling label, it is expected that the product be cooked prior to consumption." Her recommendation for cooking, therefore varies according to the type of product that might be purchased. She suggests, "If the smoked pork chop is not fully cooked, thereby being prepared for the 'first' time, then cooking to a minimum of 160°F. is recommended. If the product is fully cooked and is only going to be reheated for serving, the temperature should be 165°F." To be on the safe side, cook smoked pork chops to 165°F.

Note: The Food Code (which has been adopted by Kansas) requires that restaurants reheat foods to 165°F. internal temperature prior to serving.

Chicken Breasts in Basil Cream *Yield: 4 servings*

1/4 cup milk
1/4 cup dry bread crumbs
4 chicken breast halves, skinned and boned (about 1 pound)
3 tablespoons butter

Place milk and bread crumbs in separate shallow bowls. Dip chicken in milk, then coat with crumbs. In a skillet over medium-high heat, cook chicken in butter on both sides until juices run clear, about 10 minutes. Remove to a baking dish; cover with foil and place in 350° oven while preparing sauce. Breasts should bake until an internal temperature of 170° is reached.

Sauce

1/2 cup chicken broth
1 cup whipping cream
1 jar (4 -ounces) sliced pimientos, drained
1/2 cup grated Parmesan cheese
1/4 cup minced fresh basil (about 1 tablespoon dried, or to taste)
1/8 teaspoon pepper

Add broth to the skillet used to cook the chicken. Bring to a boil over medium heat; stir to loosen browned bits from pan. Stir in cream and pimientos; boil and stir for 1 minute. Reduce heat. Add Parmesan cheese, basil and pepper; cook and stir until heated through. Pour over the chicken.

Basil—Called the "royal herb" by ancient Greeks, this annual is a member of the mint family. Fresh basil has a pungent flavor that some describe as a cross between licorice and cloves. It's a key herb in Mediterranean and Italian cooking, and is becoming more and more popular in American cuisine. Most varieties of basil have green leaves. Basil is a summer herb but can be grown successfully inside during the winter in a sunny window. It's plentiful during summer months, and available year-round in many markets. Choose evenly colored leaves with no sign of wilting. Refrigerate basil, wrapped in barely damp paper towels and then in a plastic bag, for up to 4 days. Or store a bunch of basil, stems down, in a glass of water with a plastic bag over the leaves. Refrigerate in this manner for up to a week, changing the water every 2 days. To preserve fresh basil, wash and dry the leaves and place layers of leaves, then coarse salt, in a container that can be tightly sealed. Or, finely chop the cleaned basil and combine it with a small amount of olive oil. Freeze in tiny portions to flavor sauces, salad dressings, etc. Dried basil, though it bears little resemblance in either flavor or aroma to the fresh herb, can be purchased in the spice section of most supermarkets. Store dried basil airtight in a cool, dark place.and made it their own.

Chicken Kiev *Yield: 4 servings*

This entree can be made the day ahead and baked at the last minute.

4 chicken breast halves, skinned and boned (about 1 pound)
1/2 teaspoon garlic powder
1 tablespoon chopped chives or parsley (or a combination of both)
4 tablespoons grated Mozzarella cheese
2 tablespoons butter, cut into small chunks
Toothpicks

1 large egg, beaten with 1 tablespoon water
1 tablespoon all-purpose flour
1/2 - 1 cup bread crumbs
1/4 cup Parmesan cheese, finely grated

1/4 to 1 cup butter

Place each chicken breast between two pieces of waxed paper or plastic wrap (or try a food-grade plastic bag that has been cut open along the seams and folded in half). With a flat meat mallet or heavy plate, pound chicken to 1/8" thickness, working from the center outward.

Measure out the garlic powder, chives or parsley, Mozzarella cheese and butter onto a sheet of waxed paper; place 1/4 of each item down the center of each chicken breast. Roll up the chicken jelly-roll style, enclosing the contents; press ends to seal, and secure with toothpicks.

In a shallow dish, combine egg and water. In another shallow dish, combine flour, bread crumbs and Parmesan cheese. Roll prepared chicken in egg and then coat by rolling in bread crumb mixture; place in a shallow baking dish. They may be refrigerated at this point until ready to bake; these may be prepared a day in advance or even frozen for later use (thaw before proceeding with the baking).

When ready to bake, melt the butter and pour over chicken breasts.

Bake in 350° oven for 20 minutes and then increase to 450° for 10 to 15 minutes making sure an internal temperature of 170° is reached. Cover with foil if the breasts begin to get too brown.

Grilled Barbecued Chicken *directions are for preparation of 1 chop*

1 chicken breast, skinned and boned
Jack Daniels Barbecue Sauce, p. 182

Butterfly chicken breast by cutting horizontally through the center of the breast so that it will open like a book. Prepare grill surface by spraying with non-stick pan coating. Add chicken breast to a hot grill--a prepared outdoor charcoal or gas grill OR a grill pan heated to medium-high on the indoor range top. Allow about 4 to 6 minutes grilling time per side; brush both sides with barbecue sauce about halfway through the cooking. Cook until golden brown and an internal temperature of 170° is reached, turning at least once during the cooking time.

Grilled Southwestern Chicken *Yield: 4 servings*

4 chicken breasts, skinned and boned

Add the chicken breasts to the marinade; marinate for 4 to 6 hours in the refrigerator. (For more information on marinating, see p. 186.)

Prepare grill surface by spraying with non-stick pan coating. Add chicken breast to a hot grill--a prepared outdoor charcoal or gas grill OR a grill pan heated to medium-high on the indoor range top. Grill breasts for about 4 to 6 minutes per side or until an internal temperature of 170° is reached.

<u>Southwestern Chicken Marinade</u>
1/3 cup soy sauce
1/3 cup olive oil
1/3 cup lime juice
2 garlic cloves, minced and mashed

Combine ingredients in a mixing bowl and whisk to mix.

Lemon Tarragon Chicken *Yield: 6 servings*

6 chicken breasts, skinned and boned
Water to cover chicken breasts
About 3 tablespoons honey
About 1 teaspoon pepper

Place chicken breasts in a shallow pan and cover with water. Mix in honey and pepper (amounts may be adjusted to personal taste). Bake at 350° for 25 to 30 minutes or until tender and cooked through (170°). Drain and spoon Lemon Tarragon Sauce over the baked chicken breast.

<u>Lemon Tarragon Sauce</u> *Yield: about 3 cups*

1/4 cup butter
1 1/3 cup hot water
1 tablespoon + 1 teaspoon lemon juice
Pinch salt (to taste)
2/3 cup white wine
1/2 teaspoon dried tarragon
2 tablespoons + 2 teaspoons cornstarch
2 egg yolks (use large eggs)
1/2 cup heavy whipping cream

1/3 cup mayonnaise

Mix together the butter, hot water, lemon juice, salt, white wine and tarragon in a medium saucepan and bring to boil.
In a mixing bowl, whisk cornstarch with cold egg yolks and then add whipping cream. Slowly drizzle up to half of the hot wine mixture into egg yolks whisking constantly; then, blend the tempered egg mixture into the hot ingredients in saucepan. Stir constantly until thickened.
Remove from heat and add the mayonnaise. Stir until smooth. Store any leftover sauce in refrigerator.

About Tarragon
Tarragon is an aromatic herb known for its distinctive anise-like (licorice) flavor. Tarragon is widely used in classic French cooking and complements chicken, fish and vegetable dishes. However, care should be taken when using this herb since its assertiveness can easily dominate other flavors.

Mexican Chicken with Calico Corn Salsa *Yield: 6 serving*
Serve with Black Beans and Tomato Salsa for a complete meal.

Chicken Rolls

3 whole chicken breasts, skinned, boned and halved (or 6 chicken breast halves)
1/2 - 3/4 teaspoon salt
1/2 - 3/4 teaspoon ground cumin
1/2 - 3/4 teaspoon chili powder
6 -ounces Monterey Jack cheese, thinly sliced
Toothpicks
1/4 cup all-purpose flour
2 tablespoons vegetable oil

Place 1 chicken breast half, boned side up, between 2 pieces of waxed paper & pound to 1/4" thickness. Repeat with 5 remaining breasts. In a small bowl, combine salt, cumin & chili powder; sprinkle on exposed side of chicken breasts. Place cheese on chicken and roll up; secure with toothpicks. Roll in flour that has been placed in a low, flat bowl. Heat oil in large non-stick skillet over medium heat. Cook chicken rolls 15 to 20 minutes or until browned on all sides. Remove and bake in 350° oven while preparing the rest of the ingredients. Breasts should bake until an internal temperature of 170° is reached.

Calico Corn Salsa

1 small to medium zucchini, thinly sliced
2 garlic cloves, minced
1/2 teaspoon black pepper
1/2 cup sliced green onions
1 11 -ounce can Mexicorn (Green Giant® whole kernel corn with red & green peppers), undrained

In same skillet that was used to brown chicken, combine zucchini, garlic, pepper & onions over medium heat; cook and stir 2 to 4 minutes or until vegetables are tender. Add corn, gently stir, and cook until thoroughly heated. Remove from heat.

Serve with: Black Beans and Tomato Salsa

Black Beans:

1 - 15 ounce can black beans
1 to 2 teaspoons Tex Joy® Steak Seasoning

Season beans with Tex Joy®, heat on stove top or microwave until heated through.

Tomato Salsa: (make your own or substitute 1 cup chunky-style purchased salsa)

1 cup chopped and peeled tomatoes
1 tablespoon chopped fresh cilantro
1 tablespoon vegetable oil

Combine tomatoes, chopped cilantro and oil.

Garnishes: Fresh cilantro sprigs or tomato rose (see p. 172 for instructions)

To serve: Arrange Calico Corn Salsa on plate & top with one Chicken Roll; garnish with cilantro sprigs or a tomato rose. Arrange black beans and tomato salsa on the side.

Teriyaki Chicken *directions are for preparation of 1 chicken breast*

I chicken breast, skinned and boned
Teriyaki Marinade, p. 186
Fresh Fruit Salsa with Lime Dressing, p. 191

Marinate chicken breast overnight in Teriyaki Marinade. When ready to cook, drain and discard the marinade.

Prepare grill surface by spraying with non-stick pan coating. Add chicken breast to a hot grill--a prepared outdoor charcoal or gas grill OR a grill pan heated to medium-high on the indoor range top. Allow about 4 to 6 minutes grilling time per side. Cook until golden brown and an internal temperature of 170° is reached, turning at least once during the cooking time.

Top the grilled chicken breast with the Fresh Fruit Salsa.

Testing Chicken for Doneness

The most accurate way to tell when chicken is properly cooked is to use a meat thermometer.

Cooking Temperature Guide for Chicken

Ground chicken . . . . 170° F.
Chicken breasts, wings. . . . . .170° F.
Chicken legs, thinghs, drumsticks . . . .180° F.
Whole chickens, Cornish hens. . . . . . .180° F.

To check visually to see if chicken is done, pierce it with a fork. You should be able to insert the fork with ease, and the chicken juices should run clear. When in doubt, remove the chicken to a plate and cut with a knife to be sure the flesh is opaque throughout. (information from Tyson Chicken)

Egg Strata *Yield: 9 x 13 -inch dish; about 6 servings*
A strata is a bread pudding soufflé that's not sweet. This make-ahead entree is perfect for brunch.

6 large eggs
2 cups whole milk
1 1/3 cups shredded Cheddar cheese
2/3 cup chopped ham
2 slices bread, cubed
1/2 to 3/4 teaspoon salt
1 teaspoon dry mustard

Prepare a 9 x 13" baking dish by greasing or spraying with non-stick pan coating.
Mix all ingredients together in a large mixing bowl and pour into prepared baking dish. Refrigerate overnight. Set out at room temperature for about 30 minutes before baking. Preheat oven and then bake at 350° for 1 hour. Let stand for 10 minutes before serving.

Macadamia or Almond Oven-Baked French Toast *Yield: about 6 servings if used as the only offering at a breakfast or brunch. This overnight French toast recipe is from Marla Newell Payne.*

4 large eggs, lightly beaten
1/4 cup granulated sugar
1/4 teaspoon ground nutmeg
2/3 cup orange juice
1/3 cup whole milk
1/2 teaspoon vanilla
1 16 -ounce loaf French or Italian bread, cut into 1" slices
2/3 cup butter, melted
1/2 cup macadamia nuts, chopped or
1/2 cup slivered or sliced almonds
Garnishes: powdered sugar and nutmeg

In a mixing bowl, combine eggs, sugar, nutmeg, orange juice, milk and vanilla; stir well. Fit bread slices in a single layer into a 13 x 9" baking dish. Pour egg mixture over bread slices and turn bread to make sure that slices are completely covered with the egg mixture; cover and refrigerate 8 hours or overnight. When ready to bake, pour melted butter into a jelly roll pan; place bread slices in a single layer. Bake at 400° for 10 minutes; sprinkle with nuts and bake another 10 minutes. Garnish and serve with maple syrup.

QUICHE: *A popular luncheon item at The Kirby House, it is served with a cup of soup or a choice of side orders. Grilled Coconut Walnut Bread, p. 119, is a great accompaniment to this main dish made fresh daily at The Kirby House.*

Quiche Dough Crust

Makes (12) 8 or 9 -inch quiche crusts
4 cups vegetable oil
12 cups all-purpose flour
1 cup milk
1 tablespoon salt

Makes (1) one 8 or 9 -inch quiche crust
1/4 cup + 1 tablespoon + 1 teaspoon vegetable oil
1 cup all-purpose flour
1 tablespoon + 1 teaspoon milk
Pinch of salt

Mix above ingredients together in a mixing bowl. Press into pie pan(s). If making crust in large quantities, store any remaining unused dough in refrigerator and use within a couple of days.

Seasoned Fillings

Vegetarian Quiche
Preheat oven to 375 °
2 canned artichoke hearts, quartered
3 sun-dried tomatoes, soaked in hot water, drained & cut into fourths
2 - 3 slices green pepper, chopped
1 cup shredded Swiss cheese
1 recipe Egg Filling (see below)

Place vegetables in crust-lined pie pan. Top with cheese. Pour filling over top. Bake at 375° for 45 minutes until golden on top and custard is set.

Heartland Quiche
Preheat oven to 375 °
1/4 cup ham, cubed
1/2 cup fresh broccoli, finely chopped
1 cup shredded Cheddar cheese
1 recipe Egg Filling (see below)

Place ham and broccoli in crust-lined pie pan. Top with cheese. Pour filling over top. Bake at 375° for 45 minutes until golden on top and custard is set.

Egg Filling

Yield: filling for (3) three 8 or 9" quiches
4 cups half-and-half
9 large eggs
1/4 teaspoon black pepper
1/2 teaspoon each--dry mustard, salt & ground nutmeg
2 tablespoons fresh parsley, chopped

Yield: filling for (1) one 8 or 9" quiches
1 1/3 cups half-and-half
3 large eggs
Pinch black pepper
Pinch each--dry mustard, salt & ground nutmeg
2 teaspoons fresh parsley, chopped

Scrambled Egg Casserole *Yield: one 11 x 7 -inch baking dish or about 8 servings. A crunchy topping adds a different texture to this make-ahead brunch dish. This casserole is labor intensive but worth the effort.*

1/2 cup butter + 1 tablespoon , divided
2 tablespoons all-purpose flour
1/2 teaspoon salt
1/8 teaspoon pepper
2 cups whole milk
1 cup (4 -ounces) shredded Cheddar cheese
1 cup fully cooked ham (optional)
1/2 cup sliced mushrooms
1/3 cup sliced green onions
12 large eggs, beaten
1 1/2 cups soft bread crumbs
Additional sliced green onions for garnish, if desired

* Don't be tempted to scramble the eggs in the same skillet used to sauté the ham and vegetables--the mushroom juices will discolor the eggs resulting in an unappetizing color.

Grease a 11 x 7" baking dish.
In a medium saucepan, melt 2 tablespoons butter. Add flour, salt and pepper; cook and stir until mixture begins to bubble. Gradually stir in milk; cook until thickened and bubbly, stirring constantly. Remove from the heat. Add cheese; mix well and set aside. In a small skillet, sauté ham (if using), mushrooms and onions in 2 tablespoons butter until tender; set aside. *In another large skillet, heat 2 tablespoons butter; add eggs and cook and stir until they begin to set. Then, add the sautéed ham and vegetables plus the cheese sauce; mix well. Pour into prepared baking dish. Cover and refrigerate for 2 to 3 hours or overnight. Bake, uncovered, at 350° for 30 minutes; add buttered breadcrumbs and bake an additional 10 to 20 minutes or until bubbly, hot throughout and top is golden brown. Sprinkle with sliced green onions to garnish.
Breadcrumbs: In another skillet (could reuse the one used for the ham and vegetables), melt remaining butter; add bread crumbs and toss. Sprinkle over top of casserole.

Variations--add herbs of choice to eggs as they are scrambled. A liberal sprinkling of Tex Joy® also makes a tasty addition to this dish.

Brunch
A combination of breakfast and lunch, usually eaten sometime between 11 a.m. and 3 p.m. Brunch became quite popular in England around 1900 . . . long before it reached the United States.

One egg = 1 ounce of lean meat, fish or poultry. A large egg provides 10 to 13% of the Daily Reference Value for protein and varying amounts of many other nutrients, too.

Fettucine Alfredo *Yield: 5 cups sauce; allow about 1/2 cup per main dish serving or less for side dish.*

Alfredo Sauce

1/2 cup butter (1 stick)
3/4 cup all-purpose flour
1/4 teaspoon ground nutmeg
dash black pepper
1/2 teaspoon salt
1/4 teaspoon Italian seasoning
1/4 teaspoon minced garlic
1/4 cup Parmesan cheese, grated
2 cups heavy whipping cream (1 pint)--or less
2 cups half-and-half (1 pint)--or less

Melt butter in medium saucepan over medium-high heat. Add flour and stir with wire whisk until smooth. Add seasoning (nutmeg, pepper, salt, Italian seasoning, garlic) and cheese; stir until the cheese starts to melt. Add part of the liquids slowly, stirring constantly to keep mixture smooth. Add more as needed. Sauce should be thick like gravy. Add more salt if needed.
Serve with Fettuccine pasta.

To prepare Pasta
Allow 2 -ounces dried pasta for a first-course or side dish and at least 4 -ounces dried pasta for a main-course serving. (One pound dried pasta serves about 6 to 8 as a first-course or side dish and 4 or 5 as a main course.)
Cook 1 pound of pasta in about 6 quarts of boiling salted water (about 1 tablespoon salt).
A few drops of vegetable or olive oil helps keep the pasta from sticking together.
Follow package directions for length of cooking time; fettucini generally takes about 7 to 9 minutes to achieve al dente while more fragile varieties, such as angel-hair pasta, take less time.

al dente (Italian for "firm to the tooth")
Pasta is more flavorful al dente--tender yet slightly resistant to the bite.

Reading the pasta label: Look for pasta made from "semolina" flour. Semolina is the golden-yellow, coarsely ground flour made from hard durum wheat; it creates a firm pasta that does not disintegrate when cooked in large amounts of boiling water. Most commercially produced pastas are "enriched" which simply means B vitamins (thiamine, niacin, and riboflavin) and usually iron, are added during the production process.

Pasta History--Thomas Jefferson is credited with introducing pasta to America. He became fascinated with it on a trip to Italy and brought back cases of dried macaroni and a machine for its preparation.

Pork and Sage Pasta *Yield: serves approximately 8*
This recipe was created by Barry L. West for The Kirby House.

1/4 pound butter
1 pound pork loin, trimmed and cubed (about 1/4" cubes)
1 tablespoon minced garlic
1 cup chopped onions
1 teaspoon dried sage, crushed
1 tablespoon Italian seasoning (available as a commercial blend)
1 teaspoon dried basil, crushed
1/2 teaspoon black pepper
1 teaspoon salt
1/2 cup all-purpose flour
3/4 cup whole milk or half-and-half
8 cups cooked Penne Rigate pasta, cooked according to package directions

In a large skillet, melt butter over medium-high heat. Add pork cubes and garlic, onions, sage, Italian seasoning, basil, pepper, and salt. Sauté until pork is brown and onions are tender, stirring frequently. Slowly add flour, stirring to prevent lumping. Gradually add milk (or half-and-half) while stirring, to make sauce.
Serve with cooked Penne.

Southwestern Pasta *Yield: 8 servings*
This recipe was created by Barry L. West and adapted to use on the line at The Kirby House.

3/4 cup butter
1 1/2 cups chopped onions
1 1/2 cups chopped mushrooms
1 1/2 cups *mesquite-grilled chicken, cubed
1 cup diced tomatoes
2 tablespoons chili powder
1 tablespoon powdered cumin
1 teaspoon black pepper
1 tablespoon minced garlic
4 cups tomato sauce
1 - 2 cups water
8 cups cooked Penne Rigate pasta, cooked according to package directions

In a large skillet, melt butter over medium-high heat. Sauté onions and mushrooms until tender. Add chicken, tomatoes, seasonings (chili powder, cumin, pepper, & garlic), and tomato sauce. Thin with water as needed.
Serve with cooked Penne.

*Mesquite-grilled pre-cooked chicken may be purchased in the frozen food section of many grocery stores.

Tumbleweed Pasta--*a general guide*

Angel-hair pasta--allow 4 -ounces dried pasta per person (see directions on p. 97 for cooking).
Top the cooked pasta with any of the following:

- ❖ Boiled Shrimp
- ❖ Mesquite flavored Chicken
- ❖ Sautéed Mushrooms, p. 107
- ❖ Steamed Broccoli Flowerettes
- ❖ Alfredo Sauce, p. 97
- ❖ Marinara Sauce

A SPECIAL TOUCH!
Plate Presentation

An important part of food preparation is presentation. Even the simplest foods can become special when presented attractively. Traditionally food is plated with the starch at a 10 o'clock position; the vegetable at 2 o'clock and the entree in a 4 to 8 o'clock position. However, today foods are often stacked instead of laid out and vegetables and starches often become part of a composition of intertwined presentation. Check out plate presentation photos in food magazines or try some of the following tips:

- ❖ Gravy doesn't always have to top your meat or potatoes. Try spooning gravies and sauces in the center of the plate and placing your entree on top.
- ❖ To create height, fan meat slices around a mound of potatoes or rice.
- ❖ Sprinkle finely minced parsley on both the food and the plate rim for an interesting touch.

Vegetables during the Victorian era . . .

Vegetables rarely appeared "naked" as evidenced in these Victorian era selections:

Ladies' Cabbage

"Boil a firm white cabbage fifteen minutes, changing the water then pour more from the boiling tea-kettle. When tender, drain and set aside until perfectly cold. Chop fine and add two beaten eggs, a tablespoon of butter, pepper and salt, three tablespoonfuls of rich milk or cream. Stir well together, bake in a pudding dish until brown. Serve very hot. The dish resembles cauliflower."[55]

Sweet Potato Pie

"Boil the potatoes very soft, then peel and mash them. To every quarter of pound put one quart of milk, three tablespoons of butter, and four beaten eggs, together with sugar and nutmeg to taste. It is improved with a glass of wine."[56]

Baked Beets

"Beets are far better baked than boiled, though it takes a longer time to cook properly. French cooks bake them slowly six hours in a covered dish, the bottom of which is lined with well-moistened rye straw; however, they may be baked on the oven grate, like potatoes. Wipe dry after washing, and bake slowly. They are very nice served with a sauce made with equal quantities of lemon juice and whipped cream, with a little salt. *Science in the Kitchen*, 1892."[57]

Kirby House Vegetables and their Sauces

Add these vegetable sauces to frozen vegetables cooked according to package directions. The amount of sauce added to the cooked vegetable can vary according to personal preference but general guidelines are provided with each recipe. The Kirby House makes these sauces in large quantities (the original Green Beans Amandine sauce calls for 9 sticks of butter) but the following recipes have been adjusted for home use.

Brown Sugar Glazed Veggies *Yield: about 1 1/2 cups*

1 cup brown sugar (packed)
1 cup butter (2 sticks)
2 tablespoons white distilled vinegar
1 teaspoon salt

Mix all ingredients together in a saucepan. Cook over medium-high heat until mixture becomes smooth, thickened, and caramel colored. Spoon heated sauce over cooked vegetables such as carrot coins, mixed frozen vegetables, etc.

Cream Corn Sauce *Yield: This should be enough sauce to cover a 16 to 20 -ounce bag of frozen corn. This can be made up in advance and refrigerated.*

4 -ounces cream cheese, softened
3 tablespoons granulated sugar
2 tablespoons butter
1/2 teaspoon Tex Joy® Steak Seasoning
1/4 teaspoon white pepper (or substitute black pepper if you don't mind the black specks)
1 1/3 cups whole milk
1/3 cup heavy whipping cream, chilled
1/4 cup cornstarch

Mix together--cream cheese, sugar, butter, Tex Joy®, pepper and milk--in medium size saucepan and heat over medium temperature, stirring frequently with a spoon or whisk to blend and to avoid scorching.
To thicken this mixture . . . add the cream that has been thoroughly combined with cornstarch; cook until the mixture is thick and bubbly. (FYI: To prevent the cornstarch from becoming lumpy, place cornstarch in a small bowl and slowly drizzle in cold cream whisking until mixture is smooth.) Chill sauce until ready to use. Pour heated sauce over cooked and drained corn when ready to serve.

Green Beans Amandine *Yield: This should be enough sauce to cover a 20 -ounce bag of frozen green beans. Or, use canned or fresh green beans.*

1/2 cup (1 stick) + 2 tablespoons butter
2 tablespoons lemon juice
1 3/4 to 2 teaspoons salt
1/2 teaspoon white pepper (or substitute black pepper if you don't mind the black specks)
Toasted almonds to sprinkle over green beans (guide for toasting almonds on p. 176)

Soften butter in medium saucepan on top of the range, using medium heat. Then add remaining ingredients, except for almonds. Spoon over cooked and drained green beans when ready to serve. Sprinkle with toasted almonds.

<u>Other Green Bean Variations</u> . . .
Green Beans with Sautéed Mushrooms--add Sautéed Mushrooms, p. 107 to prepared green beans.

Southern-Style Green Beans--add Sautéed Onions, p. 107 and crumbled, cooked bacon to prepared green beans.

Vegetable Allowances: generally allow 4 -ounces (1/2 cup) cooked vegetable per person.

What's the difference between white pepper and black pepper?
Black pepper comes from berries that are picked before they are fully ripe. They turn black and shrivel when dried, creating a hot, biting and very pungent flavor.
White pepper comes from the same vine, as black, but the berries are allowed to ripen before harvesting. The outer shell is removed resulting in a milder flavor.
Thus white pepper is interchangeable with black pepper, but a larger quantity may need to be used, due to its milder flavor.

Baked Cabbage Wedges *Yield: approximately 8 to 10 servings*

1 medium head cabbage, about 2 pounds
2 tablespoons all-purpose flour
1 teaspoon salt, or to taste
1/4 teaspoon pepper, or to taste
1 teaspoon dried chervil
1/2 teaspoon dried chives
2 tablespoons granulated sugar
1/4 cup butter, cut into small pieces
1 cup hot whole milk
1/2 cup shredded Cheddar cheese

Preheat oven to 350°. Butter a 9 x 13" glass baking dish.
Cut cabbage into wedges about 1/4" thick and steam over boiling water about 15 to 20 minutes or until fork tender. Drain thoroughly and place in prepared baking dish.
Mix flour, seasonings (salt, pepper, chervil & chives) and sugar together and sprinkle over cabbage.
Dot or distribute the butter pieces over cabbage and then pour hot milk over the top.
Sprinkle the cheese over cabbage and bake at 350° for 35 to 40 minutes until golden on top.

Brandied Mushrooms *Yield: 1 serving*
Brandied mushrooms garnish the 10 -ounce Grilled Sirloin at The Kirby House.

1/2 cup sliced mushrooms
1 - 2 tablespoons butter
Splash of Brandy

In a skillet, sauté mushrooms in butter over a gas burner. Add brandy to hot skillet; rotate the pan to control the flame. When flame is out, the mushrooms are ready to serve.

Carrot Bundles *Yield: 12 bundles*

Although time consuming to prepare, these bundles can be made ahead (even a day in advance) and make an impressive addition to a dinner plate. Or, add pizzaz to a picnic (see p. 195) by putting Carrot Bundles on the menu.

2 pounds fresh carrots
1 - 2 tablespoons olive oil

Clean the carrots and cut into matchstick pieces 3 to 4" long (you should have a total of about 48 to 60 pieces). Cook them in boiling water until just crisp tender, about 5 minutes. Drain immediately and place the hot carrots in 1 to 2 tablespoons olive oil and coat well.

<u>Marinade</u>
2 teaspoons fresh lemon juice
2 teaspoons fresh chopped parsley or oregano
salt & pepper, to taste
3 tablespoons wine vinegar (white or red)
1 1/2 teaspoons granulated sugar
1 teaspoon minced garlic

12 fresh chives, cleaned and trimmed

In a mixing bowl, whisk together all the ingredients for the marinade. Add the carrots (in olive oil) and toss well; set aside.

<u>To Assemble</u>: Take 4 or 5 carrots at a time, place them in the center of a chive. Tie the chive around the bundle of carrots. Continue until all carrots are bundled and tied; refrigerate until ready to use.

Serve cold or steam just long enough to heat through. Note: if you plan to serve these bundles hot, be sure to slightly undercook in the beginning.

Green Bean Bundles *Yield: 6 servings (allowing 1 bundle per person)*

This is an adaptation of a recipe in Debbie Meyer's cookbook, "Good Friends Great Tastes" which is available at The Kirby House restaurant.

36 - 60 frozen green beans
1 -2 teaspoons Tex Joy® Steak Seasoning, divided use
3 strips bacon, cut in half, partially cooked but still limp and flexible
Garlic salt
4 tablespoons butter, melted
3 tablespoons brown sugar (packed)

<u>To make ahead</u>--complete all but last step. Put in a glass baking dish and refrigerate overnight. Add extra baking time if bundles are cold). Before putting in oven, pour melted butter over bundles and sprinkle with brown sugar.

In steamer or saucepan, steam beans until tender-crisp in water seasoned with 1/2 to 1 teaspoon Tex Joy® seasoning. When cool, wrap approximately 6 to 10 beans with bacon halves that have been partially cooked. Place bundles in a 9 x 13" baking dish. Sprinkle bundles with garlic salt and 1/2 to 1 teaspoon Tex Joy® seasoning. Pour melted butter over bundles and sprinkle with brown sugar. Bake at 350° for 15 to 20 minutes or until bacon is crisp.

Onion Rings *Yield: 1 to 2 servings*

The Kirby House serves these with Tequila Lime Sauce, p. 184.

1 large white onion, sliced 1/4" to 3/8" thick and separated into rings
Buttermilk for dipping
Seasoned flour for dredging (see p. 196)
Oil for deep-fat frying (see tips on p. 72)
Salt to taste

***Dredge**--To thoroughly coat a food with flour or other fine substance.

To prepare for the *dredging of the onion rings--place enough buttermilk for dipping in a shallow bowl (large enough in diameter to accommodate the onion rings) and place some seasoned flour in another similar size bowl. Dip the onion rings first in the buttermilk and then into the seasoned flour. Repeat, again dipping in the buttermilk and ending with the flour mixture.

Meanwhile fill a deep skillet or deep-fat fryer with enough oil to completely cover the onion rings; heat to approximately 350 to 365°. Pick up several rings at once on a fork, and drop them into the oil; fry until light brown. Drain on paper towels. Sprinkle with salt to taste and serve with Tequila Lime Sauce.

Lena's Onion Rings

Terry Tietjens used to make Lena's Onion Rings. The recipe that follows was given to Nancy Gugler by Lena Benson.

Mild Bermuda or white onions -- 6 medium, sliced paper thin
2 cups milk
3 eggs
All-purpose flour

Separate onion slices into rings. Combine milk and eggs; beat thoroughly. Pour into a shallow pan. Drop onion rings into the pan and with your fingers, swish rings round to make sure each is well coated. Lift onions out to drain. Then drop in a pan of flour, a few rings at a time, coating each well. Shake off excess flour. Put into a french frying basket. Have temperature of hot fat at 375°. Just fill the basket 1/4 full so rings brown evenly. Stir once with fork to separate. Drain on paper towels. To keep onions crispy, don't salt until just before serving.

Sautéed Onions ❖ Sautéed Green Peppers ❖ Sautéed Mushrooms

Yield: 1 serving

Lightly browned and moist, these vegetables are perfect sandwich or steak toppers. Or, try the sautéed onions on top of mashed potatoes.

Approximately 1 - 2 tablespoons butter
A handful of onion slices (from a medium onion), thinly sliced or a handful of green pepper strips, thinly sliced or a handful of thinly sliced mushrooms
Salt & pepper to taste

In a skillet, sauté onions (or peppers, or mushrooms) over high heat until lightly browned around the edges (this takes only minutes). Season with salt and pepper.

Sauté: [saw-TAY] In French, sauté means "to jump." That describes this method of cooking in which food is cooked quickly in a small amount of butter or oil. The food "jumps" as it is either rapidly stirred or shaken over heat.

Baked Potato Casserole *Yield: 6 to 8 servings*

This casserole can be assembled early in the day and refrigerated until time to bake. Remove from refrigerator and let it come to room temperature prior to baking (or add extra baking time for a cold casserole).

6 medium unpeeled potatoes, baked
1/4 teaspoon salt
1/4 teaspoon pepper
6 - 8 slices bacon, cooked and crumbled
1 cup (8 -ounces) sour cream (or more, if desired)
1 cup (4 -ounces) shredded Cheddar cheese (or more, if desired)
2 green onions, chopped

Spray a 13 x 9 x 2" baking dish with non-stick pan coating or grease lightly with solid shortening.

Cut baked potatoes into 1" cubes. Place half in a prepared baking dish; sprinkle with half of the salt, pepper and bacon. Top with half of the sour cream & cheese. Repeat layers. Bake, uncovered, at 350° for 20 minutes or until cheese is melted. Sprinkle with chopped green onions to garnish.

Mashed Potatoes *Yield: about eight 3/4 cup servings*
Yes! Real mashed potatoes are made daily at The Kirby House!

2 pounds white *russet potatoes, about 6 medium, peeled & cut into large chunks
1 teaspoon salt
1/4 - 1/2 cup whole milk (or substitute lower fat milk if desired)
3 tablespoons butter
Salt and pepper to taste

***Note**: The best potatoes for mashing are starchy varieties such as russet and Idaho. Round white or red potatoes can become glue-like when mashed so should be avoided.

Place potatoes in a large pot and add enough cold water to cover. Add salt and bring to a boil (then reduce heat to medium or medium-low) and cook until tender when pierced with a knife tip. (Allow approximately 20 to 25 minutes cooking time.) Drain thoroughly in a colander.

Meanwhile, heat the milk in a small saucepan (on low heat).

Mash potatoes using an electric mixer (a ricer or hand masher may also be used but never use a food processor as the sharp blades break down the the potato's starch granules, making them gluey) working out the lumps. Pour in the hot milk, add butter and seasonings. Continue to whip the mixture (about 1 more minute) until fluffy.

Serve at once or hold (at home) by . . .

- ❖ placing in an aluminum or stainless steel mixing bowl with a rim, cover with aluminum foil and set over a larger pan of hot water (with rim of mixing bowl resting on edge of pan creating a double-boiler effect). Warm over heat for up to 30 minutes.
- ❖ place prepared potatoes in a buttered baking dish, dot with butter or a little cream, cover loosely with foil, and keep in a 300° oven about 30 to 45 minutes.

Holiday Mashed Potatoes *Yield: 6 to 8 serving*

A mashed potato variation that can be made 1 to 2 days in advance. It is ideal for the holidays (or any other dinner) as it lessens the number of dishes that must be prepared at the last minute. This recipe came from Jane Medina.

2 pounds white russet potatoes, about 6 medium, peeled & cut into large chunks
1 teaspoon salt
1 pint sour cream
1/2 - 1 bunch green onion, chopped and divided
1 - 1 1/2 cups grated Cheddar cheese
1/2 teaspoon salt
1/4 teaspoon pepper
Paprika to sprinkle over the top, if desired

Butter a 2 -quart casserole dish.
Follow directions on p. 108 (Mashed Potatoes) for cooking potatoes in salt water. Also mash potatoes according to the same recipe (omitting the addition of the milk, butter and seasoning). Mix sour cream, green onions (reserve 1/3 cup of the green section for sprinkling over the top of the casserole), cheese, salt and pepper. Place mixture in prepared casserole dish; potatoes may be refrigerated 1 to 2 days at this point. Remove potatoes from refrigerator, allow to come to room temperature, sprinkle with paprika (if desired) and bake at 350° for about 45 minutes or until hot all the way through. Sprinkle with the remaining green onions before serving.

Potato Fans *Yield: 3 servings*

3 medium russet potatoes
1 teaspoon coarse salt
3 tablespoon melted butter
Coarse salt for sprinkling
1/2 cup shredded Cheddar cheese
1/4 cup shredded Parmesan cheese
Optional--chopped parsley and chives for garnish

Variation--omit cheeses and add a sprinkling of your favorite herbs to the potatoes as they bake.

Preheat oven to 450°.
Scrub and dry the potatoes. Cut each potato crosswise into thin slices, being careful not to cut all the way through--using the handle of a wooden spoon behind the potato will help with the cutting process.
Arrange potatoes, cut side up, in a baking dish. Carefully drizzle each potato with melted butter and coarse salt being sure that butter and salt seep into the slices.
Bake for 1 hour. Remove from the oven, sprinkle with Cheddar and Parmesan cheeses and bake for another 10 to 15 minutes, or until potatoes are tender. Garnish with parsley and chives if desired.

Potato & Yam Gratin *Yield: one 9 x 12 -inch baking dish; serves about 8*
Recipe from LaVetra Brown.

3/4 teaspoon salt
3/4 teaspoon white pepper
Dash ground nutmeg
3/4 cup whipping cream

1 pound russet potatoes
1 pound yams or sweet potatoes
1/3 cup fresh chives, snipped
1/2 cup freshly grated Parmesan cheese

Preheat oven to 350°. Butter a 9 x 12" baking dish.
Combine salt and pepper with nutmeg and cream in a small bowl and set aside.
Peel potatoes and slice thinly; place in ice water; drain and pat dry. Cover bottom of prepared baking pan with single layer of slightly overlapping russet potato slices. Drizzle lightly with cream mixture. Cover with single layer of thinly sliced yams. Drizzle lightly with cream. Sprinkle with about half of the chives and Parmesan cheese. Repeat layering ending with Parmesan cheese. Cover with foil (dull side out). Bake 30 minutes. Remove foil and continue baking 30 to 40 minutes or until potatoes are tender and cheese is brown.

Roasted Potatoes *Yield: 4 servings*

12 new potatoes, halved, or 4 medium potatoes, cut into eighths
2 large shallots or 4 green onions, finely chopped
3 - 4 tablespoons olive oil
1/4 - 1/2 teaspoon coarse salt

Preheat oven to 450°.
Combine cut-up potatoes and shallots or onions in a 9 x 12" baking dish. Drizzle oil over potatoes, toss gently to coat. Sprinkle with salt. Bake, uncovered, in a 450° oven about 25 minutes or until potatoes are tender and light brown.

Variation: Herb Roasted Potatoes
add (about 1/2 teaspoon) crushed rosemary, basil or other herbs of choice to the potatoes as they bake.

Sweet Potato Soufflé *Yield: 13 x 9 -inch baking pan or 8 to 10 individual souffle dishes*

- 4 medium sweet potatoes or yams, peeled
- 1/2 - 1 cup whole milk
- 1 1/2 cups granulated sugar
- 4 large eggs
- 1/2 cup butter
- 1 teaspoon ground nutmeg
- 1 teaspoon ground cinnamon
- 1 tablespoon vanilla

Preheat oven to 400°. Butter baking pan or dishes.

Place sweet potatoes in a large pot and add enough cold water to cover. Bring to a boil (then reduce heat to medium or medium-low) and cook until tender when pierced with a knife tip. (Allow approximately 30 to 35 minutes cooking time.) Drain thoroughly in a colander.

Drain and mash potatoes in a mixing bowl, using an electric mixer. Add remaining ingredients (milk through vanilla) and blend well. Spread into prepared pan or dishes. Bake at 400° for 20 minutes or until set. Spread with Crunchy Praline Topping and bake 10 more minutes.

<u>Crunchy Praline Topping</u>

- 1/2 cup butter, softened
- 1 cup corn flakes, crushed
- 1 cup chopped pecans
- 3/4 - 1 cup brown sugar (packed)

Mix all ingredients together in a mixing bowl.

Sweet Potatoes or Yams? Although the terms tend to be used interchangeably, there are differences . . .

<u>Sweet potatoes</u> have a yellow-gray to brown skin and yellowish to white, dry mealy flesh. <u>Yams</u> have copper to purple skins and very sweet, moist, orange flesh. The simple difference between the two is variety. And if that's not confusing, there is also a "true" yam which is a tropical tuber . . . unrelated to the sweet potatoes and yams generally found in grocery stores.

Breads from the Victorian era. . .

Berry Toast

Canned strawberries, blueberries, and blackberries may be made into an excellent dressing for toast. Turn a can of well-kept berries into a colander over an earthen dish, to separate the juice from the berries. Place the juice in a porcelain kettle and heat to boiling. Thicken to the consistency of cream with cornstarch rubbed smooth in a little water; a tablespoonful of flour to the pint of juice will be about the right proportion. Add the berries and boil up just sufficiently to cook the flour and heat the berries; serve hot. If cream for moistening the zwieback is not obtainable, a little juice may be reserved without thickening, and heated in another dish to moisten the toast; or if preferred, the fruit may be heated and poured over the dry zwieback without being thickened, or it may be rubbed through a colande as for Apricot Toast. *Science in the Kitchen*, 1892.[58]

French Bread

With a quarter of a peck of fine flour mix the yolks of three and the whites of two eggs, beaten and strained; a little salt, half a pint of good yeast, that is not bitter, and as much milk, made a little warm, as will work into a thin, light dough. Stir it about, but do not knead it. Have ready three quart wooden dishes, divide the dough among them, set it to rise, then turn them out into the oven, which must be quick. Rasp when done. *Our New Cook-Book, Peterson's Magazine*, 1868.[59]

Flour Mills in Dickinson County

According to the 1886 County Directory, there were no fewer than fourteen grist and flour mills in the county. Abilene had three mills all doing extensive business: the City Mills, located on the Smoky Hill River, south of the city; The Abilene Mills and Elevator Company, located on North Third street, between Buckeye and Olive on the north side of the railroad track; and the Dickinson County mills of the Johntz & Rice Mill Company. The Johntz & Rice Mill had an invested capital of $75,000 and more than double that amount as annual product with a capacity of 225 barrels of flour per day. The company, located on Mud Creek, south of the railroad track, later became The Security Milling Company.[60]

Meanwhile, in the nearby town of Enterprise, Christian Hoffman built the first flour mill in the county to use steel rollers. This mill also has the distinction of being the first in Kansas to ship flour overseas. The mill grew and merged, and by the 1930's had become the 7th largest flour milling concern in the United States. By then, Flour Mills of America, Inc. was headquarted in Kansas City with Hoffman family members still heading the company.[61]

Kirby House Breads

Buttermilk Biscuits *Yield: 8 to 10 large biscuits or use a smaller cutter for a higher yield*

Made into mini biscuits, and filled with thin slices of ham and apricot preserves (p. 66), these are a nice addition to a tea table.

2 cups all-purpose flour
2 teaspoons baking powder
1/4 teaspoon baking soda
1/4 teaspoon salt
1/2 cup butter, chilled
3/4 cup buttermilk
1 tablespoon butter, melted

Preheat oven to 450°.
In large bowl combine flour, baking powder, baking soda and salt; mix well. Using a pastry cutter or electric mixer, cut in the butter until the mixture is crumbly; then rub mixture with fingertips until it resembles coarse crumbs. (Note: small, chilled butter pieces in the dough create spaces which produce a flaky biscuit.) Stir in buttermilk just until moistened. Turn dough onto lightly floured surface; knead 8 to 10 times or just until well mixed. Roll out dough to 3/4" thickness on a floured work surface. With 2 1/2" biscuit cutter, cut out 8 to 10 biscuits; place 1" apart on baking sheet. Brush biscuits with melted butter. Bake for 10 to 14 minutes or until lightly browned.

Cinnamon Raisin Biscuits: Omit salt. Stir in 2 tablespoons granulated sugar and 3/4 teaspoon ground cinnamon with flour. Stir in 1/3 cup raisins with buttermilk. Brush with melted butter and sprinkle biscuits with additional granulated sugar before baking. Drizzle with powdered sugar glaze (p. 134) if desired.

Savory Herb Biscuits: Substitute 1/4 to 1/2 teaspoon garlic salt for salt and stir in 1 tablespoon fresh or 1 teaspoon dried herbs, such as dill weed, chives or crushed rosemary leaves.

Apricot Orange Muffins *Yield: about 12 muffins (2 1/2 -inch diameter)*

2 cups all-purpose flour
1 1/2 teaspoon baking soda
1 teaspoon orange peel
1/4 cup brown sugar (packed)
Pinch salt
8 -ounces (1 cup) plain yogurt
1/2 cup dried apricots, chopped
1/3 cup orange juice
1/4 cup vegetable oil
1/4 cup honey
2 egg whites, slightly beaten (use large eggs)

Preheat oven to 375°. Grease muffin tins. Combine flour, baking soda, orange peel, brown sugar and salt in a medium size bowl and set aside.

In another bowl, combine the yogurt, dried apricots, orange juice, vegetable oil, honey and egg whites. Add the flour mixture to the wet ingredients and stir just until batter is moistened. Fill each greased muffin tin about 2/3 full with batter. Bake for 14 to 18 minutes (until tops are golden brown and muffins have pulled away slightly from the sides of the pan). Remove and cool pans on cooling racks for a few minutes before depanning.

Tip for Measuring Honey

To avoid honey sticking to the measuring cup, simply measure the oil first. The honey will then slide right out of the measuring cup. Or, spray a measuring cup or spoon with non-stick pan coating prior to measuring sticky substances such as honey or molasses.

Cherry Muffins *Yield: about 12 muffins (2 1/2 -inch diameter)*

- 1 1/2 cups whole bran cereal
- 1 cup plain yogurt
- 1/2 cup low-fat milk
- 1 1/4 cups all-purpose flour
- 1/2 cup granulated sugar
- 3 teaspoons baking powder
- 1/4 teaspoon salt
- 1 teaspoon ground cinnamon
- 1 large egg
- 1/4 cup vegetable oil
- 3 -ounce package dried cherries (or dried, sweetened cranberries)

Preheat oven to 350°. Grease muffin tins. Stir together bran cereal, yogurt and milk in a medium size bowl and set aside.
In another bowl, mix the flour, sugar, baking powder, salt and cinnamon; set aside. Add egg and oil to cereal mixture; beat well to blend. Add cherries and flour mixture and stir just until batter is moistened. Fill each greased muffin tin about 2/3 full with batter. Sprinkle topping (recipe follows) over muffins. Bake for 10 to 20 minutes (until tops are golden brown and muffins have pulled away slightly from the sides of the pan). Remove and cool pans on cooling racks for a few minutes before depanning.

Topping:

- 1 tablespoon granulated sugar
- 1/4 teaspoon ground cinnamon
- 1/4 cup sliced almonds

Mix all ingredients together in a small bowl.

Tips for Muffins:

- ❖ When the liquid and dry ingredients are combined for muffins, they should be stirred only until moistened. Otherwise, the muffins will be tough and full of tunnels due to over development of the gluten in the flour.
- ❖ Good muffins should be straight-sided and rounded on top. The grain should be fine and the crumb moist.
- ❖ If the dough does not fill every muffin cup, fill the empty cups about 1/2 full of water--this will keep the rest of the muffins moist and aid in pan clean-up.
- ❖ If muffins remain in the muffin cups a few minutes they will be easier to remove. However, avoid leaving them too long or they may become soggy on the bottom (due to heat condensation) and also stick.

Apple Walnut Loaf with Maple Cream Glaze *Yield: one 9 x 5 -inch loaf or 2 smaller loaves (4 x 7 inch)*

This recipe is actually a combination and variation of several recipes compiled by Meta Newell West for the December, 2000 Christmas tea served at The Kirby House. Not only is it delicious served with tea, it makes a nice treat for friends.

1 1/4 cup applesauce
1 cup granulated sugar
1/2 cup vegetable oil
2 large eggs
3 tablespoons whole milk
2 cups all-purpose flour
1 teaspoon baking soda
1/2 teaspoon baking powder
1/2 teaspoon ground cinnamon
1/4 teaspoon each salt, ground nutmeg & allspice
1/2 cup chopped walnuts

Preheat oven to 350°. Generously grease pan(s).
In a mixing bowl, combine applesauce, sugar, oil, eggs and milk. In another bowl, combine flour, baking soda, baking powder, and spices. Add dry ingredients to the wet ones and fold in the walnuts.
Bake loaf for 50 minutes to 1 hour (depending on size of pan) or until browned and a toothpick stuck in the center comes out clean. Let cool in pan that has been placed on a wire rack. When cool, run a table knife around pan edges and remove bread. Wrap and store in refrigerator or freeze up to 2 months. Glaze prior to serving.

<u>Maple Cream Glaze</u>:
1/2 cup powdered sugar
1 tablespoon cream cheese
1 tablespoon maple syrup
Pinch salt

Combine ingredients for the glaze in the work bowl of a food processor. Process until smooth and creamy.

Allspice is often believed to be a blend of spices; its aroma and flavor resemble those of several spices (nutmeg, cinnamon, and cloves). However, allspice berries actually grow on trees belonging to the evergreen family. Native to tropical America, it has the distinction of being the only spice produced exclusively in the Western Hemisphere.

Apricot Bread *Yield: one 9 x 5 -inch loaf*

- 1 1/4 cups dried apricots, chopped
- 1/4 cup all-purpose flour
- 1/2 cup chopped pecans (optional)
- 2 tablespoons butter, softened
- 1 cup granulated sugar
- 1 large egg
- 1 3/4 cups all-purpose flour
- 1/4 teaspoon baking powder
- 1/4 teaspoon salt
- 3/4 cup orange juice

Preheat oven to 350°. Spray bottom of loaf pan with non-stick pan coating.

In bowl, add warm water to the dried apricots--enough just to cover--let soak for 30 minutes, then drain. Stir the 1/4 cup flour and pecans into drained apricots and set aside. Cream butter and sugar in a large mixing bowl. Add egg and beat.

In another bowl mix dry ingredients (1 3/4 cup flour, baking powder & salt) and add alternately with orange juice to butter/sugar mixture. Stir in apricot mixture.

Pour into prepared pan. Bake for 1 hour or until toothpick, inserted in the center of loaf, comes out clean. Let cool in pan that has been placed on a wire rack. Run a table knife around pan edges and remove bread. Wrap and store in refrigerator or freeze for up to 2 months.

Confused about "Cream"?

When this is used as an action term in recipes it simply means . . . to beat an ingredient or combination of ingredients until the mixture is soft, smooth and "creamy." Often a recipe calls for creaming a fat, such as butter, or creaming a mixture of butter and sugar. When creaming two or more ingredients together, the result should be a smooth, homogeneous mixture that shows neither separation nor evidence of any particles (such as sugar). Electric mixers and food processors may be used for the task or mix by hand with the back of a spoon.

Coconut Walnut Bread

Yield: one 9 x 5 -inch loaf

This is The Kirby Houses' signature bread and a favorite among diners. The original recipe for this bread came from Eleanor Correll but it has been modified and adjusted over the years.

- 2 cups all-purpose flour
- 1 3/4 teaspoons baking powder
- 1/4 teaspoon salt
- 1 1/3 cups granulated sugar
- 1/4 teaspoon baking soda
- 2/3 cup vegetable oil
- 2/3 cup buttermilk
- 1/2 cup flaked coconut
- 2 large eggs
- 1 1/2 teaspoons coconut flavor (such as Stirling® Hawaiian Coconut gourmet syrup)
- 1/2 cup chopped walnuts

Preheat oven to 325° and spray bottom of loaf pan with non-stick pan coating.

Mix the dry ingredients (flour, baking powder, salt, sugar, & baking soda) in large mixing bowl.

Add oil, buttermilk, coconut, eggs, coconut flavor & walnuts to flour mixture. Mix with electric mixer just until dry ingredients are moistened. Pour into prepared pan and bake for 1 hour and 15 minutes or until done (toothpick, inserted in the center of loaf, comes out clean). Do NOT open oven door during the baking process (to avoid causing the bread to sink in the center).

Let cool in pan that has been placed on a wire rack. When cool, run a table knife around pan edges and remove bread. Wrap and store in refrigerator or freeze for up to 2 months. Do NOT cut until chilled and firm.

After slicing, The Kirby House butters this bread and grills it lightly on both sides.

Tips: Coconut

Coconut comes in a variety of different sizes, plus, shredded and flaked coconut comes frozen, canned or in bags. Below is a list of equivalents that will make shopping for coconut a little easier.

8 -ounce bag, shredded = 2 1/2 cups
3 1/2 -ounce can, flaked = 1 1/3 cups
4 -ounce can, shredded = 1 1/3 cups
1 medium-sized fresh coconut = 5 cups freshly grated

Once packaged coconut has been opened, it should be closed tightly and stored in the refrigerator.

Wondering what to do with leftover buttermilk?

Buttermilk is usually available only in quart cartons but recipes invariably call for a smaller quantity. Try freezing what's left and thawing it for the next use. For convenience, measure the needed amount (2/3 cup for Coconut Walnut Bread), pour into a plastic freezer container, label, and freeze. If you need the container, simply pop the frozen buttermilk into a plastic freezer bag thus freeing up the plastic container. Thaw frozen buttermilk prior to use.

Lemon Blueberry Bread *Yield: one 9 x 5 -inch loaf or 2 smaller loaves (4 x 7 -inch)*

A delicious, moist bread; great with coffee or serve with afternoon tea.

2 cups all-purpose flour
2 teaspoons baking powder
2 teaspoons grated lemon rind
1/4 teaspoon salt
2/3 cup granulated sugar
1/2 cup (1 stick) butter
2 large eggs
1/2 cup whole milk
1/2 teaspoon lemon flavoring (such as Stirling® Lemon Meringue gourmet syrup)
2/3 cup blueberries

1/4 cup lemon juice
1/3 cup granulated sugar

Preheat oven to 350°. Generously grease pan(s).

In small bowl, stir together flour, baking powder, lemon rind, and salt.

In large bowl, with electric mixer on high speed, beat together 2/3 cup sugar and the butter until light and fluffy. Then add the eggs, one at a time, until thoroughly mixed. Add flour mixture, milk, and lemon flavoring; beat just until combined. Fold in blueberries by hand being careful not to over mix and discolor the dough.

Transfer mixture to prepared pan(s) and bake until the center springs back when gently pressed (and toothpick comes out clean)--50 to 60 minutes (about 30 minutes for smaller loaves).

Meanwhile, in small saucepan, combine lemon juice and remaining 1/3 cup sugar. Bring to a boil; cook 1 minute. As soon as bread comes out of the oven, insert a toothpick into loaf 10 to 12 times. Slowly pour hot syrup over bread to coat completely. Let bread cool in pan that has been placed on a wire rack. When cool, run a table knife around pan edges and remove bread. Wrap and store in refrigerator or freeze for up to 2 months.

Lemon Poppy Seed Bread *Yield: one 9 x 5 -inch loaf*

- 2 teaspoons grated lemon peel
- 1 1/2 teaspoons water
- 2 tablespoons granulated sugar
- 1 1/2 cups all-purpose flour
- 1 cup + 2 tablespoons granulated sugar
- 3/4 teaspoons salt
- 1 1/2 teaspoons baking powder
- 1/2 teaspoon poppy seeds
- 2 large eggs
- 1/2 cup + 1 tablespoon vegetable oil
- 3/4 cup whole milk
- 3/4 teaspoon butter extract

Preheat oven to 350°. Spray bottom of loaf pan with non-stick pan coating.

Heat lemon peel, water and 2 tablespoons sugar just until sugar dissolves in a small saucepan.

Mix remaining ingredients together in a large mixing bowl. Add dissolved sugar mixture and mix just until blended.

Pour into prepared pan. Bake for 1 hour 15 minutes or until toothpick, inserted in the center of loaf, comes out clean. Let bread cool in pan that has been placed on a wire rack. When cool, run a table knife around pan edges and remove bread. Wrap and store in refrigerator or freeze for up to 2 months.

Variation: Use batter to make muffins but reduce baking time to about 20 to 25 minutes.

Lemon Peel--One average lemon yields approximately 3 tablespoons grated lemon peel. When grating the peel of any citrus fruit, avoid the white pith underneath the skin as it has a bitter taste.

Sunshine Bread *Yield: one 9 x 5 -inch loaf*

A heavy, dense bread with a crispy crust.

- 1 1/2 cups all-purpose flour
- 1 1/2 cups granulated sugar
- 1/2 teaspoon salt
- 1/2 teaspoon baking soda
- 1/2 teaspoon ground cinnamon
- 2 large eggs
- 1/2 cup vegetable oil
- 1 cup shredded carrots (1/4 pound of carrots will yield approximately 1 cup shredded)
- 4 -ounces crushed pineapple, drained (1/2 cup)
- 1 teaspoon vanilla
- 1/2 cup chopped walnuts (optional)

Preheat oven to 350°. Spray bottom of loaf pan with non-stick pan coating.

In a large bowl, mix by hand, all ingredients just until blended. Pour into prepared pan. Bake about 1 1/2 hours or until toothpick, inserted in the center of loaf, comes out clean. Let bread cool in pan that has been placed on a wire rack. When cool, run a table knife around pan edges and remove bread. Wrap and store in refrigerator or freeze up to 2 months.

Whole Wheat Banana Bread *Yield: one 9 x 5 -inch loaf*

- 1 cup whole wheat flour
- 1/2 cup all-purpose flour
- 1 cup granulated sugar
- 1 teaspoon baking soda
- 1/2 teaspoon salt
- 1/4 teaspoon baking powder
- 1 cup mashed bananas (3 medium bananas equal about 1 -cup mashed)
- 1/3 cup vegetable oil
- 2 large eggs
- 1/4 cup chopped walnuts (optional)

Preheat oven to 350°. Spray bottom of loaf pan with non-stick pan coating.

In a large bowl, mix by hand, all ingredients just until blended. Pour into prepared pan. Bake for 50 to 60 minutes or until toothpick, inserted in the center of loaf, comes out clean. Let bread cool in pan that has been placed on a wire rack. When cool, run a table knife around pan edges and remove bread. Wrap and store in refrigerator or freeze for up to 2 months.

Variation: Use batter to make muffins but reduce baking time to 10 to 20 minutes (or bake just until done).

Whole Wheat Flour

Whole wheat flour, also called graham flour, contains the whole wheat kernel--bran, germ and endosperm--finely ground. This produces a distinctive nut-like flavor but produces a coarser texture. Stone ground whole wheat flour involves a process creating an even coarser flour. Since the germ contains oil, whole wheat flour can become rancid and thus should be stored in a cool place. The paper sack of flour can be transferred to a large plastic bag and stored in the refrigerator or even placed in the freezer.

Tips for Quick Bread Loaves:

Baking: Quick bread loaves may be baked in mini loaf pans or even in recycled 6 to 8 ounce metal cans (a tomato paste can, for instance). Fill these not more than two-thirds to three-fourths full to allow for expansion of the dough, and bake for less time than a regular sized loaf.

Pan Selection: Foods bake faster and crusts brown more quickly in dark or dull pans as the dull surface absorbs heat. For a more delicate, tender crust, use a shiny metal pan which reflects heat.

Ways to tell if loaves are done:

- ❖bread will slightly pull away from the sides of the pan
- ❖a golden brown color is characteristic in most quick breads
- ❖bread will feel firm and springy to the touch
- ❖a toothpick, inserted in the center of the loaf, will come out clean

Characteristics: A quick bread loaf may actually crack on top. This is due to the fact that most are very dense and as steam builds up, it has to be released.

Slicing: Quick breads containing nuts and fruits slice better if, after baking and cooling, they are wrapped in foil or plastic wrap and refrigerated about 12 hours.

Do you have trouble with your quick breads sticking to the bottom of the pan?
Even though loaf pans are carefully greased, sometimes the finished bread still sticks to the bottom. To avoid this problem--cut a piece of parchment paper to fit the bottom of the loaf pan; grease the pan as usual, then insert the paper and coat it with another thin layer of shortening.

 **A SPECIAL TOUCH!** 

Quick Bread waxed containers--A unique packaging idea for quick breads

You'll need:

Household paraffin wax (available at most grocery stores)	Cotton fabric scraps
Recycled coffee can	Loaf pan for draping
Saucepan	Pinking shears (to cut decorative edging)
Newspapers	Non-stick pan coating
	Tongs
	Kitchen knife

To prepare: Place wax in a clean, recycled coffee can (for easy clean up); place coffee can in a saucepan of water and heat over low heat watching carefully to make sure it doesn't smoke. Meanwhile, spread work surface with newspapers. Drape fabric over loaf pan and cut to fit. Remove fabric and spray a light coating of non-stick pan coating over the surface of the container. When wax is melted, use tongs to dip the cut fabric into the hot wax. Drape the fabric over the loaf pan. Work quickly to mold the fabric to the container, folding or gathering sides as desired. Allow fabric to dry completely before removing from container. Use a kitchen knife to loosen any sides that might stick.

Sour Cream Cinnamon Coffee Cake

Yield: one 5 x 9 -inch loaf

1/4 cup + 1 tablespoon, butter, softened (but NOT melted)
1/4 cup + 1 tablespoon shortening
3/4 cup granulated sugar
1 large egg
2/3 cup sour cream
3/4 teaspoon vanilla
1 1/2 cups all-purpose flour
3/4 teaspoon baking powder
1/4 teaspoon baking soda
1/4 teaspoon salt

Cinnamon Sugar Mixture
Mix together:
3/4 teaspoon ground cinnamon
3 tablespoons granulated sugar

Preheat oven to 350°. Spray bottom of loaf pan with non-stick pan coating.
Mix butter and shortening (in a large bowl) at medium speed with electric mixer 2 minutes until smooth and creamy. Gradually add sugar, beating 5 minutes. Add egg and beat just until yellow disappears. Add sour cream and vanilla, mixing just until blended. Mix remaining dry ingredients together in another mixing bowl, then gradually add to sour cream mixture, mixing just until blended. Be careful not to over mix! Add one-third of the batter to prepared pan. Sprinkle with cinnamon-sugar and then spoon remaining batter on top. Run a knife through loaf pan to swirl the batter. Bake for about 1 hour or until a toothpick inserted in the center comes out clean. Let coffee cake cool in pan that has been placed on a wire rack. When cool, run a table knife around pan edges and remove bread. Wrap and store in refrigerator or freeze for up to 2 months.

Currant Scones *Yield: 12 large scones*

4 cups all-purpose flour
1/2 cup granulated sugar
4 teaspoons baking powder (or 1 tablespoon + 1 teaspoon)
3/4 cup dried currants
1 1/4 cups (2 1/2 sticks) chilled butter, cut into 1/2" pieces
2 large eggs, lightly beaten
1 cup chilled half-and-half
Additional half-and-half and sugar for brushing and sprinkling before placing in oven

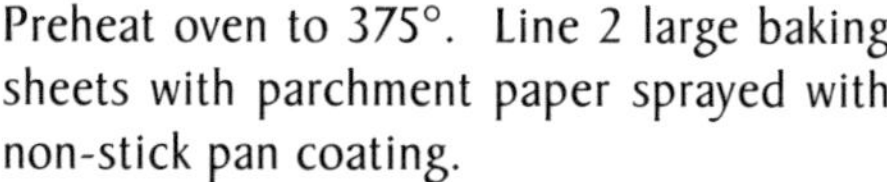

Preheat oven to 375°. Line 2 large baking sheets with parchment paper sprayed with non-stick pan coating.

Whisk flour, sugar, baking powder and currants in large bowl to blend. Rub in butter with fingertips until flour mixture resembles coarse crumbs.

Beat eggs and half-and-half in medium bowl to blend. Stir half-and-half mixture into flour mixture, tossing until dough comes together (dough will be soft and moist). Turn dough out onto lightly floured work surface. Knead gently, about 6 turns. Divide dough into half; shape each half into a 7" round. Cut each round into 6 wedges. Transfer wedges to prepared baking sheets allowing space between wedges for expansion. Brush wedges with half-and-half and sprinkle with additional sugar.

Bake scones until golden on bottom and beginning to color on top, about 25 minutes. Serve scones warm or let stand at room temperature up to 3 hours. Can also be frozen.

Shaping Variation: Scone dough may also be cut into individual rounds using a biscuit cutter.

Meta's Buttermilk Scones *Yield: about 18 small triangle shaped scones*
After testing and experimenting with several scone recipes, Meta Newell West created this variation. Buttermilk makes these scones tangy, moist, and crisp crusted.

2 cups all-purpose flour
1 teaspoon cream of tartar
1/2 teaspoon baking soda
pinch of salt
1/4 cup granulated sugar
1/2 cup cold butter, cut into small pieces
1/4 cup raisins, currants or dried, sweetened cranberries, optional
3/4 - 1 cup buttermilk
Extra granulated sugar for sprinkling
Optional: brush top of scones with butter, cream, or milk before baking

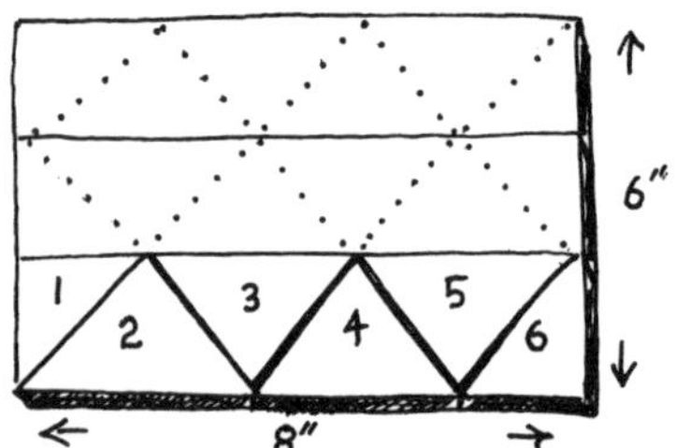

Preheat oven to 350°. Line a large baking sheet with parchment paper sprayed with non-stick pan coating.

In a medium bowl, stir the flour, cream of tartar, baking soda, salt and sugar together until well blended. Using a pastry cutter or electric mixer, cut in the butter until the mixture is crumbly; then rub mixture with fingertips until it resembles coarse crumbs. Stir in the dried fruit (if desired) and add buttermilk, a little at a time, stirring just until the mixture is moist enough to cling together. Too much mixing or too much liquid will make the scones tough.

With floured hands, round the dough into a ball. On a lightly floured work surface, pat the dough into an approximately 6 x 8" rectangle (about 1/2" thick). Cut the dough into 3 lengthwise strips, then cut each strip into six triangle shapes.

Sprinkle the surface lightly with sugar and brush with butter, milk, or cream, if desired.

Transfer the separated wedges to a greased baking sheet (allow at least 1/2" between wedges) and bake for 15 to 20 minutes or until nicely browned.

Tasty accompaniments for these scones are ...
Lemon Curd on p. 193
Devonshire-Style Cream on p. 189

Meta's Chocolate Chip Scones with Chocolate Honey Butter *Yield: about 18 small triangle shaped scones*

Meta Newell West created this Americanized variation of scones which have been quite popular on tea menus among both adults and children. The scones can be shaped, frozen and then baked fresh as needed. They're great with the Chocolate Honey Butter!

2 sticks butter, cut into chunks
1/2 cup + 2 tablespoons granulated sugar
3 large eggs
3 - 4 cups all-purpose flour
1 tablespoon baking powder
1/2 cup buttermilk
1/2 cup semi-sweet chocolate chips
Additional granulated sugar for sprinkling

In the large bowl of an electric mixer, beat butter on high speed until creamy. Add sugar and beat 3 to 5 minutes until pale and fluffy. Add eggs, one at a time, beating after each addition. Scrape sides of bowl and add 3 cups flour and the baking powder; mix only until blended using the low speed of the mixer. Then add buttermilk and again mix only until blended. Dump dough onto a lightly floured surface; work in enough additional flour to create a non-sticky dough (do not add too much flour and do not overwork!). Sprinkle chocolate chips over the batter and quickly work in with a light kneading motion. With floured hands, round the dough into a ball. On a lightly floured work surface, pat the dough into an approximately 6 x 8" rectangle (about 1/2" thick). Cut the dough into 3 lengthwise strips, then cut each strip into six triangle shapes (refer to diagram on p. 126). Arrange on a baking sheet and sprinkle the surface lightly with sugar. Loosely cover dough with plastic wrap and refrigerate about 45 minutes (or freeze, and when hard, remove to a freezer bag and freeze for up to 6 weeks).

Preheat oven to 350°. Uncover scones and bake (arrange on parchment lined baking sheets sprayed with non-stick pan coating--allow room for expansion between scones) about 25 minutes or until golden brown. Cool, uncovered, on a wire rack. Serve with Chocolate Honey Butter.

Chocolate Honey Butter
Yield: 1 cup

1/2 cup butter, softened
8 -ounces cream cheese
2 tablespoons chocolate syrup
2 tablespoons honey

In small bowl, combine all ingredients. Beat at highest speed until light and fluffy.

Orange Cranberry Scones *Yield: 12 large scones*

Bakers at The Kirby House came up with this variation and it is a favorite in the coffee shop.

- 4 cups all-purpose flour
- 1/2 cup granulated sugar
- 4 teaspoons baking powder (or 1 tablespoon + 1 teaspoon)
- 1 1/4 cups (2 1/2 sticks) chilled butter, cut into 1/2" pieces
- 1 whole orange
- 1/2 to 1 cup dried, sweetened cranberries
- 2 large eggs, lightly beaten
- 1 cup chilled half-and-half
- Additional half-and-half and sugar for brushing and sprinkling before placing in oven.

Preheat oven to 375°. Line 2 large baking sheets with parchment paper sprayed with non-stick pan coating.

Whisk flour, sugar, and baking powder in large bowl to blend. Rub in butter with fingertips until flour mixture resembles coarse crumbs.

Process entire orange, including peel, in the work bowl of a food processor until peel is fine and pulp is well grated. Incorporate into above flour/butter mixture. Add dried cranberries.

Beat eggs and half-and-half in medium bowl to blend. Stir half-and-half mixture into flour mixture, tossing until dough comes together (dough will be soft and moist). Turn dough out onto lightly floured work surface. Knead gently, about 6 turns. Divide dough into half; shape each half into a 7" round. Cut each round into 6 wedges. Transfer wedges to prepared baking sheets allowing space between wedges for expansion. Brush wedges with additional half-and-half and sprinkle with additional sugar. Bake scones until golden on bottom and beginning to color on top about 25 minutes. Serve scones warm or let stand at room temperature up to 3 hours. Can be frozen.

Shaping Variation: Scone dough may also be cut into individual rounds using a biscuit cutter.

Scones--similar to a biscuit but generally contain more sugar and some recipes add eggs; currants or raisins are typically added. Scones are thought to have originated in Scotland.

Lavash *Yield: about 40 crackers*

Lavash is a Middle Eastern cracker-bread. Although Lavash is traditionally rolled out with a rolling pin, this recipe has been adapted (by the author) for use with a pasta machine (directions that follow are for use with a hand-cranked Atlas Marcato® pasta machine). This shaping technique will create a long, narrow cracker while Lavash, rolled out with a rolling pin, is generally shaped in a circle formation. Lavash can take the place of bread at mealtime, can be used as a cracker, or as a dipper for relatively loose dips.

1 1/2 cups whole wheat flour
1 cup water, lukewarm (110°)
1 (1/4 -ounce) package or scant 1 tablespoon yeast (active dry instant)
1 teaspoon salt
2 cups all-purpose flour
Assorted seeds and seasoning (celery seed, caraway seed, fennel seed, Italian seasoning, dill weed, parsley flakes, onion powder, etc.)

In a mixing bowl, blend whole wheat flour, water, yeast and salt until moistened and well blended. Using an electric mixer, beat 3 minutes on medium speed. Work in all-purpose flour and develop dough by hand kneading, or with dough hook. until smooth and elastic (about 8 to 10 minutes).

Place dough in greased bowl and cover with plastic wrap or damp towel.

Let rise 1 hour at 80° or until double in bulk (to test--press fingers gently into dough; if indentations remain, dough has risen enough.) Divide dough into 40 pieces, shape into smooth balls; cover with damp towel and let rise again for another 30 minutes. Meanwhile prepare work surface by sprinkling a little flour in one area and selections of various seeds and seasoning in other areas. When dough rising time is up, remove about 10 balls of dough at a time; press dough balls into various seeds/seasoning for flavor and into flour if sticky areas are evident on the dough. Set up pasta machine and turn the dial to level 1--run each dough ball through the machine, returning flattened ball to floured surface. Next, turn dial to 2 and repeat; continue until Lavash is paper thin--this usually occurs at level 7. Note: if Lavash begins to tear, you have flattened the dough too much. Place an ungreased baking sheet in the oven and preheat oven and baking sheet to 500°. Remove baking sheet and arrange Lavash on the hot surface. Bake, watching carefully, for about 5 to 6 minutes (or less). Crackers should be lightly browned on top of the small bubbles that will appear on the surface. (If bread puffs excessively, it needs to be rolled thinner.) Remove bread with spatula to a cooling rack. Continue above procedure until all Lavash is baked.

 **A SPECIAL TOUCH!** 

A Champagne Brunch with Cocktail Sticks

Greet your guests with a glass of champagne and an array of cocktail sticks (such as Lavash, Puff Pastry Straws, p. 130, and, Tomato-Cheddar-Pepper Sticks, p. 130) standing in baskets and jars. This is a fun way to "take the edge off hunger," without filling up your guests as they wait for brunch. Cocktail sticks are also a nice addition to an hors d' oeuvre table or a welcome accompaniment to soups and salads.

Puff Pastry Straws *Prepare as many of these as you want . . . use one sheet of the puff pastry or several depending on how many of these tasty treats you want to create. Note: Puff pastry dough is usually sold in the freezer section of the grocery store. Plan ahead when making this recipe as the dough must be thawed.*

1 17 1/4 -ounce package frozen puff pastry, thawed according to package directions
Melted butter
Assorted toppings (Parmesan cheese, sesame seeds, poppy seeds, etc.)
Preheat oven to 375°. Line a baking sheet with parchment paper and lightly spray with non-stick pan coating.

Alternative baking method--Instead of immediately baking the cut and twisted straws, cover with plastic wrap and refrigerate the baking sheet; bake later in the day, as time allows.

Open one sheet of puff pastry on a cutting board. Brush the surface lightly with butter and then sprinkle on the toppings of your choice. Roll a floured rolling pin over the dough surface to gently press the toppings into the puff pastry and to extend the size of the pastry slightly. Using a sharp knife or Bench knife, cut the puff pastry into long 1/4" wide strips (Note: if these seem too long, cut strip in half, thirds, etc.); gently twist each strip several times. Position strips about 1" apart on the prepared baking sheet; press the ends onto the baking sheet to hold in place as they bake. Bake in oven for 12 to 14 minutes or until the straws are golden in color. Cool on a wire rack (they firm up as they cool). Best served the same day but can be stored overnight in an air-tight container. These can also be frozen.

Tomato-Cheddar-Pepper Sticks *Yield: about 3 dozen sticks*

2 cups all-purpose flour
1/2 teaspoon salt
1 1/2 teaspoons baking powder
1/2 - 1 teaspoon coarsely ground black pepper (vary amount depending on your taste)
3 tablespoons shortening
3 tablespoons tomato sauce
1/2 - 3/4 cup water, ice-cold
1/2 cup+ Cheddar cheese (vary amount depending on your taste)
Non-stick pan coating

Preheat oven to 350°.
Combine flour, salt, baking powder and pepper in a mixing bowl. Add shortening and mix, using an electric mixer, until mixture resembles coarse meal. Add tomato sauce and 1/2 cup water and mix only until the dough comes together (use the extra 1/4 cup water only if needed). Transfer the dough to a lightly floured surface; pat dough into a smooth rectangle and sprinkle surface with cheese. Using a rolling pin, roll dough into an 8 x 10" sheet as you press the cheese into the dough. Using a sharp knife or Bench knife, cut dough lengthwise into 1/4" strips. Using your hands, twist each length until the strip measures approximately 16" in length. Arrange the sticks on baking sheets, side by side but not touching. Press the ends onto the baking sheet to hold sticks in place as they bake. Spray with a light coating of non-stick pan coating and bake for 15 to 18 minutes, or until sticks are browned and firm. Place baking sheet on a cooling rack. When cool, store sticks in an air-tight container for 2 to 3 days or freeze.

By the time Terry Tietjens got involved in the restaurant business, the famous Lena's Restaurant had closed but Lena Benson shared her renowned light-as-a-feather roll recipe with him. Thereafter, Terry dutifully began his day at 4 o'clock a.m. making Lena's delicious rolls at The Kirby House from August 17, 1987 to the summer of 1996.

Lena's Rolls *Restaurant Quantity*

Cut the half batch in half again to yield 3 dozen rolls for home use; or Terry recommends using the extra dough to make cinnamon rolls. These rolls freeze well.

Full Batch *(Yield: about 12 dozen)*	**Half Batch** *(Yield: about 6 dozen)*
3/4 cup shortening	1/2 cup shortening
5 cups granulated sugar	2 1/2 cups granulated sugar
1/4 cup salt	1/8 cup salt (2 tablespoons)
6 cups boiling water	3 cups boiling water
6 cups cold water	3 cups cold water
1 cup yeast (active dry instant)	1/2 cup yeast (active dry instant)
9 eggs	5 eggs
37 - 50 cups all-purpose flour (up to 12 1/2 pounds)	18 - 25 cups all-purpose flour (up to 6 1/4 pounds)
Vegetable oil for shaping	Vegetable oil for shaping
Melted butter for brushing	Melted butter for brushing

Spray muffin tins with non-stick pan coating.

In a large mixing bowl of a Hobart-style mixer, combine the shortening, sugar, salt and boiling water. Using a dough hook, mix the shortening and water mixture until shortening is completely melted. Add cold water and continue to mix until temperature of the mixture is about 120°. Add yeast and eggs and continue mixing (allowing yeast time to begin proofing). Then add approximately half of the flour and mix thoroughly; continue adding flour about 1 cup at a time until dough begins to round up into a ball and is no longer sticky (avoid adding too much flour; the dough should be soft just not sticky.)

Pour enough oil into a pan to allow for oiling your hands as you shape dough. With well oiled hands, pinch off a large quantity of dough and smooth the surface. Using the thumb and fore-finger, pinch off 1" diameter balls and place 2 balls in a prepared muffin tin. (Note: Terry placed 2 balls of dough in each tin; Lena made smaller balls and placed 3 in each tin.) Continue shaping rolls, reoiling hands and smoothing the dough surface as needed. When pan is full, place in a warm, draft-free spot until rolls have doubled in volume--this will take 1 to 2 hours (see note that follows on proofing rolls at home; also, avoid over-rising as this could cause the rolls to go flat). During this resting period, rolls may be covered with flour-sack type towels.

Preheat oven to 350 to 375°. Bake (position rolls in oven for maximum air circulation; a convection oven is ideal for baking these rolls) for 8 to 10 minutes, rotating pans at least once during the baking period for even browning. When rolls are golden brown, remove from oven and brush with melted butter. Completely cool pans on a cooling rack. To release rolls, rap pans against a counter top and run a table knife gently around the muffin tins, if needed.

Proofing Rolls at Home
Restaurants use "proof boxes" that create the perfect climate for dough to rise. A similar environment can be created at home by placing the pans of rolls (covered with a towel) in a gas oven warmed by a pilot light or in an electric oven that has been turned on at 200° for one minute, then turned off. To create a moist "hot box," set a pan of hot water on the bottom rack and place the rolls on a rack above the water.

Origin of Lena's Roll Recipe: Terry Tietjens asked Lena about the origin of her recipe and she said an army cook gave it to her many years ago. The army cook had extolled it's virtues as a bread recipe that was easy to make and would rise fast.

Lena's Career in Restaurant Management--in brief : Lena Benson graduated from Abilene High School in 1923 and after a short stint in California came back to Abilene and went into the restaurant business with her brother-in-law. They leased the cafe in Detroit, Kansas, but during the Depression he left the business. Despite hard times, she continued and at one time also ran the Indian Hill Restaurant in Chapman. In 1933 she took over the operation of Gunzelman's restaurant on Old Highway 40. By 1939, she made the short move to the house on the hill located on the winding curve of U.S 40. She served president Dwight David Eisenhower and countless other well-known figures. When she retired, she was honored by local businesses, the Greyhound Industry and the State Restaurant Association. By the way, "Ike" always liked Lena's rolls![62]

About Yeast
Temperature is an important factor in the leavening ability of yeast. Either too hot or too cold temperatures can kill or inhibit the yeast. The optimum temperature for yeast actually depends on the activation method . . .

- ❖ When yeast is added directly to warm water, the water temperature should be about 105 to 115°. A pinch of sugar added at this time will also aid in the initial rising action. This method is often referred to as Conventional or Traditional.
- ❖ When using the Rapidmix method, where the dry yeast is mixed with part of the dry ingredients, warmer liquids (120 to 130°) are needed.
- ❖ And, if using Rapid or Quick Rise Yeast (which is more granulated), directions on the package, specify heating the liquid to 130°.

What is the difference between Active Dry, Instant, and, Rapid or Quick Rise Yeast?
Active Dry Yeast is commonly found in strips of three packets or in jars at the grocery store. This type of yeast is activated shortly after being hydrated or combined with water. Active dry yeast starts working more slowly than instant yeast, but eventually catches up with the instant.
(Active Dry) Instant Yeast becomes active the "instant" it contacts moisture. It is ideally suited to the Rapidmix method of yeast dough preparation but will not be harmed if added directly to water in the Traditional mixing method. Instant yeast does make the bread rise a bit faster than plain active dry yeast.
Rapid or Quick Rise Yeast is more granulated and can cut the rising time in half. Like instant yeast, it is ideally suited to the Rapidmix method but can be used in the Traditional mixing method of yeast dough preparation as well.

Cinnamon Rolls *Yield: 3 dozen rolls*

Prepare all in one day or since this is a refrigerator dough, make ahead & have fresh baked cinnamon rolls the next day! (For additional information about refrigerator dough, see p. 134.)

- 1 cup mashed potatoes (The Kirby House always uses real mashed potatoes, but instant may be substituted.)
- 1 cup granulated sugar
- 2 teaspoons salt
- 1/2 cup butter (or 1 stick)
- 3 3/4 cups whole milk (or you may substitute reduced fat milk)
- 2 scant tablespoons or 2 (1/4 -ounce) packages yeast (active dry instant)
- 1 1/2 teaspoons granulated sugar
- 1/4 cup + 2 tablespoons water (105 to 115°)
- 4 cups all-purpose flour
- 2 teaspoons baking powder
- 1 teaspoon baking soda
- 5 - 6 cups all-purpose flour
- 1/2 cup butter (or 1 stick), soft but not melted

In a microwave safe bowl. mix together the mashed potatoes, 1 cup sugar, salt , butter and milk; microwave on high until hot--about 5 minutes checking every 2 minutes. In a small bowl, mix together the yeast, 1 1/2 teaspoons sugar and water; let stand until yeast activates and is bubbly. In another large bowl, mix together the 4 cups flour, baking powder & soda; add the milk mixture. When temperature of this mixture has cooled to 105 to 115°, add the yeast mixture and thoroughly combine.

Add additional 4 to 5 cups of flour and softened 1/2 cup butter. Mix into dough until fairly stiff but elastic, using dough hook or mix by hand. Add enough remaining flour until dough loses its stickiness.

Put in large bowl, cover and refrigerate. This can be chilled up to 3 to 4 days. Or, instead of refrigerating the dough . . . place in a greased bowl, turning to grease top. Cover; let rise in warm place, free from drafts until doubled in bulk (about 20 minutes to 1 hour). Punch dough down and shape (according to directions that follow). Then cover and let rise again until double (about 20 to 30 minutes). Bake at 350° for 20 to 30 minutes.

<u>To make 1 dozen rolls</u> *(using 1/3 of the dough)*

2 - 3 tablespoons butter, melted
Cinnamon-Sugar mixture (p. 134)
Preheat oven to 350°.
Grease a 13 x 9" baking pan.

Scoop out 1/3 of the dough and let it relax at room temperature about 15 to 20 minutes for easier handling. Using a rolling pin, shape dough into a 10 x 14" rectangle on a lightly floured surface. Brush with 2 to 3 tablespoons melted butter and sprinkle with Cinnamon-Sugar Mixture. Roll up tightly from the long side, pinch dough to seal. Use a sharp knife or Bench knife to slice into twelve 1 1/2" thick pieces. Place cut-side down in prepared pan. Then cover and let rise again until double (about 20 to 30 minutes). Bake for 20 to 30 minutes or until lightly brown and done (when tapped, rolls should have a hollow sound).

Cool on a rack. Frost as desired with Quick Powdered Sugar Glaze (p. 134) or White Buttercream Frosting on p. 175.

Cinnamon-Sugar Mixture--Combine 1/2 cup brown sugar (packed) and 2 tablespoons ground cinnamon. This is enough to cover approximately 1 dozen rolls or 1/3 of the Cinnamon Roll dough on p. 133. This mixture can also be used on cinnamon toast, etc. Note: granulated sugar may be substituted for the brown sugar.

Quick Powdered Sugar Glaze--Blend together 1 cup powdered sugar (sift if lumpy), 1 teaspoon flavoring (vanilla, maple, lemon, etc. depending on desired flavor), 1 tablespoon milk or half-and-half and 1 tablespoon softened butter. Beat until smooth. Drizzle over rolls, breads, etc.

Refrigerator Dough or "Ice Box" Rolls

"Ice box" or refrigerator doughs may be refrigerated right after mixing. Refrigerator doughs generally have more sugar than regular doughs; this allows the yeast to remain viable for up to 3 days in the refrigerator and allows the flexibility of baking fresh dough in a shorter time period . As an added benefit, the dough actually becomes stiffer and easier to shape after refrigeration.

But, did you notice that ***baking soda was added to the Cinnamon Roll recipe*** on the previous page? The cool refrigerator temperatures helps control and slow down the rising process, but the yeast continues to cause the dough to expand by producing bubbles of carbon dioxide gas. Since this process is extended over a much longer period (compared to shaping and baking the dough immediately), sometimes an excess of carbon dioxide or an acid build-up occurs with this extended fermentation creating a sour odor and taste. Since baking soda is a base, it is often added to a refrigerator dough to counteract this acid build-up--it does this because the base neutralizes the acid, thus keeping the dough sweet and fresh tasting.
The Cinnamon Roll dough also contains baking powder, and although we might speculate on its function, it remains unclear. As a matter fact, even the bakers and staff at King Arthur Flour® were stumped about its function.

Cranberry Bread--shaped and twisted loaves *Yield: 1 loaf*

Cranberry Filling *Yield: enough for l twisted loaf*

l/2 cup chopped dried, sweetened cranberries
2 tablespoons chopped pecans
l/4 teaspoon ground cinnamon
l/8 teaspoon ground cloves
l/4 cup brown sugar (packed)
2 teaspoons freshly grated orange peel
l/4 teaspoon ground nutmeg

Combine above ingredients mixing well in a small bowl.

Prepare a standard sweet bread dough (see Rapidmix CoolRise Sweet Dough that follows). After letting dough rise once, punch down, turn out onto lightly floured surface and roll into a l0 x l4" rectangle; brush with 3 to 4 tablespoons melted butter. Spread cranberry filling over dough. Cut dough in half (so that you have two l0 x 7" sections) and roll up, starting with long side. Pinch seams to seal. Position halves side-by-side on a greased jelly roll pan. Loosely twist halves together being careful to keep sealed sides down. Pinch both ends to seal and tuck end under the twisted dough. Cover and let rise till nearly double (about 30 minutes). Bake in a preheated oven at 375° for 25 minutes or until done. Cool and drizzle with orange icing (use recipe for Quick Powdered Sugar Glaze on preceding page but use orange juice to replace the water) or frost with White Buttercream Frosting on p. l75.

Rapidmix CoolRise Sweet Dough *Yield: This will make enough dough for 2 cranberry breads. If you only want to make one cranberry bread, use the other half of this dough for dinner rolls.*

5 - 6 cups all-purpose flour
2 packages (l/4 -ounce) or scant 2 tablespoons yeast (active dry instant)
l/2 cup granulated sugar
l l/2 teaspoon salt
l/2 cup butter (l stick), cut into pieces
l l/2 cups hot water (l20 to l30°)
2 large eggs
Cooking oil

Combine 2 cups flour, undissolved yeast, sugar and salt in large bowl. Stir well to blend. Add butter. Add hot water. Beat with electric mixer at medium speed for 2 minutes. Scrape bowl occasionally. Add eggs and 2 cups more flour. Beat with electric mixer at high speed for 2 minutes or until thick and elastic. Gradually stir in just enough of remaining flour with wooden spoon (or dough hook of mixer) to make a soft dough which leaves sides of bowl. Turn out onto floured board and knead 5 to l0 minutes or until dough is smooth and elastic (or continue process in mixing bowl, using a dough hook, if preferred). Place dough in a greased bowl, turning to grease top. Cover; let rise in warm place, free from drafts until doubled in size, about 30 minutes.Punch down and proceed with directions at the top of the page.

Kolaches *Yield: 24 kolaches*

Plan ahead when making these rolls as the dough is prepared and refrigerated overnight. You'll also need to save some leftover mashed potatoes for this recipe. (The Kirby House always uses real mashed potatoes, but instant may be substituted.)

- 2/3 cup butter
- 1 cup scalded milk (heated to 150°)
- 4 - 5 cups all-purpose flour
- 1 scant tablespoon or 1 (1/4 -ounce) package yeast (active dry instant)
- 1 teaspoon salt
- 2 large eggs
- 2/3 cup mashed potatoes
- 2 - 3 tablespoons melted butter for brushing

In a large mixing bowl, stir butter into scalded milk until melted. Cool this mixture to between 120 to 130°. In a medium bowl, mix dry ingredients (4 cups flour, yeast, salt); add to milk mixture and then add the eggs and mashed potatoes. Mix to make a soft dough, adding enough additional flour to create a soft dough that is not sticky. Cover and let rise until double. Punch down (add more flour if dough appears sticky), cover with plastic wrap & a damp cloth and chill overnight.

Preheat oven to 350° and grease baking sheets (clean up will be easier if you line the pans with parchment paper and then spray with non-stick pan coating). On a lightly floured surface, knead dough about 4 to 5 turns and then divide into 24 balls; place small portions of dough onto prepared baking sheet. Brush with melted butter and let rise until light. (Test for lightness by pressing softly with your little finger near the edge of the dough. If the dent stays, it has risen enough.)Make indentation in center of each bun with the back of a spoon. Fill with fruit filling, then bake about 20 to 25 minutes or until golden brown and hollow-sounding when thumped.

Kolaches or Ceske Kolace--a popular Czechoslovakian sweet roll that has international appeal.

Pineapple Filling:

- 5 1/2 -ounce can crushed pineapple, undrained
- 1/3 cup granulated sugar--reduce or eliminate sugar (to taste) if pineapple is packed in heavy syrup
- 2 teaspoons butter
- 1 1/2 tablespoon all-purpose flour
- 1/4 teaspoon ground nutmeg

Stir ingredients together and cook in small saucepan (on top of the range or, in microwave using a microwave safe dish) until thick and bubbly.

Variation: For apricot filling, substitute apricots for pineapple.

Sun-Dried Tomato & Basil Bread *Yield: 2 loaves (9 x 5 -inch)*

2 scant tablespoons instant or 2 (1/4 -ounce) packages yeast (active dry or instant)
1 cup + 2 tablespoons water (105 to 115°)
3/4 teaspoon granulated sugar
1 cup + 2 tablespoons whole milk
1/4 cup honey
1 tablespoon + 1 teaspoon shortening
7 - 8 cups bread flour (high gluten flour) or all-purpose may be substituted
1 1/2 teaspoons dried basil leaves
1/4 cup chopped sun-dried tomatoes (soak in hot water prior to chopping; drain)
1 tablespoon salt
1/2 cup Italian herbed cheese, grated or use Mozzarella + about 1 teaspoon of Italian seasoning
1 large egg

In a small bowl, mix together the yeast, water and sugar. Let stand until yeast activates and is bubbly. Put milk, honey and shortening into a microwave safe bowl. Microwave just until shortening melts (check every 1 minute). Mix 2 /12 to 3 cups of the flour, basil, tomatoes, salt and cheese in large mixing bowl. Add the yeast mixture, milk mixture and egg. Mix with dough hook on low speed of electric mixer (or mix in bowl by hand). Gradually add as much of the remaining flour (1 cup at a time), until dough becomes smooth and elastic. (Or knead by hand--usually about 8 to 10 minutes to achieve the desired smoothness and elasticity.) Place dough in a greased bowl, turning to grease top. Cover; let rise in warm place, free from drafts until doubled in size, about 30 minutes (see guide below). Preheat oven to 350° and grease 2 loaf pans. Punch down dough and divide in half; shape into loaves. (see instructions below) Cover loosely and let rise again until double in size (about 30 minutes).

Bake for 30 to 40 minutes or until nicely browned. Remove from pan and cool on a cooling rack.

Bread flour . . . is milled from hard wheat which contains high levels of protein. When mixed with water, these proteins form gluten--the substance which gives elasticity to the dough and enables it to rise.

Why variable amounts of flour? In very humid weather, yeast recipes often require more flour because the extra moisture in the air keeps the dough soft.

Testing for double in size ... Press the tips of two fingers lightly and quickly 1/2" into the dough. If the dent stays, it is double.

To shape yeast bread loaves ... With a rolling pin, roll dough into a sheet about a 9 x 12" rectangle (roll gently but firmly to get rid of gas bubbles in the dough as well as to shape). Using your hands, roll up dough like a jelly roll, starting at long side. Pinch edges to seal, and then fold sealed ends under. Place, seam-side down, in greased pans.

Another check for doneness ... When the baking time is up, remove one loaf and tap the bottom or sides. It is done if it sounds hollow.

Croissants *Yield: 32 rolls*

Jean Lee introduced this recipe to Abilene in the 1980's when she conducted cooking classes for area residents. It is a quick variation of the traditional croissant recipe. The batter must be refrigerated at least 4 hours before use, but can remain in the refrigerator up to 4 days ... allowing for fresh baked rolls days after combining the ingredients.

5 cups all-purpose flour, unsifted
1 cup chilled butter (unsalted)
1 - 2 (1/4 -ounce) packages or scant 1 - 2 tablespoons yeast (active dry or instant)
1 cup warm water (110°)
3/4 cup evaporated milk
1 1/2 teaspoon salt
1/3 cup granulated sugar
1 large egg
1/4 cup melted and cooled butter
1 large egg beaten with 1 tablespoon water for brushing rolls prior to baking

 **A SPECIAL TOUCH!** 

Butter Rosettes

Whip butter in the work bowl of an electric mixer until light and fluffy. Use a spatula to pack butter into a pastry bag fitted with a medium to large size star tip. Cover a cookie sheet with waxed paper and pipe star shaped rosettes onto the waxed paper surface. Freeze rosettes until firm and then transfer to a freezer safe container using waxed paper to separate layers. Freeze until ready to use. Offer these butter rosettes with rolls for a special event.

Fit food processor with metal blade--add 4 cups flour and 1 cup butter (that has been cut into squares) to the work bowl. Process in bursts (using the "pulse" option) until butter ranges from the size of peas to dried beans. Transfer to a large bowl.

In the work bowl of the food processor--process yeast and water in 2 bursts. Add milk, salt, sugar, egg, remaining 1 cup flour and melted butter; process until batter is smooth. Pour this yeast mixture into the large bowl of flour mixture. Mix with spatula until flour is moistened. Cover with plastic and refrigerate overnight (or from 4 hours to 4 days). Remove dough to floured board and press into compact ball. Knead about 6 turns to release air bubbles. Divide dough into 4 equal parts. Shape one part at a time, leaving remaining dough wrapped, in plastic wrap, in refrigerator. To shape, roll one quarter of the dough on floured board into a 14" circle. With a sharp knife, cut circle into 8 pie-shaped wedges. For each croissant, loosely roll wedges toward the point. Shape each roll into a crescent and place on ungreased cookie sheet with the point down. Allow at least 1 1/2" space around each croissant. Cover lightly and let rise at room temperature in a draft free place--about 2 hours. Do NOT speed the rising by placing in a warm spot. When almost doubled in bulk, brush rolls with egg and water.

Bake in preheated 325° oven for about 25 to 35 minutes or until golden brown and blistered. Note: Baked rolls freeze well.

Test Your Knowledge of Spices

1. What is the world's most popular flavor?
2. Vanilla is a native of what country?
3. What famous explorer helped popularize the vanilla flavor?
4. Name three categories of vegetable material having flavoring value.
5. What were some of the other uses for spices in ancient times?
6. Do spices improve with age?
7. On what do spices depend for their potency?
8. Name a spice used to sweeten the breath.
9. What are some of the attributes of spices?

(Answers to Test Your Knowledge of Spices on page 148.)

Spice Storage

- ❖Store all spices in a cool, dry place. Heat can destroy flavor and may tend to "cake" some spices and blends.
- ❖Keep containers tightly closed after every use.
- ❖Check spices frequently. Spices will retain their aroma and flavor for some time under proper storage conditions, but nevertheless should be checked regularly. Generally speaking, whole spices will keep longer than ground ones.
- ❖The following is a general outline of the shelf life for products stored under ideal conditions. These guidelines were provided courtesy of Jean Sampson, McCormick Food Service @ http://www.mccormick.com

Spices, Whole	3 to 4 years
Spices, Ground	1 to 2 years
Herbs	1 to 2 years
Blends	1 to 2 years
Capsicums (Red Pepper, Paprika, Chili Powder)	1 year -(In hot or humid climates, refrigeration is recommended)
Onion & Garlic (Dehydrated)	3 years
Minced Garlic	18 to 21 months
Extracts, Colors	4 years

Fresh versus Dried Herbs

Dried herbs are more potent because they have less moisture. Therefore when substituting dried herbs for fresh ones, use 2 to 3 times less. On the other hand, if substituting fresh oregano for dried in a recipe, use 2 to 3 times more of the fresh. Crush or chop fresh herbs to release their oils and the utmost flavor. Dried herbs are best added to broth or oil for ultimate flavor release.

"May lightning strike very soon
The cook who measures herbs by tablespoon."

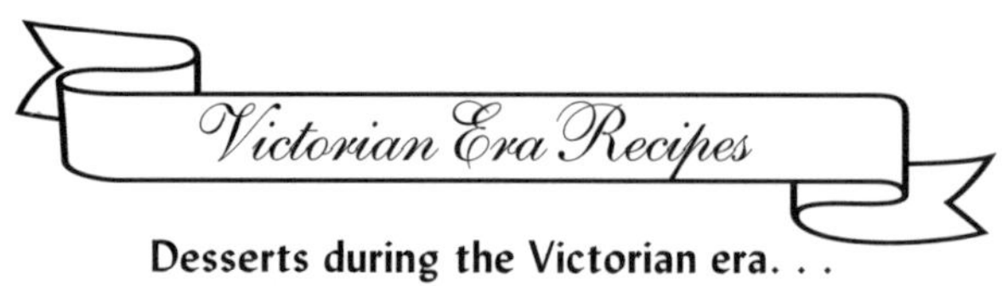

Desserts during the Victorian era. . .

Victorians were extravagantly fond of puddings, pies, and all kinds of sweets! And desserts could be quite varied including fruits-in-liquor lavishly spooned over ice cream or cake, mince pies, and steamed pudding, to mention a few. They also acquired a taste for figs . . . served up in fig cake, fig pudding, fig jam and even fig ice cream. Shortcake, too, was popular and this recipe appeared in the *Abilene Gazette* newspaper on January 23, 1885 under the heading "COOKING SCIENCE":

Lemon Shortcake

> If your family likes a good strong lemon flavor it will be a delicious dish. Make a shortcake dough exactly like a strawberry shortcake. While that is baking grate the peel and squeeze every drop of juice from it into a bowl then take half a cup of sugar and half a cup of molasses, a teacupful of water, a little lump of butter, and a tablespoonful of flour. Let this boil until it is just about as thick as boiled custard. When the shortcake is baked cut it into two parts and pour the mixture over the lower one; then lay the upper part on this, bottom side up, and cover that also with the custard.

Victorian Extracts and Spices

The A.B. Seelye Medicine Company was started in Abilene, Kansas in 1890 and eventually printed a series of informational booklets, *"Seelye's Health Guide and Cook Book."* Recipes, provided by Mrs. Seelye, promoted their extensive line of extracts, essences, spices, seasonings and food colorings. The following recipe and explanation come from one of those booklets and is provided courtesy of Terry Tietjens.

Chocolate and Rice Pudding.

Four tablespoons rice, 2 cups milk, 1 teaspoon of salt, 2 tablespoons butter, 1 teaspoon of Seelye's Vanilla, 1/2 cup of beaten cream, 1/2 cup sugar, 2 squares of chocolate, 3/4 cup seeded raisins and 2 egg whites. Soak rice in milk 1/2 hour; add salt and cook in double boiler until rice is tender. Mix butter, sugar, chocolate, raisins and Seelye's vanilla; add cooked rice, cream and beaten whites. Fill buttered baking dish, cover with a meringue, brown in a moderate oven, serve either hot or cold.

"The Vanilla Beans that are used in Seelye's Vanilla are of excellent quality and flavoring strength and cost a great deal more than cheap substitutes, consequently the customer has the satisfaction of knowing he is using pure Vanilla Extract when he buys Seelye's. Makers of cheap flavors use 'Vanillin' and 'Coumarine,' both coal tar products." Prepared from the choicest vanilla beans of Mexico and the West Indies, carefully cured and manufactured by an original process and then allowed to age, this vanilla was pronounced as having excellent flavor, aroma, and color.[63]

Kirby House Desserts

Apple Cake With Praline Sauce *Yield: one 9 -inch round cake; approximately 12 to 16 servings*

A moist apple cake with a really rich sauce. Serve as a coffee cake for brunch or as a delicious dessert.

Note: Cake keeps well, at room temperature or in the refrigerator. If making cake in advance, wrap and freeze. Thaw just prior to serving; cake is also easily cut while still frozen.

2 1/2 cups all-purpose flour
1 1/2 cups brown sugar (packed)
3/4 cup butter, softened
1 cup chopped pecans, toasted
1 teaspoon baking soda
1 teaspoon ground cinnamon
1/2 teaspoon salt
1 large egg
3/4 cup sour cream
1 teaspoon vanilla
2 apples--peeled, cored and chopped

Praline Sauce, p. 176
Optional--Whipped Cream

Preheat oven to 375°. Grease a 9" round cake pan or springform pan.

In a large bowl, using a fork, mix flour with brown sugar and butter until crumbly. Stir in nuts. Divide mixture in half. Evenly press half into pan bottom to form a crust.

Stir baking soda, cinnamon, and salt into remaining crumb mixture until blended, then make a well in the center. In a small bowl, lightly beat egg with sour cream and vanilla until smooth. Add to center of the crumb mixture, stirring just until combined. Fold in apples. Evenly spread batter over crust in the baking pan. Bake until a toothpick inserted into center comes out fairly clean, about 1 hour and 20 minutes. If top gets too brown before cake is baked, lightly lay a piece of foil over top for last 10 to 20 minutes of baking. Cool in pan on a rack. Serve with Praline Sauce. Whipped Cream is also good on this cake.

"One of the goldenest of the golden rules in making up a menu . . . is to pay special attention to the dessert course. . . . Nobody seems able to resist a delicious dessert. "

-Wolfgang Puck

Chocolate Espresso Cake *Yield: 1 three-layer 9 -inch cake*

2 cups all-purpose flour
3/4 cups unsweetened baking cocoa powder
1 teaspoon baking powder
2 cups granulated sugar
1 teaspoon salt
2 teaspoons baking soda
1 cup vegetable oil
1 cup hot, brewed Espresso or substitute strong coffee
1 teaspoon vanilla
1 cup whole milk
2 large eggs

Preheat oven to 325°. Grease three 9" round cake pans; line the bottom of each with parchment or waxed paper, cut to size. Thoroughly stir together all dry ingredients (flour, cocoa, baking powder, sugar, salt & baking soda) in a large mixing bowl. Add all of the liquid ingredients (oil, coffee, vanilla, milk & eggs) and mix on low speed for 2 minutes. Pour into prepared pans; the batter will be runny. Run a table knife through batter to break large air bubbles and to evenly distribute batter. Bake for 30 to 40 minutes or until toothpick inserted in center comes out clean. (The cakes will appear dark in color.) Frost cake, after it has cooled, using the frosting recipe that follows.

Frosting
5 tablespoons all-purpose flour (or use 1/4 cup + 1 tablespoon)
1 cup whole milk
1/2 cup butter
1/2 cup shortening
1 cup granulated sugar
1 teaspoon vanilla

Place flour in the bottom of a saucepan; slowly add milk using a wire whisk to blend and to avoid lumping. Cook over medium heat until thick. Cover and refrigerate until cooled.
Cream the butter and shortening into the sugar and vanilla using an electric mixer. Add the chilled milk mixture and beat for 10 minutes until light and fluffy.

About Cocoa:
Cocoa powder (or unsweetened baking cocoa) is what is left after most of the cocoa butter has been removed from chocolate. Dutch-process or European-style cocoa has been treated with a mild alkali such as baking soda to reduce the natural acidity of chocolate. It has a darker color and mellower flavor than regular unsweetened baking cocoa.
To substitute cocoa for unsweetened baking chocolate, use three level tablespoons of cocoa plus one tablespoon of vegetable shortening or oil for every one -ounce square of chocolate.

Black Forest Mocha Tower *Yield: 1 three-layer 9 -inch cake*
Follow directions, on preceding page, for Chocolate Espresso Cake, except use the White Buttercream Frosting (on p. 175). Frost the first layer and then spread with half of the Brandied Cherries. Repeat procedure after placing the second layer on top of the first. Finally add the third layer and frost top only (leaving sides unfrosted). Pipe extra frosting around outer edge using star tip, if desired. Chocolate curls would add a decorative touch to this cake--see "A Special Touch" tip that follows.

<u>Brandied Cherries</u>
14.5 -ounce can pie cherries, drained
About 2 to 3 tablespoons granulated sugar--enough to sweeten cherries
2 - 4 tablespoons Kirsch (cherry flavored brandy)

To drained cherries, add the sugar and Kirsch; thoroughly blend in a medium size bowl.

Black Forest Parfait *One more dessert variation using the Chocolate Espresso Cake on p. 143. Make as much (or as little as you want).*

<u>Whipped Cream Mixture</u> *Yield: about 6 cups*
3 tablespoons cold water
1 package (1/4 -ounce) Knox® plain gelatin
3 cups heavy whipping cream
1/2 cup powdered sugar
1/4 teaspoon vanilla

Pour cold water in the bowl of an electric mixer, and sprinkle the gelatin on top. Let stand for 5 minutes until dissolved. Add remaining ingredients and whip until mixture forms soft peaks.

Chocolate Espresso Cake, cut into chunks, (see recipe on p. 143)
Brandied Cherries (see recipe above)

<u>To assemble</u>: Assemble several layers of Chocolate Espresso Cake, Brandied Cherries and the Whipped Cream Mixture.

 **A SPECIAL TOUCH!** 

Chocolate Curls add a fancy touch to just about any special recipe. Simply run a vegetable peeler across the long side of a large bar of semi-sweet or bittersweet chocolate. For best results the surface of the chocolate should be just warm. You can achieve the perfect temperature by zapping the chocolate bar in the microwave for no more than 3 seconds on high.

Chocolate Ganache *Yield: one 9 -inch (one layer) cake; serves 10 to 12*
This flourless chocolate cake with chocolate glaze is frequently offered at teas served at The Kirby House.

Cake

12 -ounces semi-sweet chocolate chips
3/4 cup (1 1/2 sticks) butter, cut into pieces
6 large eggs, separated
12 tablespoons granulated sugar, divided
2 teaspoons vanilla

Preheat oven to 350°. Butter 9" diameter springform pan. Line bottom of pan with parchment paper or waxed paper, cut to size; butter paper. Wrap outside of pan with foil. Stir chocolate and butter in heavy, medium size saucepan over low heat until melted and smooth. Remove from heat. Cool to lukewarm, stirring often.
Using electric mixer, beat egg yolks and 6 tablespoons sugar in large bowl until mixture is very thick and pale, about 3 minutes. Fold lukewarm chocolate mixture into yolk mixture, then fold in vanilla. Using clean, dry beaters, beat egg whites in another large bowl until soft peaks form. Gradually add remaining 6 tablespoons sugar, beating until medium-firm peaks form. Fold whites into chocolate mixture in 3 additions. Pour batter into prepared pan.
Bake cake until top is puffed and cracked and toothpick inserted into center comes out with just a few moist crumbs attached, about 50 minutes. Cool cake in pan on rack (cake will fall). Gently press down crusty top to make an evenly thick cake. Using small knife or spatula, cut around pan sides to loosen cake. Remove pan sides. Invert cake onto a serving plate and peel off parchment paper. Glaze and decorate, if desired.

Glaze

1/2 cup heavy whipping cream
1/2 cup light corn syrup
9 -ounces semi-sweet chocolate chips (1 1/3 cup + heaping 2 1/2 tablespoons)

Bring cream and corn syrup to simmer in medium saucepan. Remove from heat. Add chocolate and whisk until melted and smooth. Place cake on rack set over a baking sheet. Spread 1/2 cup glaze smoothly over top and sides of cake. Freeze until almost set, about 3 minutes. Pour remaining glaze over cake; smooth sides and top. Place cake on platter. Chill until glaze is firm, about 1 hour. (Can be made 1 day ahead. Cover with cake dome; store at room temperature.) Serve at room temperature. Optional: Decorate with chocolate leaves or decorations--see "A Special Touch!" tip on p. 146.

 **A SPECIAL TOUCH!** 

Chocolate Leaves are impressive but easy!

Chocolate Leaves:
You'll need--3 to 4 ounces semi-sweet chocolate chips, and a few drops of vegetable oil, plus waxy leaves (such as Camellia or Philodendron). Be sure to wash leaves in soapy water and dry thoroughly prior to covering with chocolate.
Melt chocolate and oil in the microwave at 50% power. Use a spoon or pastry brush to coat the back of leaves with a substantial layer of melted chocolate. Refrigerate or freeze until firm. When completely cool, carefully peel the leaf from the chocolate to reveal a veined leaf shape. Refrigerate or freeze leaves until ready to use. Group several leaves in the middle of a cake for an especially effective presentation.

Chocolate Decorations:
Follow directions above for melting chocolate. Trace a simple design (such as a lightening bolt or figure 8) on a sheet of paper. Set design on top of a cookie sheet (or other flat surface); cover design with waxed paper. Assemble a pastry bag with a medium-size writing tip; fill with the melted chocolate and pipe chocolate onto waxed paper following the paper design; repeat until you have sufficient quantities. Refrigerate or freeze decorations until firm. When completely cool, carefully peel decorations from waxed paper. Refrigerate or freeze until ready to use. Place a decoration on top of individual slices of dessert for added height and interest.

Tips for beating egg whites
For maximum volume, egg whites should be at room temperature. If any egg yolk (which contains fat) or any other fat is present in the mixing bowl, the egg white will not foam correctly. Therefore, be careful when separating the white from the yolk--it is recommended to break each egg into a small bowl before adding the white to the larger mixing bowl (if one white is contaminated with yolk, the whole batch will be affected.) Also, be sure the mixing bowl(s) and mixer beaters are grease free.

German Sweet Chocolate Cake *Yield: 1 three-layer 9-inch cake*

- 4 -ounces Bakers® German Sweet Baking Chocolate
- 1/2 cup water
- 2 cups all-purpose flour
- 1 teaspoon baking soda
- 1/4 teaspoon salt
- 1 cup butter, softened
- 2 cups granulated sugar
- 4 egg yolks (from large eggs)
- 1 teaspoon vanilla
- 1 cup buttermilk
- 4 egg whites

Preheat oven to 350°. Prepare three 9" cake pans by lining bottom with parchment paper, or waxed paper, cut to size; spray the sides with non-stick pan coating.

Microwave chocolate and water in large microwave safe bowl on high 1 1/2 to 2 minutes or until chocolate is almost melted, stirring halfway through heating time. Stir until chocolate is completely melted. Mix flour, baking soda, and salt in another bowl; set aside. Beat butter and sugar in a large bowl with electric mixer on medium speed until light and fluffy. Add egg yolks, one at a time, beating well after each addition. Stir in chocolate mixture and vanilla. Add flour mixture alternately with buttermilk, beating after each addition until smooth. Beat egg whites in another large bowl with electric mixer on high speed until stiff peaks form. Gently stir into flour batter. Pour into prepared pans and bake 30 minutes or until cake springs back when lightly touched in center. Immediately run spatula between cakes and sides of pans. Cool 15 minutes; remove from pans. Remove parchment paper and cool completely on wire racks.

Frost with Fudge Frosting on p. 175, and decorate with Chocolate Leaves, p. 146, if desired.

Cake Pan Size: For best results use the pan sizes recommended in the directions when baking cakes. If pans are too large, the cakes may look small and flat. If pans are too small, the batter may spill over the sides of the pan. Be sure to fill pans only half full and bake any left-over batter in muffin pans to create cupcakes.

Test for cake doneness--Cakes are completely baked when the center, touched lightly with a finger, springs back and leaves no imprint or when cakes begin to pull away from the sides of pans.

Miss Ellie's Carrot Cake *Yield: 1 three-layer 9 -inch cake*

This cake is one of the signature items at The Kirby House. The recipe came from Eleanor Correll and bears her name.

2 1/2 cups all-purpose flour
2 1/2 cups granulated sugar
2 1/2 teaspoons baking soda
1 1/4 teaspoons salt
2 1/2 teaspoons ground cinnamon
5 large eggs
1 1/4 cups vegetable oil
5 cups shredded carrots (approximately 1 1/4 lb.)

The recipe for carrot cake didn't appear in American cookbooks until the second half of the 1900's. Today, carrot cake is one of the most frequently requested desserts.

Preheat oven to 350°. Prepare three 9" cake pans by lining bottom with parchment paper, or waxed paper, cut to size; spray the sides with non-stick pan coating.

In a mixing bowl, mix together the flour, sugar, baking soda, salt and cinnamon. Set aside.

In another large mixing bowl, using an electric mixer, beat the eggs until frothy. Gradually add the oil while beating. Next, gradually add the flour mixture. Add the shredded carrots and mix just until blended.

Pour into prepared pans. Run a table knife through batter to break large air bubbles and to evenly distribute batter. Bake for 30 minutes or until toothpick inserted in center comes out clean. Cool and frost with Maple Cream Cheese Frosting.

<u>Maple Cream Cheese Frosting</u>

1/4 cup butter, softened (1/2 stick)
6 -ounces cream cheese
1 teaspoon maple flavoring
4 1/3 cups powdered sugar
(1 tablespoons water)
Ground nutmeg for garnish

Cream together butter and cream cheese. Add maple flavoring and gradually add powdered sugar (sift if lumpy) until spreading consistency is reached. Add water if frosting is too stiff. After cake is cool, frost between the layers and on top only.

Sprinkle nutmeg over the top of the frosted cake. The Kirby House, offers this tip to get a fine, even sprinkling: place about 1/2 to 1 teaspoon nutmeg in the palm of one hand and then run both palms together over surface of the cake.

Answers to Test Your Knowledge of Spices on page 139.

1. Vanilla. 2. Mexico. 3. Cortez. 4. Spices, herbs and seeds. 5. For money, drugs, embalming and burial. 6. No, they actually begin to lose their flavor with age. 7. Oils in spices give them potency & it is these oils that evaporate when exposed to air or heat. 8. Cloves. 9. If used properly, spices stimulate the appetite, bring out full natural flavor of the foods to which they are added, and can aid digestion.

Kirby House Cheesecake *Yield: 1 cheesecake*

The Kirby House uses a Quick Shortbread Crust recipe as a means of saving time. This crust is easy to cut yet still complements the cheesecake filling.

Quick Chocolate Shortbread Crust

Thoroughly mix the following:

1/3 cup shortbread crumbs (see recipe for shortbread on p. 150, or use purchased shortbread)
2 tablespoons powdered sugar
1 tablespoon unsweetened baking cocoa powder

Quick Shortbread Crust

1/3 cup shortbread crumbs (see recipe for shortbread on p. 150, or use purchased shortbread)

Preheat oven to 350°. Prepare a 9" springform pan by spraying it with non-stick pan coating. Sprinkle crust ingredients (select either the chocolate or basic shortbread variation) over bottom of the springform pan.

Basic Filling

24 -ounces of cream cheese, softened (equivalent to three 8 -ounce packages)
1 cup granulated sugar
2 tablespoons + 2 teaspoons cornstarch
1 1/2 teaspoons clear vanilla or substitute dark vanilla
1/3 cup sour cream
3 large eggs

Using an electric mixer, beat cream cheese and sugar in large mixing bowl using a wire whip attachment, if available. Continue to beat with the mixer until ingredients are smooth and creamy. Beat in cornstarch. Add vanilla and sour cream. Add eggs, one at a time, beating only until combined; be careful not to over beat. (Over beating can lead to cracking on the surface of cheesecake.)

Assembly: *Enclose the bottom & sides of the springform pan (containing the crust) in aluminum foil; pour the cheesecake filling into prepared crust. Place the springform pan in a large roasting pan set on an oven rack; add 1/2 to 1" hot water to roaster, creating a water bath. Bake the cheesecake 1 to 1 1/2 hours at 350° or until set.

For safety . . . when baking time is up, carefully remove the cheesecake from the roasting pan; leave the roasting pan of hot water in the oven removing only after water has cooled.

Cool the cheesecake on a wire rack. Cover and chill.

*The bottom & sides of the springform pan are wrapped in foil to insure that moisture from the water bath does not permeate the cheesecake as it bakes.

Tip from Vangie--Despite all efforts, sometimes a cheesecake still develops a crack in the center. Vangie Henry (owner and operator of The Kirby House) suggests laying a sheet of plastic wrap over the crack while the cheesecake is still warm. Use fingertips to apply just enough pressure to close the crack and smooth the surface.

Shortbread

Cream together:
- 2 cups butter
- 1 cup powdered sugar

Add and mix thoroughly:
- 4 cups all-purpose flour
- pinch salt
- pinch baking powder

Press dough into an even, thin layer on a standard cookie sheet that has been sprayed with non-stick pan coating. Prick dough with fork and bake at 350° in a preheated oven until evenly browned and crisp. Cool and break apart enough to use for the cheesecake crust. Remaining pieces can be cut into bite-size cookies and are delicious with fresh fruit, ice cream or alone!

 **A SPECIAL TOUCH!** 

Cheesecake Toppings

Of course, cherry (or other fruit) pie fillings always make a nice cheesecake topping, but here are a few other ideas:

- ❖ Arrange cut or whole, fresh strawberries over the top and drizzle with melted strawberry jam.
- ❖ Cover with The Kirby Houses' Raspberry Sauce on p. 177, top with fresh raspberries and drizzle with chocolate sauce.
- ❖ Or, offer a "Cheesecake Bar" where an assortment of toppings are available (sauces, nuts, fresh fruits, whipped cream, melted jams, etc.) and let each person select their favorites to garnish, decorate and flavor their cheese cake slice.

The Kirby House creates a multitude of cheesecake variations . . . all using the same basic filling. Following are some of those variations:

Blackberry Swirl Cheesecake *Yield: 1 cheesecake*

- 1 cup white chocolate chips
- 1/2 cup blackberry jam
- 1 teaspoon to 1 tablespoon Kirsch (cherry flavored brandy)

Prepare the Basic Cheesecake Filling (p. 149) adding the white chocolate chips to the mixture. Add filling to a 9" springform pan sprinkled with the Chocolate Shortbread Crust (p. 149). Meanwhile heat the blackberry jam thinning with a little cherry brandy. Swirl the heated jam through the cheesecake filling and bake as directed.

Caramel Apple Cheesecake *Yield: 1 cheesecake*

- 3 tablespoons butter
- 1 cup sliced, peeled apples (see p. 43 for information on apple selection)
- 1 teaspoon ground cinnamon
- 1 teaspoon granulated sugar
- 2 tablespoons Amaretto (an almond based liqueur)

Melt butter in a skillet over medium heat. Add apples, cinnamon and sugar; cover and simmer to soften apples. Remove cover and continue to cook and stir to reduce liquid. Sprinkle the Shortbread Crust (as directed on p. 149) in the bottom of a 9" springform pan; add caramel apples.Prepare the Basic Cheesecake Filling (p. 149) adding the Amaretto to the mixture and place on top of the apple mixture; bake as directed.

Coconut Cheesecake *Yield: 1 cheesecake*

2 tablespoons coconut syrup (such as Stirling® Hawaiian Coconut gourmet syrup)
1 1/2 cups flaked coconut

Topping

1 cup sour cream
3 tablespoons granulated sugar
1/2 to 1 cup toasted coconut (see p. 163 for tips on toasting coconut)

Prepare the Basic Cheesecake Filling (p. 149) adding the coconut syrup to the cream cheese mixture. After beating in eggs, fold in the flaked coconut. Add filling to a 9" springform pan sprinkled with the Shortbread Crust and bake as directed.

For topping: mix sour cream and granulated sugar. Top with sour cream mixture after cheesecake is baked and completely cool. Sprinkle with toasted coconut.

French Silk Cheesecake *Yield: 1 cheesecake*

1/4 cup semi-sweet chocolate chips
2 tablespoons butter
2 tablespoons hot water
1/4 cup unsweetened baking cocoa powder

Melt the semi-sweet chocolate chips and butter in a small saucepan.

In a small bowl, slowly add the hot water to the cocoa powder, stirring constantly, until cocoa is completely dissolved. Mix this with the chocolate chips and butter.

Prepare the Basic Cheesecake Filling (p. 149) adding the above mixture slowly to the basic filling; mix until thoroughly combined. Add filling to a 9" springform pan sprinkled with the Chocolate Shortbread Crust and bake as directed.

German Chocolate Cheesecake *Yield: 1 cheesecake*

2 tablespoons butter
1/4 cup + 2 tablespoons semi-sweet chocolate chips
2 tablespoons hot water
1/4 cup unsweetened baking cocoa powder
3/4 to 1 cup flaked coconut
1/2 to 3/4 cup chopped pecans

In a small saucepan, melt the butter and chocolate chips. In a small bowl combine a small amount of the water with the cocoa; once it is thoroughly mixed, add the remaining water. Add both the chocolate and cocoa mixture to the cream cheese mixture in the Basic Cheesecake Filling (p. 149). After beating in the eggs, fold in the coconut. Add filling to a 9" springform pan sprinkled with the Shortbread Crust; sprinkle top with chopped pecans and bake as directed.

Hazelnut Cheesecake *Yield: 1 cheesecake*

2 - 3 teaspoons hazelnut flavor (such as Stirling® Rocky Mountain Hazelnut gourmet syrup)
1 double shot of brewed espresso or substitute strong coffee (about 1/4 cup)

Prepare the Basic Cheesecake Filling (p. 149) adding 2 to 3 teaspoons hazelnut syrup to the mixture. Add filling to a 9" springform pan sprinkled with the Chocolate Shortbread Crust (p. 149) and swirl a double shot of espresso through the filling; bake as directed.

Kahula® Fudge Cheesecake *Yield: 1 cheesecake*

3/4 cup Kahlua® (a Mexican coffee liqueur with herbs and vanilla)

Prepare exactly the same as the French Silk Cheesecake (p. 151) but add Kahula to the mixture; bake as directed.

Lime Cheesecake *Yield: 1 cheesecake*

1/3 cup key lime juice (or use fresh lime juice)
2 - 3 drops green food coloring

Topping
1 cup sour cream
3 tablespoons granulated sugar

Prepare the Basic Cheesecake Filling (p. 149) adding the lime juice. Add filling to a 9" springform pan sprinkled with the Shortbread Crust and bake as directed.
For topping: Mix sour cream and granulated sugar. Top with sour cream mixture after cheesecake is baked and completely cool.
Note: Key Lime juice is actually yellow in color. To achieve a characteristically green color, food coloring is added.

Pumpkin Cheesecake *Yield: 1 cheesecake*

This is a wonderful addition to your Thanksgiving or Christmas feast.

To the Basic Cheesecake Filling (p. 149) add:
1 cup canned pumpkin
1 teaspoon ground cinnamon /
3/4 teaspoon ground ginger
1/4 teaspoon ground cloves
1 1/2 tablespoons Captain Morgan Original Spiced Rum® (Puerto Rican Rum with Spice and Other Natural Flavors)
2 tablespoons heavy whipping cream
1/2 cup granulated sugar
1/2 cup brown sugar (packed)

Add to a Gingersnap Crust--made by sprinkling the bottom of a 9" springform pan with 1/3 cup finely crushed gingersnap cookies. Bake as directed.

Strawberry Wave Cheesecake *Yield: 1 cheesecake*

Fresh or frozen strawberries--puree in the blender or food processor to equal about 1/2 cup of puree

Prepare the Basic Cheesecake Filling (p. 149); add half of the filling to a 9" springform pan sprinkled with the Shortbread Crust (p. 149) and then swirl the strawberry puree through the filling. Add the rest of the cheesecake filling and continue to swirl. Bake as directed.

Turtle Cheesecake *Yield: 1 cheesecake*

Praline Sauce, p. 176

Chocolate Chips (preferably mini chocolate chips)

Prepare the Basic Cheesecake Filling (p. 149); add filling to a 9" springform pan sprinkled with the Chocolate or Plain Shortbread Crust (p. 149) and bake as directed. Drizzle with praline sauce and sprinkle with chocolate chips when cheesecake is cool.

Eggnog Cheesecake *Yield: 1 cheesecake*

Shortbread Crust, prepare as directed on p. 149

Filling:

24 -ounces of cream cheese, softened (equivalent to three 8 -ounce packages)
1 cup granulated sugar
3 tablespoons cornstarch
3 tablespoon Captain Morgan Original Spiced Rum® (Puerto Rican Rum with Spice and Other Natural Flavors)
1 teaspoon vanilla
2 large eggs
1 cup heavy whipping cream
4 large egg yolks
Ground nutmeg to sprinkle over top

Beat cream cheese and sugar in large mixing bowl using a wire whip attachment, if available. Continue to beat with the mixer until ingredients are smooth and creamy. Beat in cornstarch. Add Spiced Rum and vanilla. Add eggs and beat just until combined; be careful not to over beat. (Over beating can lead to cracking on the surface of cheesecake.) Whip the cream and then fold into the above mixture. Mix egg yolks and fold into mixture. *Enclose the bottom & sides of the springform pan (containing the prepared crust) in aluminum foil; pour the cheese-cake filling into prepared crust and sprinkle with nutmeg. Place the springform pan in a large roasting pan set on an oven rack; add 1/2 to 1" hot water to roaster creating a water bath. Bake the cheesecake 60 minutes at 350° or until set.

For safety . . . when baking time is up, carefully remove the cheesecake from the roasting pan; leave the roasting pan of hot water in the oven removing only after water has cooled. Cool the cheesecake on a wire rack. Cover and chill.*The bottom & sides of the springform pan are wrapped in foil to insure that moisture from the water bath does not permeate the cheesecake as it bakes.

Cinnamon-Sugar Oat Cookies *Yield: about 5 dozen cookies*
Jane Medina adapted a basic recipe to create these great cookies which are now a favorite at special Kirby House functions.

- 1 1/4 cup dark brown sugar (packed)
- 1/2 cup Crisco® shortening
- 1/2 cup butter or margarine, softened
- 1/2 cup granulated sugar
- 2 large eggs
- 2 tablespoons milk
- 2 teaspoons vanilla
- 1 3/4 cups all-purpose flour
- 1 teaspoon baking soda
- 1/2 teaspoon salt
- 1/2 teaspoon cinnamon
- 2 1/2 cups uncooked, quick-cooking or old-fashioned oats
- 1 cup coarsely chopped nuts, optional (Jane uses toasted pecans)
- Extra granulated sugar for rolling

Preheat oven to 375°.
In large mixing bowl, combine brown sugar, shortening, butter and granulated sugar. Beat at medium speed of electric mixer until light and fluffy. Add eggs, milk and vanilla. Beat at medium speed until well blended. Add flour, baking soda, salt and cinnamon. Beat at low speed until soft dough forms. Stir in oats and nuts.
Place extra granulated sugar in a shallow bowl. Use a cookie scoop or teaspoon to dip out a ball of dough and then roll each ball in the sugar. Place balls about 2" apart on ungreased cookie sheets. Bake about 8 minutes. Let cool for 1 minute before removing from cookie sheets. Cool completely before storing.

Raisin Oat Cookies --Add about 1 cup raisins to the above mixture when incorporating the oats and nuts. Note: If raisins are dry, add to slightly beaten eggs and let them "plump" for a few minutes.

Chocolate Chip Oat Cookies --Omit cinnamon and add one 12 -ounce package semi-sweet chocolate chips when incorporating the oats and nuts. Also, omit rolling the cookies in sugar.

Gingersnaps *Yield: about 4 to 5 dozen cookies*
This is a prize winning recipe from Terry Switzer and a favorite at Abilene High School Honor Society receptions.

- 3/4 cup shortening (Crisco®)
- 1 cup brown sugar (packed)
- 1/4 cup molasses
- 1 large egg
- 2 1/4 cups all-purpose flour
- 2 teaspoons baking soda
- 1/2 teaspoon salt
- 1 teaspoon ground ginger
- 1 teaspoon ground cinnamon
- 1/2 teaspoon ground cloves
- about 1/4 cup granulated sugar for rolling

Preheat oven to 375°. Grease or spray cookie sheets. Cream together (using an electric mixer) shortening, brown sugar, molasses, egg. Add flour, soda, salt, ginger, cinnamon, and cloves to molasses mixture and blend. Form into small balls. Roll in granulated sugar. Place 2" apart on prepared cookie sheet. Bake about 8 to 10 minutes. Do not overbake! Additional sugar can also be sprinkled on the warm cookies.

Bob's Mocha Chocolate Cookies *Yield: about 4 to 5 dozen tea size cookies*
The recipe (with a few minor adjustments) for these delicious cookies came from Bob Riedel; it is always a big hit at Abilene High School Honor Society receptions.

1/2 cup butter (1 stick)
4 -ounces unsweetened chocolate
3 cups semi-sweet chocolate chips, divided
1/2 cup all-purpose flour
1/2 teaspoons baking powder
1/2 teaspoon salt
4 large eggs
1 1/2 cups granulated sugar
1 1/2 tablespoons espresso powder (The Kirby House grinds espresso beans to create this powder or a flavored coffee powder (such as General Foods International Coffees® could be used).
2 teaspoons vanilla
2 cups chopped, toasted pecans (see p. 176 for tips on toasting)

Preheat oven to 350°. Grease or spray (with non-stick pan coating) cookie sheets. In a saucepan, melt the butter, unsweetened chocolate and 1 1/2 cups of the chocolate chips; stir until smooth. Remove from heat and let the mixture cool slightly. In a medium bowl, combine the flour, baking powder, and salt. In a large bowl, beat together the eggs, sugar, espresso powder and vanilla. Blend in the chocolate mixture. Add the flour mixture. Stir in the nuts and the remaining chocolate chips. (Dough may be chilled at this point if it is too soft to shape.) Drop rounded mounds of cookie dough at least 1" apart on the prepared baking sheets. Bake the cookies for 10 minutes or until they are cracked and shiny on the outside yet soft on the inside. Cool completely on the baking sheet.

Frosted Carrot Cookies *Yield: 3 1/2 dozen*

3/4 cups shortening (Crisco®)
3/4 cup granulated sugar
1 cup mashed carrots (grate, then cook & mash)
1 teaspoon vanilla
2 cups all-purpose flour
1/4 teaspoon salt
2 teaspoons baking powder

Preheat oven to 350°. Grease or spray (with non-stick pan coating) cookie sheets. Cream shortening and sugar. Add mashed carrots and vanilla. Add dry ingredients--flour, salt, baking powder--to shortening mixture and mix well. Drop by teaspoons on prepared cookie sheet. Bake for 10 to 12 minutes or until set and light brown. Cool and then frost.

<u>Frosting</u>:
1/4 cup butter (1/2 stick)
2/3 - 1 cup powdered sugar, sifted
about 1 tablespoon orange juice concentrate

Blend in food processor, using cutting blade--butter and 2/3 cup powdered sugar. Add about 1 tablespoon orange juice concentrate and blend. Add more powdered sugar as needed to get a thick consistency. Spread on cool cookies.

Cranberry Shortbread Rounds *Yield: about 5 dozen*

- 1 cup (2 sticks) butter, room temperature
- 1/2 cup granulated sugar
- 2 tablespoons whole milk
- 1 teaspoon vanilla
- 1/2 teaspoon salt
- 2 1/2 cups all-purpose flour
- 3/4 cup dried, sweetened cranberries
- 1/2 cup chopped pecans
- 3/4 cup shredded coconut
- Powdered sugar for sprinkling

In the bowl of an electric mixer, beat butter and sugar on medium speed until light and fluffy, about 2 minutes. Add milk, vanilla, and salt. Beat until just combined. Gradually add flour, cranberries, and pecans. Mix on low speed until fully combined. Divide dough in half. Shape each half into 8" logs, about 2" in diameter. Roll logs in coconut, pressing lightly to coat the outside of each log. Wrap logs in plastic wrap, and refrigerate until firm, about 2 hours.

Preheat oven to 375°. Using a sharp knife, cut logs into 1/4" thick slices. Transfer to parchment lined baking sheets that have been lightly greased, place about 1 1/2" apart. Bake until edges are golden, about 12 minutes. Transfer to a rack to cool. Sprinkle with powdered sugar when cool. Store up to 2 weeks in an air-tight container.

Tips for Cookie Baking and Storage

- ❖ Select a bright cookie sheet. If using a Teflon or dull sheet, reduce the heat or the baking time slightly. (Bright cookie sheets reflect heat whereas, dull sheets absorb heat often causing the cookie to brown too quickly.)
- ❖ Be sure cookies are all the same size and shape. Small ones will burn before the other ones are done.
- ❖ Bake cookies in the center of the oven. Often it is best to bake only one sheet at a time to allow for uniform heat circulation and browning. If two cookie sheets are placed in the oven at the same time, they should be placed far enough apart to allow for even heat circulation.
- ❖ Use a cookie sheet that is small enough to allow the air to circulate around the sides of pan so that cookies will not burn on the bottom before they are brown on the top.
- ❖ Place cookies at least 1 -inch from the sides of the cookie sheet to prevent those along the edges from becoming too brown.
- ❖ Check as soon as minimum baking time is up.
- ❖ Cookie dough will melt and spread on a hot baking sheet so have a second cool sheet for the next batch.
- ❖ If cookies are left on the baking sheet too long, they will stick and be difficult to remove.
- ❖ Avoid stacking cookies while still hot or they may stick together.
- ❖ Avoid storing different kinds of cookies together. Place crisp, thin cookies in a container with a loose cover. Soft cookies keep best in an air-tight container with a tight cover.

Kolache Cookies *Yield: about 7 to 8 dozen*

This delicious recipe fuses the best of the traditional kolache yeast bread and a rolled cookie. Don't let the use of yeast and the apparent lack of sugar fool you--this is wonderful cookie and worth the extra work.

1/4 cup sour cream, room temperature
1 package active dry yeast or scant tablespoon instant yeast
1 large egg, lightly beaten
1 cup (2 sticks) butter, cut into small pieces
2 cups all-purpose flour
About 1 cup fruit jam or preserves (Apricot jam is a delicious filling in these cookies)

Preheat oven to 400°.

In a small saucepan or microwave safe bowl, heat sour cream to 110°; add yeast. Set aside until slightly bubbly, about 10 minutes. Using a whisk, stir in egg until smooth. Set aside. Add butter and flour to a medium mixing bowl and then use electric mixer to cut the butter into flour until it resembles coarse meal. Stir in sour cream mixture until dough comes together. On a lightly floured surface, roll out dough 1/4" thick. Cut into 1 to 1 1/2" rounds. Transfer to ungreased cookie sheets, placing about 1 1/2" apart. Cover with a clean kitchen towel or plastic wrap. Let sit for 15 minutes. Make a thumbprint in center of each cookie. Fill each thumbprint with about 1/2 teaspoon jam or preserves. Bake until edges are golden, 10 to 12 minutes. Transfer to a rack to cool. Let cookies cool on pans for 5 minutes. Remove cookies to a rack. While cookies are still warm, drizzle with Sugar Glaze.

<u>Sugar Glaze</u> *Makes about 3/4 cup*

1 cup powdered sugar, sifted
2 tablespoons butter, melted
2 teaspoons light corn syrup
2 to 3 tablespoons whole milk

Combine sugar and butter. Add corn syrup, stirring to combine. Drizzle in milk a little at a time until the glaze has a runny consistency.

What does the word "cookie" mean? It's derived from the Dutch word "koekje" which means "small cake." And that's just what the very first cookies were--small drops of cake batter used to test the heat of the oven.

Tea Time Tessies *Yield: 30 pastries*
Mini-muffin tins are needed for this recipe.

Pastry Base
3 -ounces cream cheese, softened
1/2 cup (1 stick) butter or margarine
1 cup sifted all-purpose flour

Preheat oven to 350°. Lightly spray the bottom on each muffin tin with non-stick pan coating.
In a small bowl, blend the cream cheese and butter with mixer. Add flour; mix until a soft dough forms. Do not over mix. Divide into 30 walnut-sized balls. Press dough into prepared mini-muffin cups shaping to fit the curve of the tin. (Note: if dough is hard to work with, cover and refrigerate for about 1 hour and continue.)

Pecan Filling
3/4 cup brown sugar (packed)
1 tablespoon butter, softened
1 large egg
1 teaspoon vanilla
Dash salt
3/4 cup broken pecan pieces

Mix the first five ingredients thoroughly in a medium mixing bowl. Add pecans.
Fill each pastry about half full with pecan filling. Bake 25 to 30 minutes or until pastry is light brown. Cool baking pans on cooling racks. When cool, remove cookies from pan by running a knife around the edge of each muffin cup; then carefully invert pan on a plate.

 **A SPECIAL TOUCH!** 

A Cookie Reception

Selecting cookies for a reception, or other event, is much like planning a meal. Be sure to consider:

- ❖Flavor--Choose cookies that offer a variety of flavors. A rich, chocolate cookie with nuts might be contrasted with a light sugar cookie. Avoid too many selections containing one particular ingredient or taste ... in other words, unless you are having a "chocolate tasting," avoid offering a cookie tray that might include Chocolate Lover's Brownies, Chocolate Chip Oat Cookies and yet, another chocolate cookie.
- ❖Color--Colorful cookie combinations are visually appealing. Chocolate Chip Oat Cookies, Kolache Cookies drizzled with a sugar glaze, and Thumbprint Cookies filled with raspberry jam, are much more interesting than a selection of all light cookies.
- ❖Texture--Balance soft cookies with crisp, crunchy cookies.
- ❖Shape--Vary the shape of the cookies. Cranberry Shortbread Rounds, bar cookies cut in rectangle shapes, and Tea Time Tessies offer an array of interesting shapes on a cookie tray.

Thumbprint Cookies *Yield: 4 dozen*

These are great cookies for an afternoon tea or cookie reception.

2 large eggs (separated)
1 cup butter
1/2 cup brown sugar (packed)
1 teaspoon vanilla
2 cups all-purpose flour
Pinch of salt
1 - 1 1/2 cup finely chopped pecans
About 1/2 - 1 cup fruit preserves or jam

Preheat oven to 350°. Grease cookie sheets or line with parchment paper and spray with non-stick pan coating.

Separate eggs; reserve egg whites by placing in a low, flat bowl. In a large bowl, cream butter, brown sugar and egg yolks. Add vanilla, flour and salt, mixing well. Shape dough into balls. Roll in egg whites, then nuts. Place on cookie sheets about 2" apart; with thumb, dent each cookie. Bake 10 to 15 minutes or until nicely browned. Remove cookies from oven and fill thumbprint with about 1/2 to 1 teaspoon preserves or jam. (Note: make additional indentation as needed when cookies are removed from oven.) Cool cookie sheets on cooling racks for a few minutes and then remove cookies to a cooling rack.

About Sugars

- **Granulated sugar** is white table sugar, made from sugar cane or sugar beets. It is available as fine granules or in cubes.
- **Brown sugar** is granulated sugar with molasses added for flavor and color. Dark brown sugar has a stronger flavor than light brown sugar.
- **Powdered sugar**, also referred to as confectioner's sugar, has been ground to a fine powder and then sifted. It contains about 3% cornstarch to prevent caking.
- **Molasses** is a by-product of making cane sugar. Both light and dark molasses are available.

Chocolate Lover's Brownies *Yield: one 17 x 13 -inch jelly roll pan*
A crisp crusted brownie with a fudgy, gooey interior. This is a delicious cookie but actually becomes a mouth-watering dessert when plated, drizzled with chocolate sauce, sprinkled lightly with powdered sugar and topped with a dollop of whipped cream or a small scoop of ice cream.

1 cup butter
1 1/4 cups semi-sweet chocolate chips
1 1/2 cup + 2 tablespoons granulated sugar
2/3 cup all-purpose flour
1 1/2 teaspoon baking powder
3 large eggs
2 teaspoons *espresso powder (The Kirby House grinds espresso beans to create this powder)
1 tablespoon + 1 teaspoon vanilla
1 cup semi-sweet chocolate chips
1 cup coarsely chopped walnuts

*A flavored coffee powder (such as General Foods International Coffees® could be substituted).

Preheat oven to 350°. Liberally grease, or spray with non-stick pan coating, a 17 x 13" jelly roll pan.
Melt the butter and 1 1/4 cups chocolate chips in a saucepan, on in a microwave safe bowl; set aside.
In a mixing bowl, combine dry ingredients (sugar, flour and baking powder) and thoroughly mix. Add eggs, espresso powder and vanilla and mix using an electric mixer; then add the melted chocolate mixture, mixing until well combined. Stir in the remaining chocolate chips and walnuts. Pour into prepared pan and bake approximately 30 minutes. Cookies will be done when set and crusty on top. Since they are fudgy and gooey in consistency, a toothpick in the center will not come out clean. Cut and serve warm or cold.

A SPECIAL TOUCH!
Offer a Coffee Bar with Dessert

For a coffee bar buffet--select small, interesting dishes (stemmed parfait glasses, martini glasses, demitasse cups, silver bowls, etc.); fill each with a different coffee flavoring. Flavorings might include:

mini chocolate chips	crushed peppermint candies	granulated sugar
cinnamon-sugar mix	crushed butterscotch candies	brown sugar
cocoa mix	crushed cinnamon candies	sugar cubes
whipped cream		colored sugars

For a smaller dinner party--fill the depressions of a deviled egg dish with the powdered flavorings and set a bowl of whipped cream in the center of the plate.
Be sure to provide small spoons for dipping and let your guests enjoy. This is a real crowd pleaser and adds "a special touch" to any event.

Fruit Bars *Yield: one 17 x 13" jelly roll pan*

Serve as a bar cookie, or "dress-up" these bars by placing on a pool of Vanilla Cream, p. 178. Serve a small dip of vanilla ice cream on the side and sprinkle the dessert plate with dried, sweetened cranberries.

Fruit

2/3 cup raisins
2/3 cup dried, sweetened cranberries
2/3 cup dried apricots, chopped
1 cup water or brandy

Mix fruit (raisins, cranberries, apricots) in a microwave safe bowl; cover with water (or brandy), then microwave until boiling. Cover with plastic wrap and let stand 20 minutes. Drain and set aside. (Save the flavored water for another use, if desired.)

Crust

2 cups all-purpose flour
2/3 cup brown sugar (packed)
1 cup butter

Preheat oven to 350°. Liberally grease, or spray with non-stick pan coating, a 17 x 13" jelly roll pan.

In medium bowl, mix flour, brown sugar and butter just until coarse crumbs form. Press into prepared jelly-roll pan. Bake for 20 minutes or until golden brown.

Topping

4 large eggs
2 cups brown sugar (packed)
1 cup all-purpose flour
2 teaspoons vanilla
2/3 cup chopped pecans

In large mixing bowl, beat eggs on low speed for 4 minutes. Add brown sugar, flour, and vanilla. Mix just until combined. Fold in drained fruit and chopped pecans. Pour over baked crust, spreading evenly. Bake 30 to 40 minutes, covering with foil the last 10 minutes to prevent over browning, if necessary. Bars should be golden brown and a toothpick, inserted into the center should come out clean. Cool completely, then sprinkle with powdered sugar. Cut as desired.

Harvest Pumpkin Bars Yield: one 17 x 13 -inch jelly roll pan

1 tablespoon ground cinnamon
1 1/2 teaspoon baking soda
1/2 teaspoon salt
3 cups granulated sugar
3 cups all-purpose flour
3 cups canned pumpkin (two 15 -ounce cans yield approximately 3 1/2 cups)
1 1/2 cups vegetable oil
6 large eggs
1 1/2 teaspoon vanilla

Preheat oven to 350°. Liberally grease, or spray with non-stick pan coating, a 17 x 13" jelly roll pan.
Sift together the dry ingredients (cinnamon, baking soda, salt, sugar and flour) and combine in a large bowl. Add the pumpkin, oil, eggs and vanilla to the dry ingredients (above) and mix just until moistened and smooth. Pour into a prepared pan. Bake at 350° for 20 to 30 minutes or until toothpick inserted in center comes out clean. Cool completely, then frost. Cut as desired.

Frosting
2/3 cup butter, softened
12 -ounces cream cheese
1 tablespoon vanilla
3- 4 cups powdered sugar (sift if it appears lumpy)

Cream together the butter, cream cheese and vanilla. Add powdered sugar, one cup at a time, beating until smooth. If too stiff to spread, add a little water.

Tips on Cutting Bars:

- Use a Bench Knife for easy cutting of bar cookies. Simply use the cutter to press directly down, then lift and move down the row. Because this involves a "lift and cut" technique, rather than the dragging of a knife, ragged edges are avoided. It is also much easier to form straight lines using a Dough Cutter.
  Note: This tip was submitted and accepted for print in *Cuisine Magazine* by Meta Newell West.
- Line baking pan with aluminum foil, allowing the edges of the foil to extend over the edge. After cookies are baked and cool, lift the foil by the edges and transfer to a cutting board. Peel off foil. Use a sharp knife to trim all four sides before cutting into bars.

Old-Fashioned Lemon Bars *Yield: One 9 x 13 x 2 -inch baking pan*

Lemon Filling
2/3 cup granulated sugar
1/2 cup butter
3 large egg yolks, beaten
1/4 cup lemon juice

Mix sugar and butter in saucepan (avoid using an untreated aluminum saucepan as the acid in the lemon juice may react with the aluminum creating a discoloration of the filling; anodized aluminum or stainless steel will NOT create this effect). Heat and stir until blended. *Temper beaten eggs and then slowly whisk eggs and lemon juice into the hot mixture. Cook and stir over medium heat for about 5 minutes or until thick and just bubbling. Transfer to a bowl, cover and let cool for at least 30 minutes.

Crust
2 cups all-purpose flour
1 cup granulated sugar
1/2 teaspoon baking soda
1 cup butter
2/3 cup flaked coconut, **toasted
1/2 cup chopped, toasted pecans
(see p. 176 for toasting tips)

Preheat oven to 375°. Grease the baking pan or spray with non-stick pan coating.
In a medium to large size bowl, using an electric mixer, combine flour, sugar and soda. Cut in butter only until crumbly (over mixing will create a dough rather than a crumbled mixture). Reserve 1 1/2 cup crumb mixture and mix with coconut and pecans; set aside. Press remaining crumbs into the bottom of prepared pan. Bake for 10 minutes; cool on wire rack for 10 minutes. Meanwhile, reduce oven to 350°.
To assemble: After 10 minute cooling, spread lemon filling over crust; then sprinkle reserved crumb mixture over top. Bake for 20 to 25 minutes or until golden brown. Chill to further set the lemon filling.
When cool, cut as desired.

* **Temper** . . . To slowly add a hot liquid to eggs: 1) place eggs in a mixing bowl and beat with a wire whisk, 2) slowly drizzle up to half of the hot mixture into egg yolks whisking constantly, 3) then, blend the tempered egg mixture into the hot ingredients in saucepan. This procedure will gradually raise the temperature of the eggs without making them curdle.

** **Toasting Coconut**
In the Oven . . . spread 1 cup flaked or shredded coconut in a thin layer in a 15 x 10" baking pan. Bake at 350° for 4 to 5 minutes or until light golden brown. For even browning, stir and turn with a pancake turner after 2 minutes, and then every minute. Keep coconut spread in a thin layer. Remove from oven and cool on paper towels.
In the Microwave . . . place 1 cup flaked or shredded coconut in a 2-cup glass measure. Microwave on high for 2 1/2 to 4 minutes or until toasted. Stir after the first minute, then every 30 seconds. Cool on paper towels.

German Chocolate Pie *Yield: one 9 -inch pie*

1 1/2 cups granulated sugar
2 tablespoons unsweetened baking cocoa powder
2 large eggs
1/2 cup (1 stick) melted butter
5 1/4 -ounces evaporated milk (1/2 cup +2 1/2 tablespoons)
3/4 teaspoon vanilla
1/2 cup chopped pecans
1 cup flaked coconut
1 9" pie shell, unbaked

Preheat oven to 325°.
In a large bowl, blend the sugar and cocoa. Add eggs, butter, milk and vanilla and blend well. Fold in the pecans and coconut. Pour into an unbaked pie shell and bake for 1 1/2 hours or until browned and puffed across the top.

Confused about the difference between Evaporated and Condensed Milk?
Evaporated milk is made of whole or skim milk with half of the water removed. It is then sealed in cans and sterilized. Evaporated milk can be used full strength, in place of cream, or mixed with water to use as milk.
Condensed milk is evaporated to reduce the water with at least 40% sugar added. Sweetened, condensed milk is generally used in candy and dessert recipes.

Maple Custard Pie with Maple Whipped Cream *Yield: one 9 -inch pie*

1 9" pie shell, unbaked
3 large eggs
2 cups whole milk
1/2 cup maple syrup

Preheat oven to 400°. Bake pie shell for 5 minutes.
In a mixing bowl, using an electric mixer, beat eggs, milk and syrup until thoroughly combined. Pour mixture into the pie shell and reduce temperature to 350° for 45 minutes or until knife inserted near edge comes out clean).
Chill pie and then top with Maple Whipped Cream. Refrigerate leftovers.

Maple Whipped Cream

1 cup heavy whipping cream
1/4 cup maple syrup

In a mixing bowl, using an electric mixer, whip cream and syrup until soft peaks form.

Plantation Pecan Pie *Yield: one 9 -inch pie*

3 large eggs
1 cup light corn syrup
1 cup granulated sugar
2 tablespoons butter, melted
1 teaspoon vanilla
1/8 teaspoon salt
3 tablespoons Jack Daniels Whiskey
1 cup pecan pieces
1/2 cup semi-sweet chocolate chips
1 9" pie shell, unbaked

Preheat oven to 400°.
Beat eggs slightly, then blend in corn syrup, sugar, butter, vanilla and salt. Stir in whiskey, pecans and chocolate chips. Pour into unbaked pie shell.
Bake at 400° for 15 minutes. Reduce temperature to 350° and bake 30 more minutes or until browned and puffed across the top.

Pie Crust or Pastry for Single-Crust Pie *Yield: one 8 or 9 -inch pie*

1 1/4 cups all-purpose flour
1/2 teaspoon salt
1/3 cup shortening (Crisco® brand is recommended)
4 - 5 tablespoons cold water

In a bowl, combine flour and salt; cut in the shortening until crumbly. Gradually add water, tossing with a fork until a ball forms. Roll out pastry to fit the specified pie pan. Transfer pastry to pie plate. Trim pastry to 1/2" beyond edge of pie plate; flute or decorate edges. Fill shell and bake according to filling directions.

Pastry is another term for pie crust. A perfect crust has a pleasant flavor, a delicate brown color, and is both "short" and flaky. A "short" pastry is one that is tender and breaks easily. A flaky pastry is layered throughout and tiny blisters show on the surface. A pastry which is "short" but not flaky is crumbly; a pastry which is flaky but not "short" is undesirably tough.

Tips for a Perfect Pie Crust

- ❖ Use ice-cold water and use only as much as it takes to hold the flour mixture together; the amount of water will vary due to weather conditions.
- ❖ Avoid over mixing or excess handling once the water is added (over mixing will develop the gluten resulting in a tough crust).
- ❖ Roll out pastry with as little additional flour as possible for a more tender crust.
- ❖ Ease the rolled pastry into the pie plate. Stretching the crust to fit will cause shrinkage during the baking process.
- ❖ Cover the edges of crust with foil strips before placing the pie in the oven to prevent excess browning. Uncover after 20 minutes of baking.

The Right Pie Pan--Glass and dark or dull finished pans allow the heat to be absorbed into the pie crust resulting in a well-baked, tender, browned undercrust. Soggy, soaked undercrusts may result when shiny metal pans are used because they deflect heat.

Sour Cream Apple Pie in Nutty Crust *Yield: 1 pie*

Nutty Pie Crust

- 1 cup all-purpose flour
- 1 stick butter, softened
- 1/4 cup powdered sugar
- 1/2 cup chopped pecans or walnuts

In a mixing bowl, thoroughly combine all ingredients. Pat into the bottom and sides (but not on top edges) of a pie pan--avoid too thick of a crust (if you have leftover dough, wrap and keep in refrigerator for another pie).

Sour Cream Apple Filling

- 2 tablespoons all-purpose flour
- 1/8 teaspoon salt
- 3/4 cup granulated sugar
- 1 unbeaten large egg
- 1 cup sour cream,
- 1 teaspoon vanilla
- 2 to 3 cups sliced and peeled apples (about 3 to 4 medium apples)

Preheat oven to 400°.
In a mixing bowl, mix the flour, salt, sugar, egg, sour cream and vanilla. Add the sliced apples and mix; pour into unbaked shell. Sprinkle evenly with the topping. Bake at 400° for 15 minutes; reduce heat to 350° and continue to bake another 30 minutes or until firm in center and nicely browned. Cool at room temperature and then refrigerate. Serve this pie chilled.

Topping

- 1/3 cup granulated sugar
- 1/3 cup all-purpose flour
- 1 teaspoon ground cinnamon
- 1/4 cup butter

Mix together the sugar, flour. and cinnamon in a bowl; cut in the butter just until mixture is crumbly.

Pies—An American Tradition

Farm wives are credited with perfecting the American art of pie baking. The English were making top-crust-only pies of sweet fruits and savory meats as long ago as the Middle Ages. But American settlers reinterpreted the pie and made it their own.

Apple Crumb Cobbler *This dessert is made in individual souffle dishes or small oven-proof baking dishes. Yield will depend on the capacity of your baking dishes. Also, ingredients for the crust and topping can be made ahead, stored in the refrigerator, and then individual desserts can be baked as needed.*
Served with Cinnamon Ice Cream and The Kirby House Praline Sauce (p.176), this dessert is a real hit!

Crust

3/4 cup all-purpose flour
3/4 cup shredded Cheddar cheese
1/4 cup chilled butter (cut into approximately 4 pieces)

Preheat oven to 350°. Grease individual dishes.
Mix ingredients for crust in a large mixing bowl until crumbly but thoroughly mixed. Press into bottom of baking dishes creating a crust approximately 1/4" thick.

Filling

1 20 -ounce (1 lb. 4 oz.) can apple pie filling
1 1/2 teaspoons ground cinnamon

Combine filling ingredients and spoon approximately 1 1/2" of filling onto each crust.

Brown Sugar Streusel Crumb Topping

3/4 cup brown sugar (packed)
1/4 cup + 2 tablespoons all-purpose flour
1/4 cup + 2 tablespoons quick-cooking oats
1/4 cup butter, softened

In a medium mixing bowl, using an electric mixer, mix crumb topping ingredients only until crumbly. Sprinkle each dessert with approximately 1/4" of the topping. Bake desserts 20 to 30 minutes or until topping is golden and filling is bubbly.

FYI: Cobblers join the other homey fruit-and-dough desserts that are typically American: pandowdy, crisp, brown betty, crunch, slump, grunt and buckles.

Chocolate Fondue *Yield: 3 1/2 cups*

1 cup light corn syrup
3/4 cup heavy whipping cream
18 -ounces semi-sweet chocolate chips (3 cups + 2 tablespoons)

Combine corn syrup and whipping cream in a heavy saucepan; heat on medium heat until warm throughout. Remove from heat; add chocolate morsels, stirring until smooth. Spoon into fondue pot or chafing dish.

Serving Suggestions: Provide platters of fresh strawberries, fresh pineapple chunks and small squares of pound cake for guests to dip into the fondue. Of course, toothpicks or skewers will also need to be provided.

Chocolate Mousse *Yield: about eight 1/2 cup servings*

1/4 cup heavy whipping cream
8 -ounces semi-sweet chocolate (1 1/3 cups chips)
1/4 cup light corn syrup
1/4 cup butter
3/4 cup heavy whipping cream
2 tablespoons powdered sugar
1/2 teaspoon vanilla
3 tablespoons Grand Marnier® (brandy based, orange flavored liqueur)

 Note: 1 pound (16 -ounces) of chocolate chips = 2 cups.

Put whipping cream, chocolate, corn syrup and butter in a microwave safe bowl. Microwave until chocolate melts*. Stir with wire whisk until smooth. Cool.

Beat cream, powdered sugar, and vanilla just until stiff peaks form. Be careful not to over beat as it will begin to turn to butter and will not blend with chocolate properly.

Gently fold whipped cream into chocolate mixture along with the Grand Marnier®. Spoon into dishes or spoon into pastry bag, then squeeze into parfait glasses, mounding slightly at the top. Cover loosely with plastic wrap and chill.

* **Melting Chocolate:** For ease--use a microwave set for 1 to 2 minute(s), stir and continue microwaving at 1 minute intervals until completely melted. Always melt chocolate using an uncovered container. Even one drop of water that falls from condensing steam on a piece of plastic wrap can make your chocolate stiffen or "seize." Containers and utensils used for melting chocolate should be completely dry. If the melted chocolate stiffens, you can soften it by quickly stirring in a little vegetable oil or shortening.

Chocolate Truffle Torte *Yield: one 9 -inch Torte*

- 1/2 cup butter (1 stick), softened, but not melted
- 1 1/2 cup granulated sugar
- 1 tablespoon vanilla
- 6 large eggs
- 10 -ounces (1 2/3 cups) bittersweet chocolate, melted and slightly cooled
- 1/2 cup all-purpose flour

Preheat oven to 350°. Grease and flour the sides and bottom of a 9" springform pan. Place first 3 ingredients (butter, sugar & vanilla) in a mixing bowl and mix with electric mixer, on medium to high speed, until well combined. Then add 2 eggs at a time, beating well after each addition; continue until all eggs are incorporated. With a rubber spatula, stir in chocolate and flour until well blended. Pour into prepared pan and bake for 1 hour or until cake cracks around edges and is firm in the center. Cool, then pour chocolate ganache over top.

<u>Chocolate Ganache</u>

- 1/2 cup heavy whipping cream
- 1/2 cup light corn syrup
- 9 -ounces (1 1/3 cups + heaping 2 1/2 tablespoons) semi-sweet chocolate chips

Bring cream and corn syrup to simmer in medium saucepan. Remove from heat. Add chocolate and whisk until melted and smooth. Place cake on rack set over a baking sheet. Spread 1/2 cup glaze smoothly over top and sides of cake. Freeze until almost set, about 3 minutes. Pour remaining glaze over cake; smooth sides and top. Place cake on platter. Chill until glaze is firm, about 1 hour. (Can be made 1 day ahead. Cover with cake dome; store at room temperature.) Serve at room temperature.

Types of Chocolate: *Semi-sweet and bittersweet* chocolate both contain at least 35% pure chocolate but vary in the amount of sugar and flavorings added. Due to their fat content, they have a good melting consistency. *Milk chocolate* is made of at least 10% chocolate and contains milk solids and milk fat. Thus, it is harder to melt and is not recommended in recipes calling for melted chocolate.

Cranberry or Raisin Bread Pudding with Creme Anglaise

Yield: Serves 8

2 cups dry bread cubes
(crusts trimmed)
4 cups milk, scalded
1 tablespoon butter
1/4 teaspoon salt
3/4 cup granulated sugar
1 teaspoon ground cinnamon
1/4 teaspoon ground nutmeg
4 slightly beaten large eggs
1 teaspoon vanilla
3/4 cup dried cranberries,
sweetened OR raisins

Creme Anglaise (see below)
Vanilla or Coffee Ice Cream
Additional cranberries or raisins
for sprinkling

Preheat oven to 350°. Grease or spray (with non-stick pan coating) a 2 -quart baking dish.

In a large mixing bowl, soak bread cubes in milk for 5 minutes. Then add butter, salt, sugar, and spices.

In another bowl, whisk eggs and vanilla and add to bread mixture, mixing well. Pour into greased baking dish. Bake in pan of hot water in 350° oven about 50 minutes, or until done.

To serve: Ladle Creme Anglaise on a large dessert plate; top with a serving of bread pudding; position a small scoop of Ice Cream on the side. Sprinkle plate with additional cranberries or raisins, if desired. Another option is to layer cubed Bread Pudding, Creme Angaliase and Ice Cream in individual parfait glasses.

Creme Anglaise *Yield: 1 2/3 cups*
A vanilla custard sauce that is a delicious accompaniment to bread pudding.

1 cup half-and-half
1/2 cup heavy cream
2 large egg yolks
3 tablespoons granulated sugar
1 teaspoon cornstarch

In a medium-size heavy saucepan bring half-and-half and heavy cream just to a boil. Meanwhile, in a bowl, whisk together yolks, sugar, and cornstarch until slightly thickened and pale, about 2 minutes. To this egg mixture, add hot cream in a stream, whisking constantly; transfer back to the saucepan. Cook custard over moderately low heat, stirring constantly until a thermometer registers 180°, about 2 minutes (do not let custard boil). Transfer custard to clean bowl and cool slightly, stirring occasionally. Creme Anglaise may be made 2 days ahead and chilled, covered. Reheat sauce if desired.

Date Pudding with Praline Sauce *Yield: one 8 " baking dish; 6 to 8 servings*
Although referred to as a pudding, this dessert actually has a very moist cake-like consistency.

Pudding

- 1 cup dates
- 1 cup boiling water
- 1/2 cup chopped pecans
- 1 tablespoon baking soda
- 2 tablespoons butter, melted
- 1 cup granulated sugar
- 1 cup all-purpose flour
- 1/2 teaspoon salt
- 1 large egg

Preheat oven to 325°. Grease or spray (with non-stick pan coating) an 8" square baking pan.
In the work bowl of a food processor, grind dates, water, pecans and soda.
In a mixing bowl, combine remaining ingredients; then add ground dates and mix thoroughly. Pour into a prepared baking dish and bake 20 to 30 minutes or until firm and cake-like in consistency (toothpick inserted in center should come out clean).

Topping

- 1/2 cup granulated sugar
- 1/2 cup chopped dates
- 1/2 cup chopped pecans
- 1/2 cup boiling water

Meanwhile, process topping mixture in the work bowl of the food processor. When cake is done, remove from oven and pour the processed topping onto pudding. Serve warm or refrigerate and cut after dessert is thoroughly chilled. This pudding can be made a day in advance.

Optional Serving Accompaniments

Praline Sauce, p. 176
Vanilla Ice Cream
Powdered Sugar for dusting plate

To serve: Ladle a thin layer of warmed Praline Sauce onto a large dessert plate. Add a piece of pudding cake with a small dip of vanilla ice cream on the side. Lightly dust plate with powdered sugar (see directions that follow listed under "A Special Touch.")

Variation: Pudding can also be topped with whipped cream and praline sauce can be omitted.

Sprinkling or dusting a dessert plate with powdered sugar is a dramatic but simple plate presentation. To make the sprinkling easy, place powdered sugar in a fine mesh sieve or colander and sprinkle over the plate surface.

Grand Marnier® Ice Cream Delight *Yield: one 8 -inch pie; serves 6 to 8*

1 1/2 quart (6 cups) vanilla ice cream, softened
1 6 -ounce can orange juice concentrate, softened
3-4 tablespoons Grand Marnier® (brandy based, orange flavored liqueur)
1 purchased chocolate crumb crust
Optional garnishes: chocolate syrup and chocolate leaves

In a mixing bowl (or work bowl of a food processor) quickly, but thoroughly, combine the ice cream, orange juice and Grand Marnier®. Spread into purchased crumb crust and freeze for several hours or until firm.

Set out at room temperature about 10 minutes before you are ready to serve.

To garnish pie, drizzle with chocolate syrup and top with chocolate leaves or other chocolate decorations (refer to p. 146).

A SPECIAL TOUCH! 

Dessert Garde Manger or "The Art of Dessert Garnishing"

Lemon Roses--Start with a lemon placed bottom side up. Carefully start cutting off a 1/2" wide continuous strip of skin beginning at the bottom of the lemon and continue to cut with a sawing motion, spiraling all the way around and around, ending at the stem of the lemon. Carefully roll this long strip into a tight coil, then let it open up slightly to create a rose-like blossom. Place your "flower" on top of a dessert or serving platter. This same technique may also be used to create a **tomato rose**.

Citrus Twists--Use the wide section of a lemon zester to peel a long strip from around the outside of a citrus fruit. Twist the peel around a pencil and refrigerate for 30 minutes of more. Remove the stick and pull off the curl.

Citrus Twists

Strawberry Fans--Using a small knife, make vertical slices about 1/2" from the leaf all the way to the bottom leaving strawberry connected at top. Spread out in a fan shape.

Gumdrop Flowers--Sprinkle a cutting board and a rolling pin generously with sugar. Roll out a gumdrop into an oval shape--to avoid sticking, continuously sprinkle and pat the gumdrop with sugar. Roll out three "petals" of one color per flower. To form the flower--roll one "petal" into a cone or bud shape flaring out the top edge, add a second and then a third layer; pinch the bottom to secure and hold the flower petals together.

Strawberry Fans

Leaves--roll out a green gumdrop and use a paring knife to cut a leaf shape.

Lemon Tart *Yield: one 11-inch tart; about 10 to 12 servings*

Meta Newell West added layers of cream cheese filling and lemon curd topping to a shortbread crust creating a welcome addition to the spring tea season at The Kirby House.

Shortbread Crust

- 1/2 cup butter, softened
- 1/2 cup granulated sugar
- 1 large egg yolk
- 1 1/2 teaspoon vanilla
- 1 1/2 cup all-purpose flour

Preheat oven to 375°. Coat a 10 or 11" tart pan (with removable bottom) with non-stick cooking spray.
In large bowl, cream butter and sugar until light and fluffy. Beat in egg yolk and vanilla. Stir in flour. Press dough into prepared pan. Prick with fork and bake until golden brown, about 15 to 20 minutes. Remove to cooling rack and cool thoroughly.
This crust freezes well and can be made in advance and frozen.

Filling: Cream Cheese layer

- 1 8 -ounce package cream cheese, softened
- 2 tablespoons granulated sugar
- 1 teaspoon vanilla

Beat cream cheese and sugar until smooth.
Stir in vanilla.

Filling: Lemon Curd topping

1 1/2 cups prepared Lemon Curd (recipe on p. 193).

To assemble the tart:

Spoon cream cheese filling evenly over shortbread crust.
Spread with lemon curd.
Chill for 2 hours prior to serving.

Garnishing ideas

Top with fresh mint and a lemon rose or gumdrop flowers (see "A Special Touch!" tip on p. 172). Serve with whipped cream, if desired.

Whipping cream doubles in volume as it is whipped. If 2 cups whipped cream is needed, begin with 1 cup heavy whipping cream. Add 1 to 2 tablespoons powdered sugar and about 1 tablespoon vanilla to flavor the 2 cups of whipped cream. For increased volume, chill the mixing bowl and beater prior to whipping the cream.

Holding Whipped Cream--Whipped cream is generally best when prepared at the last minute, but try whipping a small amount (about 2 ounces per 1 cup heavy whipping cream) of cream cheese and then adding the cream; whip as usual. Although this won't keep for long periods, it can be made several hours in advance.

Tiramisu *This dessert is prepared in individual red wine or parfait glasses. Yield will depend on the capacity of your dessert dishes.*
Traditional tiramisu uses mascarpone cheese and savoiardi (Italian ladyfingers). This version, used at The Kirby House restaurant, gets "rave" reviews from guests.

- 1 10 3/4 to 12 -ounce pound cake (available packaged on the shelf, frozen or prepare from a mix or from "scratch.")
- 1/3 cup Captain Morgan Original Spiced Rum® for sprinkling (this amount is approximate and may be varied to taste)
- 1 14 -ounce can sweetened condensed milk (not evaporated milk)
- 1 cup cold water
- 1/2 - 1 teaspoon almond extract
- 1 tablespoon hazelnut flavoring (such as Stirling® Rocky Mountain Hazelnut gourmet syrup)
- 1 3 1/2 -ounce package instant vanilla pudding mix
- 2 cups heavy whipping cream, chilled

Cut pound cake into bite-size pieces. Place in large mixing bowl and sprinkle liberally with Spiced Rum. Toss to coat, then set aside. In a medium bowl whisk together (by hand, or with a mixer) the sweetened condensed milk, water and flavorings. Add pudding mix and whisk until smooth. Set in refrigerator for 5 minutes. Place the whipping cream in a large mixing bowl (use a whisk attachment, if available) and whip until thick, stiff peaks form. Fold (gently incorporate using a hand whisk) the pudding mixture into the whipped cream and mix just until blended and smooth. Set this pudding mixture aside.
Layer, following the instructions below.

Other ingredients needed for layering the dessert:
Cocoa-Espresso Powder: Mix together: 1 cup unsweetened baking cocoa powder & 1/2 cup espresso powder (The Kirby House grinds espresso beans to create this powder but a flavored coffee powder--such as General Foods International Coffees® could be substituted). Use as needed and store leftover for later use.
Shaved Chocolate

Assemble--can combine in individual parfait glasses in the following order:

1. 2 - 3 spoonfuls of pudding mixture
2. Layer of pound cake
3. About 2 teaspoons of Cocoa-Espresso Powder, sprinkled lightly
4. 2 - 3 spoonfuls of pudding mixture
5. Layer of pound cake
6. 1 teaspoon of Cocoa-Espresso Powder
7. 2 - 3 spoonfuls of pudding mixture
8. Shaved chocolate, sprinkled lightly

Can assemble ahead; cover loosely with plastic wrap, then refrigerate until ready to serve.

Fudge Frosting *Yield: enough frosting for one 3-layer cake.*
The Kirby House uses this frosting on the German Sweet Chocolate Cake, p.147.

6 tablespoons soft butter (not melted)
2 tablespoons light corn syrup
1/4 teaspoon salt
1 teaspoon vanilla
3/4 cup unsweetened baking cocoa powder
1/4 cup + 2 tablespoons whole milk
2 2/3 cups powdered sugar (sift if lumpy)

In a mixing bowl, beat butter, corn syrup, salt, vanilla and cocoa with an electric mixer until smooth.
Add milk and powdered sugar, mixing until smooth. Add more milk if frosting is too stiff.

White Buttercream Frosting *Yield: enough frosting to liberally spread two 8 or 9-inch cake layers or one 13 x 9 -inch sheet cake.*
Prepare this frosting and keep in the refrigerator up to 2 weeks. Use to spread on cinnamon rolls, your favorite cakes or quick breads. The Kirby House uses this frosting on the Black Forest Mocha Tower, p. 144.

1/2 cup solid vegetable shortening (Crisco® recommended)
1/2 cup butter, softened (but not melted)
1 teaspoon vanilla (clear is preferable, if available)
4 cups powdered sugar (sift, if lumpy)
2 tablespoons whole milk (approximately)

In a large mixing bowl, cream shortening and butter with electric mixer until thoroughly blended. Add vanilla to above mixture and blend. Gradually add powdered sugar to shortening mixture, one cup at a time, beating well on medium speed, after each addition. Add milk a little at a time, beating until light and fluffy--use amount needed for a spreadable frosting.

Chocolate Buttercream Frosting variation . . .
Add 3/4 cup unsweetened baking cocoa powder and an additional 1 to 2 tablespoons milk to the above White Buttercream Frosting recipe.

Frosting Tips:
- ❖ Cool cake completely before frosting, unless recipe specifies otherwise.
- ❖ Lightly brush cake to remove excess crumbs (a pastry brush works well for this task).
- ❖ For two-layer cakes, the bottom layer should be upside-down and the top layer right-side up, for best shape and easier frosting.
- ❖ Fill cake layers with about 1/2 cup of frosting.
- ❖ Carefully spread a thin layer of frosting on the sides of the cake to set any remaining crumbs before frosting entire cake--this creates a professional appearance.

Praline Sauce *Yield: about 3 cups*

This is a "honey" of a sauce. At The Kirby House it is used to top the Apple Crumb Cobbler, p. 167, Apple Cake, p. 142, Date Pudding, p. 171, and Turtle Cheesecake, p. 153. Also, try it on vanilla ice cream.

1 cup honey
2 cups brown sugar, packed
1/4 cup + 2 tablespoons butter
3/4 teaspoon salt
1 cup heavy whipping cream
1 tablespoon caramel flavor (such as Stirling® Creme Caramel gourmet syrup)
1 tablespoon vanilla
1/2 cup toasted pecans

Mix honey, brown sugar, butter and salt in a medium saucepan and bring to a boil. Continue cooking and stirring until sugar is completely dissolved. Remove from heat and let cool just until sauce begins to thicken. Add cream, caramel flavor, vanilla, and pecans to above mixture stirring until blended. Sauce will appear thin at this point but will thicken as it cools. Chill until ready to use and reheat as needed.

Toasting Nuts ... Toasting crisps and brings out the flavor of nuts. To toast--place nuts in a 325° oven for about 5 to 7 minutes (time varies according to nut size) and turn frequently. Watch carefully as nuts can burn or scorch in a matter of minutes due to their high oil content. Over-toasting results in both a loss of flavor and a tough product.

Raspberry Sauce *Yield: about 1 cup*

10 -ounces frozen raspberries
1/4 cup currant jelly
2 tablespoons Kirsch (cherry flavored brandy)
1 teaspoon lemon juice (freshly squeezed is preferable)
1 tablespoon + 1 1/2 teaspoons cornstarch
Scant 3 tablespoons cold water

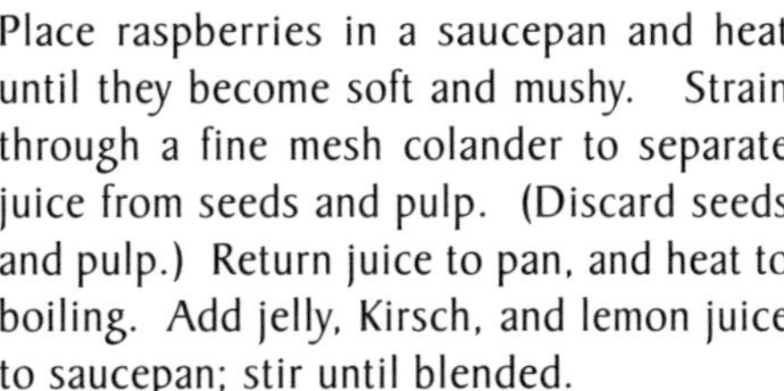
Place raspberries in a saucepan and heat until they become soft and mushy. Strain through a fine mesh colander to separate juice from seeds and pulp. (Discard seeds and pulp.) Return juice to pan, and heat to boiling. Add jelly, Kirsch, and lemon juice to saucepan; stir until blended.

Place cornstarch and cold water in a small bowl to form a paste. Add cornstarch mixture to hot raspberry juice , heat and stir until thickened. The thickened sauce will be clear red in color and should thoroughly coat a metal spoon (if the spoon is raised several inches above the saucepan, the sauce should form "sheets" as it drops off of the spoon).

Cornstarch as a Thickener

Starches are not water-soluble so care must be taken to avoid lumpy sauces that break down. Tips for working with cornstarch include:

- In recipes without sugar (such as the one above), combine cold water with the cornstarch (hot water at this point may cause the starch granules to shrink resulting in an inability to absorb water). Introduce this paste gradually into hot, but not boiling, liquid.
- Cornstarch is recommended for thickening very acid fruits because it does not lose its thickening power as quickly as (wheat) flour in the presence of an acid.
- For recipes calling for sugar, simply mix the sugar and cornstarch together prior to introduction to a liquid--this will avoid lumping.
- When thickening with cornstarch . . . constant, gentle stirring is necessary to avoid lumps and to hold the starch particles in suspension until gelatinization takes place and the mixture thickens.

A SPECIAL TOUCH!

Plate Painting

Add dessert sauces to squeeze bottles and "paint" the dessert plates . . . experiment with free-form designs, scripted names, etc. Or, squirt sauces over desserts that have been plated.

The Raspberry Sauce (p. 177) works well in a squeeze bottle. Create a squeezable caramel sauce by leaving the pecans out of the Praline Sauce on p. 176. Purchased sauces can also be used or create these simple sauces:

Vanilla Cream and Chocolate Cream Sauce

Perfect sauces for decorating dessert plates.

Vanilla Cream

In a mixing bowl, lightly whip heavy cream with powdered sugar and vanilla (see p. 173 for amounts); stop whipping before soft peaks form. Place in a squeeze bottle and use to decorate dessert plates.

Chocolate Cream

Follow directions above except mix unsweetened baking cocoa powder with the powdered sugar.

Chevron Frames

Squirt dots of sauce around plate edge; drag toothpick through dots to make a design.

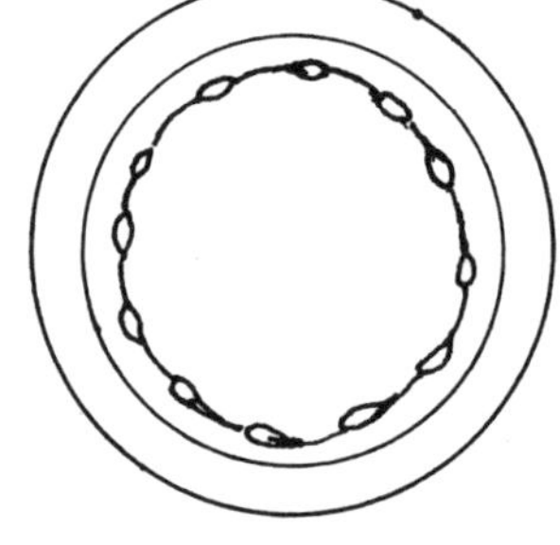

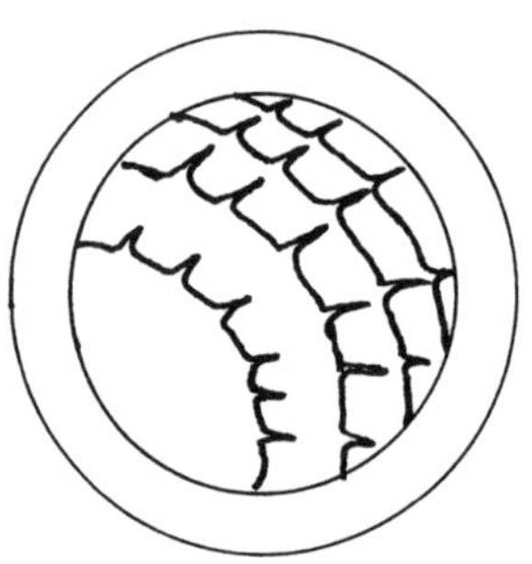

Sunburst

Squirt curved lines of sauce onto dessert plate. Drag tip of a toothpick across lines to create a design.

Chevrons

Squirt parallel lines of sauce onto dessert plate. Drag tip of a toothpick across lines to create a design, alternating toothpick first in one direction and then in the other.)

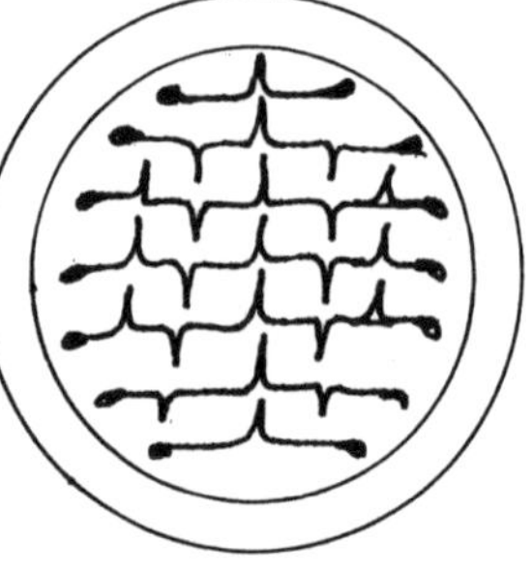

Chocolate Peanut Butter Crunch Balls *Yield: thirty-eight 3/4-inch balls*
A nice addition to a dessert buffet; great for gift giving or as a special treat.

- 1 cup chunky peanut butter
- 1/2 cup corn syrup
- 2 cups rice crispy type cereal
- 8 -ounces (1 1/3 cup) semi-sweet chocolate chips
- 1/4 cup chopped peanuts

Beat together the peanut butter and corn syrup in a medium size bowl until well blended; add rice cereal and mix thoroughly. Use a teaspoonfuls to shape mixture into 38 balls. Place on a large, foil-lined baking sheet and chill for several hours (about 2) or until firm.

Place chocolate in a medium size microwave safe bowl. Microwave on high power for 1 minute. Stir chocolate and continue heating for 1 minute intervals, until melted and smooth.

Use a fork to lift peanut butter balls; dip into chocolate, immersing completely; shake off excess chocolate by gently tapping fork on edge of bowl. Return to the baking sheet. If chocolate thickens too much, microwave at half power until soft enough to dip.

Let chocolate-coated balls start to harden for 30 minutes, or until chocolate is almost firm. Sprinkle tops with chopped peanuts. Let stand until hardened. Store in the refrigerator.

 **A SPECIAL TOUCH!** 

Fanciful Presentations for Candies

- ❖ Place candies at several heights using a mixture of stemmed glassware (martini glasses, red wine glasses, etc.) and low glass bowls. Arrange these on a mirror for a shimmering effect.
- ❖ Clean a tin can thoroughly and hot glue peppermint sticks to the outside surface. Fill the inside with candies. This makes a nice gift presentation or a unique container to use at Christmas.

Bottled Water in the Victorian era?

Not only did the Victorians have access to bottled water, it might have been bottled in Abilene.

AbileneA Water

"AbileneA," the famous cathartic water, was advertised extensively as "America's only Natural Cathartic Water." It was considered to be the ideal eliminant or laxative and was endorsed by local doctors. The AbileneA Company was the sole owner and distributor of this mineral water containing sodium sulfate and other trace substances. The water was discovered in 1898 and was located fifteen miles northwest of Abilene on a high upland knoll. In a handwritten letter, Harold P. Huffa recalls working at the plant as a youth.

". . . I worked Saturdays at the Abilene bottling plant. It was located in a store building between Buckeye and Spruce, and faced both Second and Third streets. The water well was some distance from town, and it was hand pumped into cream cans and hauled by team and wagon to the bottling plant, and poured into an overhead stock tank. Below it was a bench with a pipe along several spigots about four feet apart, and each spigot had a short piece of rubber hose attached which the girl operator inserted in each bottle to fill it. My job was to bring empty cases of bottles and take the full ones to the capper. After being capped they had to be washed as the chemicals in the water left the bottles with a white coating, and the labels would not stick." He goes on to confess, " . . . it tasted like Epson salt, and acted as bad as it tasted."[64]

Another Victorian Era Enterprise . . .

The Belle Springs Creamery--a local plant that shipped throughout the USA

The Belle Springs Creamery Company started at Belle Springs, 12 miles southeast of Abilene in 1886. Later the business expanded and moved to Abilene (located across the street east of the present day courthouse) with manufacturing plants at Salina and Emporia, Kansas. According to papers dated 1910 at the Dickinson County Historical Society, the company had over 200 collecting points, and their products were shipped (via rail) all over the United States. The "Belle Springs" brand of creamery butter was sold in air-tight packages. In addition to butter, the company specialized in cream, ice cream and ice. It was the largest and one of the most important industries in the area.[65] It was at Belle Springs Creamery in Abilene that President Dwight David Eisenhower worked as a youth.

Kirby House
Glazes, Sauces, Gravies, Marinades, Miscellaneous

Cranberry Glaze *Yield: about 2 cups*

This is the sauce used on Cranberry Glazed Pork Roast, p. 82. Or use it on ham or roasted poultry.

1 16 -ounce can jellied cranberry sauce, plain or whole berry
1 tablespoon Dijon mustard
2 tablespoons orange juice, cold
2 teaspoons cornstarch
1 tablespoon + 1 teaspoon grated orange peel
1/4 teaspoon ground cinnamon
1/8 teaspoon salt
2 tablespoons sherry (optional)

Place cranberry sauce and Dijon mustard in a medium saucepan; blend with a whisk. In a small bowl, combine cold orange juice with cornstarch to make a smooth paste. Add all the remaining ingredients to the orange juice mixture and blend with a whisk. Add this mixture to the cranberry sauce & Dijon mustard; cook on medium heat until thickened.

❀ 1 medium orange = approximately 3 tablespoons grated peel

Jack Daniels ® Barbecue Sauce *Yield: about 4 1/2 cups*

This sauce is added to a butterflied and grilled chicken breast to create the "Grilled Barbecued Chicken," p. 90, on the menu at The Kirby House.

12 -ounces tomato paste (or 1 1/2 cups)
1 cup molasses
1 cup dark corn syrup
1/2 cup white distilled vinegar
1/2 cup honey
1 tablespoon + 1/4 teaspoon paprika
1 tablespoon + 1/4 teaspoon Worcestershire sauce
1 tablespoon + 1/4 teaspoon Jack Daniels® Old #7
2/3 teaspoon Liquid Smoke
1 teaspoon hot pepper sauce (such as Tabasco®)
1/2 teaspoon garlic powder (or to taste)
1/2 teaspoon chili powder (or to taste)
1/2 teaspoon onion powder (or to taste)
1/4 teaspoon cayenne pepper (or to taste)

Mix all ingredients together in a large saucepan. Simmer over low to medium heat for 15 to 30 minutes or until flavors have a chance to blend. Taste and adjust seasonings as needed.

Store in refrigerator until ready to use.

When using glazes and barbecue sauces during baking ... Baste a ham during the last 45 minutes of baking. Depending on the size of a pork roast, chops or poultry (the smaller the size, the shorter the time), allow 15 to 20 minutes in the oven after the addition of a glaze. The same size guidelines and timing apply to the addition of sweet barbecue sauces added to steaks, ribs or poultry. The high sugar content of the glazes and sauces will cause surface burning with extended exposure to heat and this creates an undesirable flavor as well.

Béarnaise Sauce *Yield: about 2 cups*

Béarnaise is a classic French sauce made by reducing vinegar, wine, tarragon and shallots; it's finished by adding egg yolks and butter. The Kirby House version of Béarnaise Sauce is a fool-proof version that is not subject to the "beaking" that can occur in the classic version. This sauce is a nice topping on grilled salmon or serve with other types of fish, meat, eggs and vegetables.

- 5 large egg yolks
- 8 -ounces cream cheese, softened & cut into chunks
- 1/4 cup + 1 tablespoon lemon juice
- 1/2 teaspoon salt
- Scant 3 tablespoons minced onion
- 1 1/2 teaspoons tarragon leaves, crushed
- 1/4 cup + 1 tablespoon white wine (Chablis)
- 1 1/2 tablespoons water (1/2 tablespoon = 1 1/2 teaspoons)

In a medium saucepan, whisk egg yolks and then add cream cheese. Heat over low temperature, stirring constantly. Add remaining ingredients and stir vigorously until thickened.

Cocktail Sauce *Yield: about 2 1/4 cups*

Serve with boiled shrimp or other seafood.

- 2 cups ketchup
- 1 heaping tablespoon horseradish, or more to taste, as desired
- 1 teaspoon lemon juice, or to taste

Blend ingredients in a mixing bowl. Refrigerate to blend flavors. For added zest, Vangie Henry suggests adding 1/2 teaspoon Worcestershire sauce and a dash or two of hot pepper sauce (such as Tabasco®).

Dill Sauce *Yield: about 3 cups*

This is the sauce served with the Salmon Filet at The Kirby House.

- 3/4 cup dill pickle juice
- 1 pint heavy whipping cream (2 cups)
- 2 teaspoons dried dillweed
- 1/4 cup + 2 tablespoons cold water
- 1/4 cup cornstarch

In a saucepan, slowly whisk the pickle juice into the cream; add the dillweed. Heat over low to medium heat until thick and bubbly. In a small bowl, whisk cold water with cornstarch to make a smooth paste. Slowly whisk into hot (but not boiling) cream mixture and cool until thickened. Chill.

Raisin Sauce *Yield: about 1 1/2 cup*

A delicious sauce to serve with ham or other pork cuts.

1/2 cup granulated sugar
1/4 cup water
1/2 cup currant jelly
1/2 cup raisins
1 1/2 tablespoon white distilled vinegar (1/2 tablespoon = 1 1/2 teaspoons)
1 tablespoon butter
1/2 + 1/4 teaspoon Worestershire sauce
1/4 teaspoon salt
1/8 teaspoon ground cloves (to measure 1/8 teaspoon, fill the 1/4 teaspoon half full)

Cook sugar and water for 5 minutes (or until sugar completely dissolves) over medium heat in a medium saucepan.
Add remaining ingredients to the sugar-water and simmer for several minutes until it resembles a thickened sauce. Store in refrigerator.

Tequila Lime Sauce *Yield: about 2 1/2 cups*

This sauce is served with the Onion Rings, p. 106 at the restaurant.

2 cups sour cream
Zest from 1 lime (about 1 tablespoon)
Juice from 1 lime (about 2 tablespoons)
1 cup prepared Ranch Dressing
2 tablespoons Tequila

Whisk together all ingredients in a mixing bowl. Refrigerate to blend flavors.

About Tequila

Usually associated with Margarita cocktails, Tequila originated in Tequila, Mexico. It is made by fermenting the sweet sap of the agava plant.

A dash or a pinch?
Dash = scant 1/8 of a teaspoon
Pinch = 1/16 of a teaspoon

Brown Gravy *Yield: about 1 1/4 cups*

A basic brown gravy using a flour base.

2 tablespoons butter
1/4 cup all-purpose flour
1 heaping teaspoon concentrated beef base (such as Minor's® brand)
1 cup warm water
Salt to taste

Melt butter over medium heat in a saucepan. Slowly add flour, whisking until smooth.

Mix base and water together, then slowly stir into the above roux (French term for flour-fat paste). Stir with whisk until thickened and smooth.

Add salt and continue cooking 2 or 3 minutes longer to improve flavor.

White Gravy *Yield: about 2 1/2 cups*

This is the gravy The Kirby House uses over their Country Fried Steaks, p. 72.

4 tablespoons (1/2 stick) butter
1/2 cup all-purpose flour
2 teaspoons concentrated chicken base (such as Minor's® brand)
1 cup warm water
3/4 to 1 cup milk
Salt to taste

Melt butter over medium heat in a saucepan. Slowly add flour, whisking until smooth. Mix chicken base with water. Add slowly to the roux (French term for flour-fat paste) stirring constantly to keep mixture smooth. Slowly add 3/4 cup milk to gravy, stirring or whisking to keep smooth. Cook until thickened; add additional milk if needed to achieve gravy-like consistency. Add salt and continue cooking 2 or 3 minutes longer to improve flavor.

About gravies ...

Gravies are simply a variation of cream sauces and success can be achieved by:

- ❖ using correct proportions.
- ❖ cooking on low to medium heat.
- ❖ thoroughly mixing the flour and fat.
- ❖ slowly adding the liquid to the flour mixture.

Meat fats may be used in place of part of the fat and meat or vegetable juices may be substituted for part of the liquid.

A perfect gravy is a smooth, satiny, creamy mixture. It does not taste starchy; it's flavor is a pleasing combination of the blended ingredients.

Steak Marinade *Yield: about 1 1/2 cups*
This marinade is used to flavor the steak used in Grilled Steak Salad on p. 46. A versatile marinade that could be used to impart flavor to any steak.

1/2 cup Worcestershire sauce
1 cup water
1 1/2 teaspoons honey
Pinch of salt
Pinch of white pepper
Pinch of black pepper

Whisk all ingredients in a stainless, food-grade plastic, or glass mixing bowl until thoroughly combined. Refrigerate until ready to use.

Teriyaki Marinade *Yield: about 1 1/4 cups*
Chicken breasts are marinated overnight in this sauce to create the Teriyaki Chicken, p. 93 on the menu at The Kirby House.

1 cup red wine
1/4 cup soy sauce
1/4 cup brown sugar, packed
Pinch of garlic powder
Pinch of powdered ginger or grated ginger root

Whisk all ingredients in a stainless, food-grade plastic, or glass mixing bowl until thoroughly combined.
Refrigerate until ready to use.

About Marinades

- A marinade is a seasoned liquid used to add flavor. Those containing an acid (such as wine, vinegar, fruit juice, etc.) also tenderize the surface of meats and, in so doing, further encourage the transfer of flavors.
- When marinating, use a low, flat container that will allow the meat to absorb the maximum liquid. It is also important to select a material that will not react with acid. Approved materials include: glass, stainless steel, or food-grade plastic.
- Tender foods can be marinated to add flavor but avoid too long of an immersion or they may turn stringy or mushy. Tough, large cuts of meat may marinate for 12 or more hours; cubed meats (containing fibrous tissue) may marinate about 2 to 3 hours. Small, tender steaks, tenderloins, etc. may marinate a shorter time, the purpose being to flavor rather than tenderize. Always refrigerate foods as they marinate.
- A general rule is to allow about 1/4 cup marinate per pound of meat.
- If you plan to use the marinade (leftover from soaking raw meats) to baste the meat during cooking or as a base for gravies or sauces, it MUST be heated to boiling to kill any harmful bacteria that might have been present in the raw meat.

Baked Brie with Almonds *Yield: serves 16 or more people when used as an appetizer or even at a cocktail party where other food selections are offered.*

1 pound wheel Brie cheese
1/3 cup slivered or sliced almonds
1/4 cup butter
1/4 cup minced parsley

Preheat oven to 300°.
Place Brie in an oven-proof dish. Toast almonds in butter and stir in parsley. Heat cheese at 300° for 8 to 10 minutes or until just warm. Top with almond mixture and serve immediately.

Cheddar Carousel *Serves a crowd--16 to 25 and maybe more depending on what other appetizers or snacks might be offered. This unusual recipe was discovered in "Beyond Parsley," by the Junior League of Kansas City, Missouri. The original recipe calls for strawberry preserves but, we received "rave" reviews when we substituted raspberry and made a few other minor adjustments. For smaller groups, we recommend you cut this recipe in half and place it in a small round pan with a juice glass inverted in the center for the ring mold. Serve with crackers.*

1 pound Cheddar cheese, finely grated
3/4 cup mayonnaise
1 medium onion, finely chopped
1 clove garlic, pressed
1/2 teaspoon Tabasco sauce
1 cup chopped pecans
1 cup raspberry preserves

In a mixing bowl, combine all ingredients, except raspberry preserves, and mix well. Put in a ring mold that has been sprayed with non-stick pan coating. Chill thoroughly. (Mixture will set as it chills.) Unmold and fill center with the preserves.

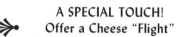

A SPECIAL TOUCH!
Offer a Cheese "Flight"

Cheeses add flavor to any gathering, from casual get-togethers to cocktail parties. Or, serve a flavorful cheese "flight"--small portions of several cheeses--before a meal as an appetizer, or at the end of the meal in place of a sweet dessert course. Cheese flights are a fun and easy way to try different cheeses and experience the subtle differences of each one.

Simple Serving Suggestions

- Serve the cheese at room temperature, removing it from the refrigerator up to two hours prior to the arrival of guests.
- Before guests arrive, type informational sheets to label the cheeses so guests know which cheese they're tasting. This is educational and, also serves as a great conversation starter.
- Present the cheese in large wedges to display its natural beauty on a large plate, wooden board or piece of marble. A "radish mouse" is a fun addition to your cheese display. (Directions for a "radish mouse" are on p. 189.)

- ❖ Provide different knives for each cheese to avoid intermingling flavors. Although it is fun to let guests cut their own portions from the wedges, we find it helpful to have some slices ready for quick pick-up.
- ❖ Nice cheese pairings include: Fruits: grapes, pears, and apples; Vegetables such as cherry tomatoes and olives; Toasted nuts; Breads--dark breads like pumpernickel match with strong cheeses or fruit breads and nut breads with blue cheeses. Crusty breads and crackers go well with most any cheese. (Allow about 3/4 to 1 pound crackers for every 25 people.)

Cheese Selections

There are no precise rules for choosing selections for a cheese "flight." Cheese offerings can all come from the same family, such as Cheddars (Cheddar, Colby, Monterey Jack); or similar textures, such as semi-soft (Brick, Muenster, Mozzarella). Or, use several cheeses (usually no more than five) with varying textures and flavors. Another idea would be to have each selection represent a different family of cheese groupings (such as Cheddar, Blue-Veined, Dutch, Provolone, Swiss). You can also let your taste buds be the guide and base selections on your own personal preferences. Although many guidelines suggest allowing one to two ounces of cheese per person, we have found that if you include the cheese recipes we offer on p. 187, small wedges of other types of cheese will be sufficient. Below you will find our recommendations, plus information that was included on the identifying labels for a Cheese "Flight" recently offered for the Eisenhower Foundation.

Brie : A good cheese to begin your sampling due to its soft texture and mild flavor. Brie originated in France and its thin, edible crust reveals a creamy interior. Made of cow's milk, this cheese belongs to the Surface-Ripened Family Cheese Group. We've teamed Brie with nuts for a tasty combination of flavors.
Gruyère: It is smooth to the touch and golden to the eye. Its complex nature makes it a cheese that is worth tasting over and over. Look for nutty and buttery flavors with a slight hint of sweetness. This cheese belongs to the Swiss Family Cheese Group and has a semi-hard texture.
Gouda: Gouda originated in Holland and is typically sold in rounds with a wax coating (which is removed before eating). It's texture is hard (but certainly not as hard as many other cheeses that fall in this same category). Look for a butterscotch flavor with nutty overtones, and a somewhat salty flavor. Gouda belongs to the Dutch Family Cheese Group and is made partly from skim milk.
Cheddar: A hard textured cheese with a smooth, firm body and characteristic yellow-orange color. It originated in England and is made from whole cow's milk; it belongs to the Cheddar Family Cheese Group (along with Colby and Monterey Jack). We've created a "Cheese Carousel" teamed with fruit preserves for your sampling pleasure (recipe on p. 187).
Blue Cheese: or Bleu belongs to the Blue-Veined Family Cheese Group. Due to its strong flavor, many cheese experts recommend sampling it last so that it will not overpower the milder flavored cheese offerings. Blue cheese originated in France; it has a semi-soft, crumbly texture with characteristic veins of mold.

A SPECIAL TOUCH!

A Radish Mouse--a "fun" addition to a cheese tray

You'll need a fresh radish with the root end attached--the root serves as the mouse's tail. Cut a thin slice off the bottom of the "mouse" so he will sit flat (reserve the slice as it will form the ears). The stem should be trimmed and shaped so it appears as a nose. With the tail at the back, hold the radish with the stem (or nose) end facing you, and for the eyes, place two small cloves on either side and slightly above the stem point. For the ears, cut the reserved slice in half, make 2 narrow slits about 1/4" deep above the clove eyes and slip the ears in place.

Devonshire-Style Cream *Yield: about 2 1/2 cups*

3 -ounces cream cheese, softened
1 teaspoon granulated sugar
1 cup heavy whipping cream, at room temperature

Beat together the cream cheese and sugar with an electric mixer in a medium-size bowl on medium-high speed until mixture is light and fluffy.

Add the heavy cream; beat with mixer on high speed until stiff peaks form when turned-off beaters are lifted from bowl. Cover and refrigerate. Will keep in the refrigerator about 1 week.

Devonshire Cream, Devon Cream or Clotted Cream-- All of these terms refer to a topping originally made in Devonshire, England by heating unpasteurized cream and then allowing it to set at room temperature until thickened. Today it is still made in England by separating the cream from unhomogenized milk and scalding it until it becomes thick. Devonshire cream is typically served with scones.

Dill Yogurt Dip *Yield: about 3 cups*

Serve this dip with fresh vegetables. Or, hollow out a round rye bread loaf and fill the center with the dip; use the bread pieces as dippers.

1 cup sour cream (8 -ounces)
1 cup mayonnaise
4 teaspoons dill weed
1 cup plain yogurt
4 tablespoons finely chopped onion
4 tablespoons dried parsley flakes

In a medium size mixing bowl, combine and mix all ingredients.

How many vegetables for a "veggie" tray?

Allow 7 to 8 pounds of fresh veggies for 50 people; 3 1/2 to 4 pounds for 25 or about 2 to 2 1/2 pounds for 16, and 1 to 1 1/2 pounds for 8. Do keep in mind that this amount is based on EP (Edible Portion) so if you are using vegetables with lots of waste (such as cauliflower--with approximately 38% waste), allow for slightly more.

Fizzy Orange Juice *Yield: about 3 cups*

A great nonalcoholic beverage for a brunch or a special treat for early morning.

1 6 -ounce can orange juice concentrate
18 -ounces (or 3 orange juice cans) chilled Club Soda
Ice

In an open-mouth pitcher, prepare orange juice according to package directions, except use club soda instead of water. Whisk the juice using a swirling motion to create the "fizz," and serve immediately with ice.

Fresh Fruit Salsa with Lime Dressing *Yield: 3 to 4 cups*

This salsa is used to top the Teriyaki Chicken, p. 93, on the menu at the restaurant. Try serving this with tortilla chips as a change from the traditional tomato salsa.

Select combinations of fruits to equal 3 to 4 cups: tomatoes, honeydew melon, cantaloupe, pineapple, kiwi, etc.
4 purple onion rings (taken from 1 small onion)
3 to 4 jalapeno pepper slices (taken from 1 jalapeno pepper)

Core, chop and seed tomatoes. Peel and seed melons. Clean and core pineapple. Peel kiwi. Chop very fine and place in a stainless steel, food-grade plastic or glass mixing bowl. Add finely chopped onions and jalapeno peppers. Toss with Lime Dressing. Use immediately or tightly cover and refrigerate for up to 5 days.

<u>Lime Dressing</u>:
1/4 cup lime juice
2 tablespoons honey
1 tablespoon olive oil

In a small mixing bowl, whisk together all the ingredients.

About Salsa: Salsa is the Mexican word for "sauce" and traditionally brings to mind a fresh tomato-pepper mixture. Today the ingredients used in salsa are limited only by the imagination.

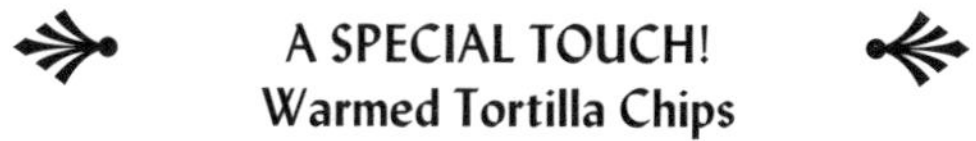

A SPECIAL TOUCH!
Warmed Tortilla Chips

Warm tortilla chips by placing in a crock pot set on low.

Guacamole *Yield: about 4 cups*

- 1 cup chopped onion
- 1/4 - 1/2 teaspoon minced garlic clove
- 1 - 2 jalapeno peppers (depending on level of heat desired); remove seeds before mincing
- 2 1/2 cups chopped tomatoes, drained
- 1 tablespoon lime juice
- 1 teaspoon each salt and pepper, or more to taste, as desired
- 2 large avocados, peeled, pitted & pits removed

In a mixing bowl, combine the chopped onions, the minced garlic and jalapeno peppers. Add the chopped tomatoes, lime juice, salt and pepper and blend until the tomatoes are partly liquefied but still lumpy. In another bowl, mash the avocados and then add to the tomato mixture. Chill in the refrigerator for 2 to 3 hours before serving to blend flavors.
Tip: Burying the avocado pit in the Guacamole until time to serve, will help the guacamole retain it's bright green color.

How to Select, Ripen, and Peel an Avocado

- ❖ When buying an avocado for immediate use, select fruit that yields to gentle pressure--if planning to use later in the week, look for firmness.
- ❖ To speed the ripening of unripe avocados, simply place the fruit in an ordinary paper bag and store at room temperature until ready to eat (usually two to five days). Including an apple in the bag speeds up the process even more.
- ❖ Avocado's are easy to peel when ripe: Start by cutting the avocado lengthwise around the seed. Rotate the halves to separate. Remove the seed by sliding the tip of a spoon gently underneath and lifting out. Next, peel the fruit by placing the cut side down and removing the skin with a knife or your fingers, or simply scoop out the avocado meat with a spoon.
- ❖ To retain a fresh green color, avocados should either be eaten immediately or should be sprinkled with lemon or lime juice and covered in an air-tight container. If guacamole turns brown on the top after storage, simply discard the top layer.

Origins of the Avocado

The fruit seems to have originated in Central America and Mexico. The Aztecs named the fruit ahuacatl; the avocado tree was growing wild in the ruins of the Aztec and Mayan temples. The English word avocado was probably derived from attempts to speak phonetically the Aztec name ahuacatl.

Lemon Curd *Yield: about 1 1/2 cups*

Lemon curd is very versatile. The Kirby House uses this recipe as an accompaniment to scones and it is used in the Lemon Tart on p. 173. It can be made in advance and stored in the refrigerator for several months.

4 large eggs
2 cups granulated sugar
1/8 teaspoon salt
1/4 cup butter, softened
1/2 cups fresh lemon juice
(approximately 2 to 3 lemons)
2 tablespoons grated lemon zest

In the top of a *double boiler (or stainless steel mixing bowl that can be set over a pan of boiling water to create a double boiler effect), mix together eggs, sugar, and salt. Stir in butter, lemon juice and lemon zest. Cook until thick (pudding like consistency), about 30 minutes, stirring frequently. Cool to room temperature; store in refrigerator. Curd becomes thicker when chilled.
Lemon Curd keeps well in the refrigerator so may be prepared in advance.

*Avoid using an untreated aluminum saucepan as the acid in the lemon juice may react with the aluminum creating a discoloration of the curd; anodized aluminum or stainless steel will NOT create this effect.

Marvelous Microwave Marmalade *Yield: about 2/3 cup*

This recipe, from Waunita Batemen, is great with scones or biscuits. It also makes a great (and quick) gift --package in an interesting jar and place in a basket with fresh breads.
Or whip equal amounts of marmalade and butter for "**Orange Marmalade Butter.**"

1 orange (unpeeled, quartered with
white membranes removed)
Granulated sugar

An Orange Cup

For a "fun" presentation, cut an orange in half, hollow it out and fill with Marmalade or "Orange Marmalade Butter."

Place orange in the work bowl of a food processor; pulse until orange is finely chopped. Transfer orange to a 1 -quart glass measuring cup. Add an amount of sugar equivalent to the amount of chopped orange; stir until thoroughly mixed. Place orange-sugar mixture in microwave and cook on medium speed until slightly thickened--about 6 minutes. Stir occasionally, about every 2 minutes. Be careful not to overcook. Cover and refrigerate until ready to use.

Mexican Rice *Yield: about 6 to 8 servings*
This makes a nice side dish to accompany a Mexican meal.

1 cup white rice
1 cup tomato sauce
1 cup water
1 tablespoon corn oil
1/4 teaspoon ground cumin
1/2 teaspoon black pepper
1/2 of a small onion or about 1/4 teaspoon onion powder
1 garlic clove, minced or 1/4 teaspoon garlic powder
1 tablespoon chicken base such as Minor's® Chicken Base)

Preheat oven to 350°. Spray a large casserole with non-stick pan coating and then mix all ingredients directly in the casserole. Place in oven and bake 45 minutes to an hour or until rice is fluffy and liquid has been absorbed.

Rice Doneness Test--Rice will be fluffy and tender when completely cooked.

Cumin is an ancient spice that dates back to the Old Testament. Shaped like a caraway seed, cumin is the dried fruit of a plant in the parsley family, Cumin is available in seed and ground forms.

Kinds of Rice
Regular Rice--The hull and the bran have been removed by polishing. Short grain rice is less expensive than long grain; it is used for casseroles, and creamy desserts. Long grain rice is an all-purpose rice and cooks fluffier and flakier; it works well in side dishes. One cup uncooked yields about 3 1/2 cups cooked.
Precooked (Instant) Rice--Commercially cooked, rinsed and dried, this rice is quick to fix and can be substituted for regular rice. One cup uncooked yields about 2 cups cooked.
Brown Rice--A vitamin-rich whole grain, with only the outer hull removed. It has a nutty flavor and is used as a side dish. Refrigeration of the raw rice is recommended (because the oil in the germ can get rancid). One cup uncooked yields about 4 cups cooked.
Wild Rice--Long grained and dark greenish-brown in color, this is not really a rice, but the seed of an aquatic grass. Expensive, it is often sold combined with brown rice. Four ounces uncooked yields about 3 cups cooked.

Miscellaneous Rice Tips
- Add seasonings and butter to rice before cooking for the most flavor.
- Don't stir rice while it is cooking unless directed to do so. (Stirring scrapes the starch off the grains & makes the rice sticky.)
- If rice is old or has been stored in a very dry place, it may take more time to rehydrate.
- Fluff cooked rice with a fork before transferring to a serving dish.

- ❖ Don't cook rice in tomatoes or other high acid liquids. It will take much longer to get tender.
- ❖ Cooked rice reheats well; cook twice as much as you need and freeze some for another meal.
- ❖ To reheat frozen rice, add 2 tablespoons water for each 1 cup rice and microwave, covered, on high power for 2 minutes, or steam it over simmering water for a few minutes.
- ❖ Long-grain rice gets crunchy when refrigerated; choose medium or short grain rice for rice salads or puddings that will be chilled.

Olive Spread *Yield: 1 1/2 cups*

This spread can be used on the classic New Orleans Muffuletta sandwich, served on toast crisps for an hors d' oeuvre, or as a relish.

1 cup green olives
1 cup black olives
1/4 cup chopped red onion
2 tablespoon freshly squeezed lemon juice
1 tablespoon prepared horseradish
1 tablespoon chopped garlic
1 tablespoon Dijon mustard
1 teaspoon Italian seasoning
Dash of hot pepper sauce (such as Tabasco®)
Dash of Worcestershire sauce
1/2 cup olive oil

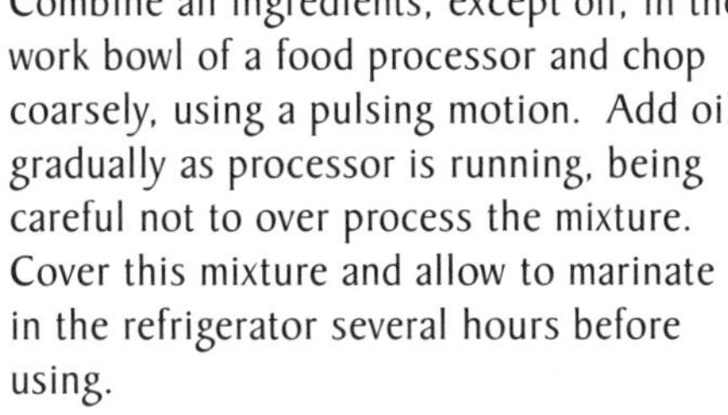
Combine all ingredients, except oil, in the work bowl of a food processor and chop coarsely, using a pulsing motion. Add oil gradually as processor is running, being careful not to over process the mixture. Cover this mixture and allow to marinate in the refrigerator several hours before using.

 **A SPECIAL TOUCH!** 

Add Pizzaz to Your Picnic

Serve a Muffuletta sandwich, Carrot Bundles, p. 105, your favorite pasta or potato salad and dessert at your next picnic.

To prepare a Muffuletta sandwich: Slice off the top 1/2" from a 9 to 10" loaf of dense round bread; hollow it out and pack with a layer of Olive Spread (above) and then layer with Italian meats and cheeses; end with a final layer of the Olive Spread. Replace the bread top; wrap in foil and and place a 3 pound weight on sandwich; refrigerate at least 6 hours. When ready to serve, cut the loaf into wedges. Serves 8.

For a festive picnic effect, use terra cotta pots and liners to hold the food. In *"Good Friends Great Tastes,"* Debbie Meyer suggests lining the terra cotta with foil and lettuce leaves before adding the food.

Seasoned Flour *Yield: about 3 cups*

This flour is used for breading on the Country Fried Steak, p. 72 and Onion Rings, p. 106.

3 cups all-purpose flour
3 tablespoons Tex Joy® Steak Seasoning
1 teaspoon garlic salt
1 teaspoon white pepper

In a mixing bowl, thoroughly combine all ingredients. Store in an air-tight container using as needed.

Tex Joy Steak Seasoning

is a commercial blend used at The Kirby House Restaurant.
It is found in . . .

Blue Cheese Salad Dressing
South of The Border Sandwich
Scrambled Egg Casserole
Pimento Cheese Spread
Salisbury Steak
Crab Tostadas
Mexican Chicken
Cream Corn Sauce
Green Bean Bundles
Seasoned Flour
Country Fried Steak
Onion Rings
Potato Soup

Tex Joy® is sold by the Texas Coffee Company which also manufactures a full line of spices, spice blends and coffee products. Tex Joy® Steak Seasoning may be purchased in the coffee shop at the Kirby House Restaurant or contact:

Texas Coffee Company
P.O. Box 31
Beaumont TX 77704
1-800-259-3400
Order products online
@ http://www.texjoy.com/spices.htm

MENUS FROM THE KIRBY HOUSE

Recipes from this cookbook were used to create the menu selections that follow. Menus, similar to these, are actually offered for "special event" and catered meals provided by the restaurant.

Beef Menus

 # 1

Cranberry-Pecan Salad with Orange Vinaigrette, p. 38
"Melt In Your Mouth Roast" with Brown Gravy, p. 74
Mashed Potatoes, p. 108
Brown Sugar Glazed Veggies, p. 102
Lena's Rolls, p. 131
Grand Marnier® Ice Cream Delight, p. 172

 # 2

House Salad with Celery Seed Dressing, p. 37 / Crouton Toasts, p. 39
Stuffed Filet Mignon with Green Peppercorn Butter, p. 77
Holiday Mashed Potatoes, p. 109
Green Bean Bundles, p. 105
Croissants,& Butter Rosettes, p. 138
Date Pudding with Praline Sauce, p. 171

Pork Menus

 # 3

Green Salad with Dijon Vinaigrette, p. 35 / Parmesan Toppers, p. 39
Herb Stuffed Pork Loin with Applesauce, p. 83
Potato Fans, p. 109
Green Beans with Sautéed Mushrooms, p. 103
Miss Ellie's Carrot Cake with Maple Cream Cheese Frosting, p. 148

 # 4

Green Salad with Bacon Dressing, p. 34 in Crisp Parmesan Baskets, p. 39
Cranberry-Glazed Pork Loin, p. 82
Sweet Potato Soufflé, p. 111
Green Beans Amandine, p. 103
Pumpkin Cheesecake with Gingersnap Crust, p. 152

 # 5

Waldorf Slaw, p. 43
Pistachio Crusted Pork Loin, p. 84
Potato and Yam Gratin, p. 110
Southern-Style Green Beans, p. 103
Lena's Rolls, p. 131
Bread Pudding with Creme Anglaise, p. 170

Menus

Poultry Menus

 # 6

Apple Salad with Poppy Seed Dressing, p. 37
Chicken Breasts in Basil Cream, p. 88
Rice Pilaf (from a packaged mix)
Carrot Bundles, p. 105
Buttermilk Biscuits, p. 114
Lemon Tart, p. 173

 # 7

Green Salad with Caesar Salad Dressing, p. 35
Chicken Kiev, p. 89
Fettucini Alfredo, p. 97
Green Beans with Sautéed Mushrooms, p. 103
Sun-Dried Tomato and Basil Bread, p. 137
Tiramisu, p. 174

 # 8

Grilled Barbecued Chicken, p. 90
Red Potato Salad, p. 44
Assorted Relishes with Dill Yogurt Dip, p. 190
Savory Herb Biscuits, p. 114
Cinnamon-Sugar Oat Cookies, p. 154

Brunch Buffet Menus

 # 9

Scrambled Egg Casserole, p. 96
Frosted Sausage Ring, p. 82
Roasted Potatoes, p. 110
Macedonia di Frutta, p. 40
Meta's Buttermilk Scones, p. 126 / Orange Marmalade Butter, p. 193

 # 10

Macadamia or Almond Oven-Baked French Toast, p. 94
Oven Baked Bacon, p. 84
Orange Ambrosia, p. 41

 # 11

Egg Strata, p. 94
Baked Potato Casserole, p. 107
Fizzy Orange Juice, p. 190
Apple Cake with Praline Sauce, p. 142
and Whipped Cream, p. 173

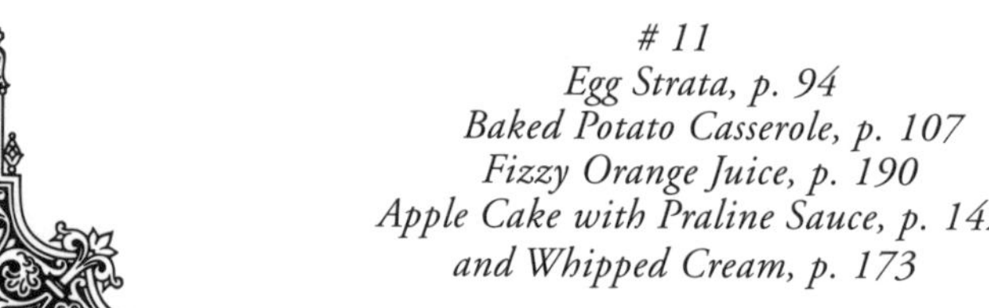

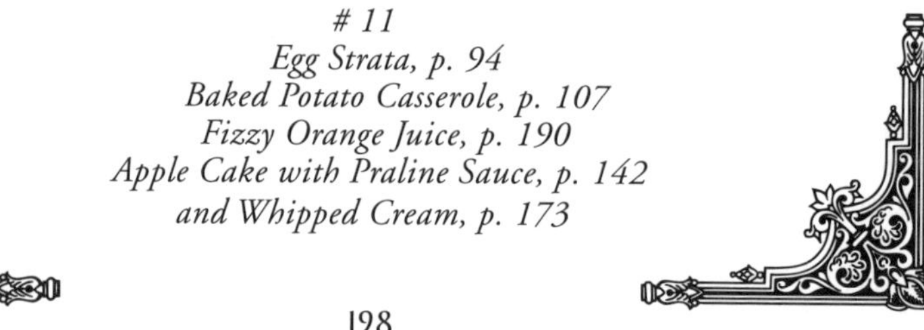

Menus

Tea Menus

 # 12

Meta's Buttermilk Scones, p. 126 with Lemon Curd, p. 193
Chicken Salad Finger Sandwiches p. 45
Ham & Apricot Tea Sandwiches, p. 66
Raspberry Thumb Print Cookies, p. 159
Chocolate Ganache, p. 145

 # 13

Currant Scones, p. 125 with Devonshire-Style Cream , p. 189
Ham & Asparagus Roll Ups, p. 66
Cucumber Sandwiches, p. 66
Old-Fashioned Lemon Bars, p. 163
Tea Time Tessies, p. 158

 # 14

Meta's Chocolate Chip Scones with Chocolate Honey Butter, p. 127
Buttery Ham Mousse Tea Sandwiches, p. 65
Pimento Cheese Sandwiches, p. 67
Apricot Kolache Cookies, p. 136

Individual inventiveness combined with Industrial Revolution technology brought an array of changes to the Victorian food supply. With the separation of food production from the consumer, the negative aspects of unscrupulous food adulteration and unsanitary production methods arose. Reputable food producers counteracted this trend by adding logos and graphic labels to their foods, and, in the process, modern day marketing and advertising were born. World Fairs became a perfect way to win product recognition. For example, the 1893 World's Columbian Exposition in Chicago was the venue for the debut of consumer products which are still familiar today--Cream of Wheat, Shredded Wheat, Pabst Beer, Aunt Jemima syrup, and Juicy Fruit gum.[66]

What follows, in the next few pages, is a chronological look at some of the Victorian era foods and food related producers.

And finally. . .

A Chronology of some of the FOODS, FOOD PRODUCERS, their PRODUCTS and ADVERTISING TECHNIQUES UNIQUE TO THE VICTORIAN ERA (1837 - 1901)

1838 Carbonated Soda

In 1838 a Philadelphia perfume dealer by the name of EugËne Roussel (an immigrant from France) developed a method that allowed him to carbonate the ever-popular lemonade. Soon "soda" was the rage, and within a few years there were at least half a dozen manufacturers providing bottled beverages to the confectioners and pharmacists.[67]

1840 Hires Root Tea!

In 1840 Charles E. Hires first experimented with combinations of roots, herbs and flavorings for a new beverage, and in 1870 he marketed his new drink, "Hires Root Tea." Friends later encouraged him to change the name to "Root Beer." [68]

1847 Beginning of Cadbury Chocolate Candy

Fry & Sons, now Cadbury, first made chocolate candy in 1847. [69]

Mid 1800's Graham Flour and later Graham Crackers

Sylvester Graham, a confirmed vegetarian, trumpeted the benefits of whole-grain wheat which in the mid 1800's became known as "Graham" flour. Mr. Graham stressed a natural, vegetarian diet in an era when "meat" ruled the menu. His followers, referred to as "Grahamites," were loyal, although others thought he had taken "leave of his senses." Nevertheless, credit for the health food cracker of the Victorian era (none other than the graham cracker) goes to Sylvester Graham. Creative advertising promoted Graham's sweetened whole-wheat cracker as not only healthy but as aiding moral restraint (supposedly acting as a suppressant of masturbation in boys). [70]

Mid 1800's Penny Candies

Sweet-making developed rapidly into an industry during the early nineteenth century through the discovery of sugar beet juice and the advance of mechanical appliances. Homemade hard candies, such as peppermints and lemon drops became popular in America during that time. By the mid 1800's, over 380 American factories were producing hard "penny candy," which was sold loose from glass cases in general stores. [71]

1850's Borden Condensed Milk

In an attempt to solve the problem of tainted milk that carried tuberculosis and smallpox germs, Gail Bordon developed a system that evaporated the water from milk. After several set backs, he eventually set up a factory in New York. His success, as well as that of his competitors, was assured with the outbreak of the Civil War. Soldiers could carry milk to the field despite the lack of refrigeration.[72]

1850 First Commercial Pretzels

In 1850, Julius Sturgis was baking bread at a stone house in Lititz, Pennsylvania. Legend has it that a man passing through the area gave Sturgis the recipe for hard pretzels in return for his generous hospitality. He added pretzels to his bread business, and in 1861 Sturgis stopped making bread and opened the first commercial pretzel bakery in America.[73]

1851 First Cheese Factory in America

An American dairyman named Jesse Williams established American's first cheese factory, near Rome, New York on January 1, 1851.[74]

1852 Baker's German Sweet Chocolate

Samuel German developed German Sweet Chocolate, in 1852, while working for the Baker's Chocolate Company. "German" chocolate is thus an all-American product and carries the name of its developer.[75]

1859 Rumford Baking Powder / Self-Rising Bread Flour

Rumford baking powder was formulated in 1859, by Eben Horsford, (a professor at Harvard University). Prior to this, baking powder formulas were based on crude combinations of cream of tartar and baking soda; this combination was expensive and fairly unpredictable. So, Rumford Baking Powder was quickly and widely accepted, as it was less expensive and had more dependable results. The calcium acid phosphate was also considered healthier than cream of tartar. [76] Rumford Chemical Works later sold a self-rising bread flour (or "bread preparation" containing their baking powder) as evidenced in an ad from the 1879 edition of Housekeeping In Old Virginia, 1884. [77]

1861 Jelly Beans

An 1861 advertisement in Boston promoted the sending of jelly beans to soldiers in the Union Army during the Civil War. Although earlier forms of the "bean" date back to Biblical times, the jelly bean, as we know it, quickly earned a place among the other "penny candies" available in general stores. Merchants sold them by weight, and they were taken home in paper bags.[78]

1868 Fleischmann's Yeast

When the Fleischmann brothers immigrated to America, they were disappointed in the breads which were made with unreliable home-brewed starters and leaveners. So, in 1868, they built a yeast plant in Cincinnati and patented a compressed yeast cake that revolutionized home and commercial baking in the United States. They introduced their product to the world at Philadelphia's Centennial Exposition of 1876. From that point on, Fleischmann's Yeast became a household name. Dedicated to manufacturing better yeast and helping bakeries improve their yeast-raised products, the Fleischmanns added a research laboratory to their Peekskill, New York plant in 1900."[79]

1869 Pillsbury Company

With no experience in flour milling, 26-year-old Charles Pillsbury bought into a run-down Minneapolis Flour Mill on the Mississippi River. He dealt with farmers personally from a little wooden shack, and by the end of the year the Pillsbury Mill showed a profit. On October 12, 1882, Pillsbury's giant "A" mill, the world's largest, set a one-day production record of 5,107 barrels. Five years later, Pillsbury was the largest flour miller in the world. "And, in 1900, Pillsbury sponsored it's first recipe contest, offering cash prizes of $680."[80]

Other New Foods available to consumers in the **1860's** included Perrier Water, canned pork and beans, canned soup, Tabasco Sauce, White Rock Spring Water. Peerless Wafer, cold breakfast food (Granula), Gulden mustard, Folgers coffee (pre-roasted and ground), and an English flour, McDougall. Peanuts were a popular snack food and a candy called "Conversation" was also popular.[81]

Other 1860's New Food Companies included Arm & Hammer, Cargill, Bassett, Schrafft, Del Monte, Bay Sugar Refining, Royal Baking Powder, Chase & Sanborn, Goodman's Matzohs, Ghiardelli, and Tobler. Armour established a meat-packing factory in 1865.[82]

1870's Infant Formula

Henri Nestle began producing "baby formula" during the mid 1800's in Switzerland. Nestle's company was purchased by Jules Monnerat in 1874, and this new company began to produce a condensed milk product. In America, they also began to market "Nestle's Milk Food," targeting infants and invalids. Meanwhile, the Anglo-Swiss Condensed Milk Company, founded in 1866 by Americans Charles and George Page, broadened its product line in the mid 1870's to include cheese and infant formulas. The two companies remained fierce competitors until they merged in 1905.[83]

1875 Nestle Milk Chocolate

Daniel Peter figured out how to combine milk and cocoa powder to create milk chocolate. Peter, a friend and neighbor of Henri Nestle, started a company that quickly became the world's leading maker of chocolate. Eventually Nestle and Peter joined forces forming the Nestle Company.[84]

1879 Hulman & Company Begins Producing Baking Powder

Through the talents and determination of Herman Hulman, a wholesale grocery operator, Hulman & Company produced a formula for the production of "Crystal" and "Dauntless" baking powder in 1879; these baking powders were promoted in a four-county area in Indiana. Hulman's company continued to refine and improve their formulas for baking powder, introducing "Milk" in 1887. From 1899 to 1923 "Clabber" baking powder was marketed until the formula was perfected and the name changed to "Clabber Girl Baking Powder." Hulman & Company acquired Rumford Baking Powder through the purchase of the Rumford Chemical Works in 1950.[85]

Other New Foods available to consumers in the **1870's** included cubed sugar, synthetic vanilla, Wheatena, and the ice cream soda became a popular treat.The commercial production of margarine began in the 1870's, and Saccharin was developed in 1879.[86]

Other 1870's New Food Companies included Lipton, F. & J. Heinz, Hills Brothers, Grand Union Tea Co., and Confectioner's Journal. William Underwood was the first to register a U.S. food trademark--Red Devil®.[87]

1880 Gold Medal Flour

Cadwallader C. Washburn built the largest flour mill west of Buffalo, N.Y. in 1866 on the banks of the Mississippi River in Minneapolis, Minnesota. It cost $100,000 to construct and was called "Washburn's Folly" by those who were sure the demand for Midwestern spring wheat flour would never grow to match the new company's supply. But Washburn was an innovator, and in 1880, shortly after he had established a partnership with John Crosby, the new Washburn Crosby Company won the gold medal at the first Millers' International Exhibition. The winning flour was renamed Gold Medal flour. In 1928 the Washburn Crosby Company merged with several regional millers to form General Mills.[88]

1880 Philadelphia Cream Cheese

In 1880 the Empire Cheese Company of New York began producing Philadelphia brand cream cheese for a New York distributor named Reynolds.[89]

1882 Red Star Yeast

Red Star Yeast & Products traces its roots back to 1882 when it was incorporated as the Meadow Springs Distilling Company in Milwaukee, Wisconsin. In 1890, the company began a research and development center, and even before 1900 their yeast wrappers carried recipes for the home baker.[90]

1882 Powdered Soup

In 1882 Swiss miller Julius Maggi created a food product utilizing legumes that was quick to prepare and easy to digest. His instant pea and bean soups helped launch Maggi & Company. By the turn of the century, his company was producing not only powdered soups, but also bouillon cubes, sauces, and flavorings.[91]

1886 Coca-Cola

Coca-Cola is the invention of Dr. John Stith Pemberton, an Atlanta pharmacist, who, in 1886, made a caramel-colored syrup--the basis of Coke--in his backyard. Pemberton's local druggist mixed carbonated water with the syrup and served it as a soda fountain drink for five cents a glass. Pemberton's associate, Frank M. Robinson, suggested the name Coca-Cola, thinking two "C"s would make for attractive advertising. In 1893, the name "Coca-Cola®" was registered with the U.S. Patent Office. Although the company changed ownership several times, the progress of Coca-Cola didn't slow down. In 1894, the first factory to manufacture Coke's syrup opened in Dallas, Texas, and, by 1895, Coca-Cola was being drunk in every state and territory in America.[92]

1889 Calumet Baking Powder

In 1889 a food salesman by the name of William M. Wright developed a "new and better" baking powder which he made at night and sold during the day. He called his new product Calumet Baking Powder. [93]

Other New Foods available to consumers in the **1880's** included malted milk, Aunt Jemima Pancake Flour, Dr. Pepper, Thomas's English Muffins, Salada Tea, Tetley Tea, Log Cabin Syrup, Morton's Salt and flaked cereal. Commercially canned meats and fruits were also in grocery stores in the 1880's.[94]

Other 1880's New Food Companies included McCormick Spices, R. T. French, B. H. Kroger, ConAgra, White Lily Foods, Lever Brothers, Diamond Crystal Salt, Manischewitz, and L'Ecole de Cordon Bleu.[95]

1891 Fig Newtons
The machine that produced Fig Newtons was invented in 1891. Originally these cakes were simply called NEWTONS, and rumors abounded about how they came by that name. Perhaps they were named after the physicist that the inventor of the machine idolized--Sir Isaac Newton, or maybe the cakes took their name from the Massachusetts town of Newton, a suburb of Boston. Whatever the case might be, they appealed to the Victorians who had acquired a taste for figs.[96]

1892 Maxwell House Coffee
A coffee blend developed by Joel Cheek for the Maxwell House Hotel in Nashville, Tennessee, became so popular that the hotel owner ordered no other coffee to be served to guests. This special blend became known as Maxwell House coffee.[97]

1894 Hershey Candy Bars
At the Columbian Exposition, the World's Fair held in Chicago, in 1893, chocolate-making machinery made in Dresden, Germany, was displayed. It caught the eye of Milton S. Hershey, who had made his fortune in caramels. He saw the potential for chocolate and installed chocolate machinery in his factory in Lancaster, Pennsylvania, where the first Hershey chocolate bar was produced in 1894.[98]

1894 Beginning of the Ralston Purina Company
The Ralston Purina Company was founded in 1894 as the Robinson-Danforth Commission, a horse and mule feed business on the banks of the Mississippi River in St. Louis, Missouri. In the early 1900's, Danforth marketed a whole-wheat breakfast cereal to St. Louis grocers under the Purina label. The cereal was later renamed Ralston Wheat Cereal after receiving the endorsement of a well-known doctor of the day, Dr. Ralston. In 1902, the "Ralston" and "Purina" names were joined, and the company was officially renamed Ralston Purina.[99]

1895 Postum
In a little white barn in Battle Creek, Michigan, C.W. Post made the first batch of Postum, a cereal beverage which served as a coffee substitute in 1895.[100]

1895 First Patent for Peanut Butter
Many health conscious individuals experimented with the production of peanut butter. However, it was Dr. John Harvey Kellogg, in 1895, who applied for and received the first patent for peanut butter. Dr. Kellogg had begun experimenting with peanut butter as a vegetarian source of protein for his patients at the Western Health Reform Institute in Battle Creek, Michigan. With the help of his brother, W. K. Kellogg, he eventually set up the Sanitas Food Company to market peanut butter and other foods

produced at the Institute to grocery stores. Joseph Lambert, a Kellogg employee who had worked on developing food processing equipment, began selling his own hand-operated peanut butter grinders in 1896. Three years later, his wife Almeeta published the first nut cookbook, "The Complete Guide to Nut Cookery," and two years later the Lambert Food Company was organized. [101]

1896 First Ice Cream Cone

After several decades of believing the ice cream cone had been invented at the St. Louis Fair in 1904, it turned out that a New Yorker had a U.S. patent on just such an item several months before the fair opened. Italo Marchiony had been selling lemon ice in cones from his push carts since 1896 and was issued a patent on his mold December 13, 1903. In his application he described his invention as being "like a waffle iron and producing several small pastry cups with sloping sides." [102]

1896 Packaged Coconut

One of the earliest foods identified in history, coconut was also one of the first early explorers brought to Europe. At the beginning of the 1800's, coconuts graced only the tables of the rich and the royal. They were rare, expensive, and tedious to split and use. That changed in 1896 when Franklin Baker devised a method for packing grated coconut that retained its freshness." [103]

1897 Smucker's Jams and Jellies

It was apples from Johnny Appleseed's trees that Orrville, Ohio, resident Jerome M. Smucker first pressed at a cider mill he opened in 1897. "Later, he prepared apple butter too, which he offered in crocks that each bore a hand-signed seal--his personal guarantee of quality. Before long, J. M. Smucker's name became well-known in its own right, as residents throughout the region--and eventually the nation--came to associate it with wholesome, flavorful fruit products."[104]

1897 Grape Nuts

In 1897, after a stint in Dr. John Harvey Kellogg's Western Health Reform Institute, C.W. Post invented Grape Nuts, one of the first ready-to-eat cold cereals. In the early 1900's, he went on to invent a flaked corn cereal called Elijah's Manna, later renamed Post Toasties. Post became known for his national advertising campaigns and was dubbed the "Grandfather of Advertising in America." His campaigns featured distinctive logos, testimonials from doctors and patients, and factory packaging.[105]

1897 Jell-O

In 1897 Pearl Wait adapted an 1845 patent for a gelatin dessert, and his wife, May Davis Wait, named the new product Jello-O. In 1899 Francis Woodward bought the rights to Jell-0 from Mr. Wait for $450.[106]

1898 The Beginnings of Nabisco

Billboards across American assured consumers that "You Need a Biscuit"! "Uneeda Biscuits" were a Victorian era addition that still grace the shelves of our modern supermarkets today. We know them simply as "soda crackers." Actually, they were a light, flaky soda cracker with a unique octagonal shape. They were introduced by Adolphus Green and heavily advertised by a chain of bakeries stretching from Maine to Louisiana to Colorado. They have the distinction of being the first product to represent the **Na**tional **Bis**cuit **Co**mpany which was incorporated in 1898. Creative advertising and moisture-proof packaging were used by the company that would later become Nabisco.[107]

Other New Foods available to consumers in the **1890's** included Minute Tapioca, condensed soup, canned pineapple, Knox's Gelatin, Canada Dry Ginger Ale, Tootsie Rolls. Swans Down Cake Flour, Entenmann bakery products, Pepsi-Cola, Wesson Oil, Cracker Jacks, Crepes Suzettes, and Oysters Rockefeller. The 1890's brought about the introduction of public school hot lunches and S&H Food Stamps, Coca-Cola was available in bottles; the first brownie recipe was published.[108]

Other 1890's New Food Companies included Beech-Nut, Beatrice Foods, Hobart, and American Beet Sugar. The F. & J. Heinz company began their "57 Varieties" ad campaign and the Campbell company adopted red and white labels inspired by Cornell football uniforms.[109]

1901 Quaker Oats

Packaged oats gave the American family a product that would be superior in quality to the oats sold in open barrels at general stores, and by the late 1800's, several companies were vying for this market. By 1901, three Midwest milling companies joined forces to form the Quaker Oats Company, bringing together the top oats-milling expertise in the country."[110]

1899 Carnation Milk

On September 6, 1899, grocer E.A. Stuart and a fellow entrepreneur founded the Pacific Coast Condensed Milk Company in Kent, Washington. Stuart became the sole proprietor in 1901 and later renamed his company "Carnation." He is credited with coining the slogan, "The Milk of Contented Cows." The slogan soon evolved into the simple phrase still present on Nestle Carnation Evaporated Milk labels today--"From Contented Cows®."[111]

Endnotes

[1] A Gem: "The City of the Plains" (1887; rpt. Abilene, Ks.: R & D Printers for Dickinson County Historical Society, 1976), p. 36.

[2] Arnold Palmer, Movable Feasts (London: Oxford UP, 1952), p. 106.

[3] Eric Swegle, e-mail to the author, July 2000. (Mr. Swegle holds a degree from Kansas State University and has worked for preservation architects and served as chairman of the architectural review board for the Union Square National Register Historic District in Baltimore, MD.)

[4] Terry Tietjens, personal interview, July 2000.

[5] A Gem: "The City of the Plains," pp. 37-55.

[6] Isabella Beeton, The Book of Household Management (1861: rpt. USA: Farrar, Straus and Giroux, 1969), p. 908.

[7] Elan & Susan Zingman-Leith and Tim Fields, The Secret Life of Victorian Houses (Wash., D.C.: Elliott & Clark Publ., 1993), p. 115.

[8] 1904-05 City Directory of Abilene, Kansas (Abilene, Ks.: Abilene Directory Company, 1904), p. 19. (Available at The Abilene Public Library.) and a publication issued by the Abilene Commercial Club, 1915 (ftom Tietjen's files at the Seeleye Mansion.

[9] Ronald S. Barlow, Victorian Houseware, Hardware & Kitchenware (El Cajon, Calif.: Windmill Publ. Co., 1992), p. 149. (Permission granted by author to reproduce illustrations from this book. Book rights are now owned by Dover Publications, 31 East 2nd Street, Mineola, N.Y., 11501.)

[10] Ibid.

[11] Dorothy T. & Ivan Rainwater, American Silverplate (Nashville, Tn.: Thomas Nelson, Inc., 1968), pp. 323-325.

[12] D.S. Defenbacher, Knife / Fork / Spoon (n.p.: Coldwell Press, 1951), pp. 41-45, 56.

[13] Cecil B. Hartley, The Gentlemen's Book of Etiquette, and Manual of Politeness: Being A Complete Guide For a Gentleman's Conduct In All His Relations Towards Society (Boston, Ma.: G.W. Cottrell, 1860), pp. 53-62.

[14] Allison Kyle Leopold, The Victorian Cupboard Catalog (Old Chelsea Station, N.Y.,: The Victorian Cupboard, 1993), p. 9, citing The New Cyclopedia of Domestic Economy (n.p.: n.p., 1871), n. pag.

[15] Henry P. Willis, Etiquette and The Usages of Society (New York: Dick & Fitzgerald Publ., 1860), p. 29.

[16] Ibid., p. 27.

[17] Ibid., p. 29.

[18] Thomas Hill, Never Give A Lady A Restive Horse: A Handbook of Etiquette From Victorian Times in America (n.d.: rpt. Berkeley, Ca.: Diablo Press, Inc., 1990), pp. 20-21.

[19] Barlow, p. 153.

[20] Willis, p. 28.

[21] Barlow, p. 181.

[22] Edmund P. Hogan, The Elegance of Old Silverplate and Some Personalities (Exton, Pa.: Schiffer Publ. Co., 1980), pp. 43-45.

[23] Barlow, p. 172.

[24] John Crosby Freeman, Victorian Entertaining (Philadelphia, Pa.: Courage Books, 1992), p. 77.

[25] Barlow, p. 175.

[26] Patricia M. Mitchell, Victorian Christmas Celebration Cookbook (Chatham, Va.: Sims-Mitchell, 1991), p. 24.

[27] Freeman, p. 38, citing Mary Henderson, Practical Cooking and Dinner Giving (n.p.: n.p., 1876), n. page.

[28] Maud C. Cooke, Social Etiquette, or Manners and Customs of Polite Society (Cinn., Ohio: W.H. Ferguson Co., 1896), pp. 279-284.

[29] Barlow, p. 170.

[30] Rainwater, pp. 95-97.

[31] Hogan, p. 43.

[32] Cooke, pp. 279-284.

[33] Barlow, p. 184.

[34] Ibid., p. 36.

[35] Hill, p. 22.

[36] Beeton, p. 910.

[37] Mrs. E.B. Duffey, The Ladies' and Gentlemen's Etiquette: A Complete Manual of the Manners And Dress of American Society (Phil., Pa.: Porter & Coates, 1877), pp. 66, 68.

[38] Zingman-Leith, pp. 13-15.

[39] Willis, pp. 27-28.

[40] Duffey, p. 148.

[41] Beeton, p. 952.

[42] Ibid., p. 960.

[43] Available WWW: http://ask.com--History of Carbonated Beverages

[44] Candace M. Volz, "The Modern Look of the Early-Twentieth-Century House: A Mirror of Changing Lifestyles," American Home Life, 1880-1930: A Social History of Spaces and Services (Knoxville, Tn.: The Univ. of Tennessee Press, 1992), p. 31.

[45] Mrs. C.C. Wyandt, My Friends' and My Own (n.p.: n.p., 1913), n. pag. (This is an original cookbook compiled for a friend by Mrs. Wyandt. The original copy--with additions--is available at The Dickinsion County Historical Society; a copy of the original is available at The Abilene Public Library.)

[46] Available WWW: http://members.home.net/starview.

[47] Aaron and Susan Armstrong, Stagecoach Inn's Collection of Gourmet Recipes (Denver, Co.: Heather Publ. Inc. 1996), p. 152.

[48] Wyandt, n.pag.

[49] Available WWW: http://www.housemouse.net/.

[50] Ibid.

[51] Available WWW: http://members.home.net/starview.

[52] Ibid.

[53] Mitchell, p. 17 citing Godey's Lady's Book (n.p.: n.p., 1885), n. pag.

[54] Available WWW: http://www.housemouse.net/.

[55] Armstrong, p. 153. (Recipe identified in text as coming from the 1880's)

[56] Available WWW: http://www.geocities.com/BourbonStreet/Quarter/2926/. (Widow Rumble's Homepage, Vickie Rumble web owner: A plethora of mid-Victorian topics of interest available at this site.)

[57] Available WWW: http://www.housemouse.net/.

[58] Ibid.

[59] Ibid.

[60] Dickinson County Directory for 1886 (Abilene, Ks.: Dickinson Co., 1886), pp. 25, 53 (photocopy of original document) and misc. photocopied articles from Historical Society files.

[61] Personal interview with Reed Hoffman, grandson of Christian Hoffman, September, 2001.

[62] Information based on miscellaneous newspaper articles displayed at Mr. K's Restaurant which now occupies the former Lena's Restaurant on Old Highway 40.

[63] Seelye's Health Guide and Cook Book (n.p.: n.p, n.d.), n. pag. (from Tietjens files at The Seelye Mansion)

[64] Miscellaneous papers and letter on file at the Dickinson County Historical Society and 1904-05 City Directory of Abilene, p. 30.

[65] Miscellaneous papers and letter on file at the Dickinson County Historical Society (Past & Present, Progress and Prosperity, 1910.)

[66] Available WWW: http://members.home.net/starview.

[67] Ibid + additional info. found @ http://ask.com (History of Carbonated Beverages).

[68] Ibid.

[69] Freeman, p. 31.

[70] Available WWW: http://www.famousveggie.com/slyvestory.cfm. and Zingman-Leith, p. 20

[71] Available WWW: http://www.candyusa.org. Information obtained from The National Confectioners Association and The Chocolate Manufacturers Association.

[72] Available WWW: http://www.lsjunction.com/people/borden.htm.

[73] Available WWW: http://sturgispretzel.com.

[74] Available WWW: http://www.ilovecheese.com.

[75] Available WWW: http://www.duncanhines.com.

[76] Available WWW: http://www.hulman.com.

[77] Marion Cabell Tyree, Housekeeping in Old Virginia (n.p.: Louisville, Ky., 1883), n. pag.

[78] Available WWW: http://www.candyusa.org. Information obtained from

The National Confectioners Association and The Chocolate Manufacturers Association.

[79] Available WWW: http://www.breadworld.com. Used with permission of Fleischmann's Yeast, a division of Burns Philp Food, Inc.

[80] Information courtesy of the Pillsbury Company; reprinted with permission.

[81] Available WWW: http://www.housemouse.net/.

[82] Ibid.

[83] Available WWW: http:///www.nestle.com.

[84] Ibid.

[85] Available WWW: http://www.hulman.com.

[86] Available WWW: http://www.housemouse.net/.

[87] Ibid.

[88] Available WWW: http://www.generalmills.com.

[89] Information drawn from http://www.kraftfoods.com, and used with permission from Kraft Foods, Inc. (http://www.kraftfoods.com/html/heritage/kraftb.html)

[90] Available WWW: http://redstaryeast.net.

[91] Available WWW: http:///www.nestle.com.

[92] Available WWW: http://www.cocacola.com.

[93] Information drawn from http://www.kraftfoods.com, and used with permission from Kraft Foods, Inc. (http://www.kraftfoods.com/html/heritage/kraftb.html)

[94] Available WWW:http://www.housemouse.net/.

[95] Ibid.

[96] Available WWW: http://www.nabiscoworld.com/newtons/.

[97] Information drawn from http://www.kraftfoods.com, and used with permission from Kraft Foods, Inc. (http://www.kraftfoods.com/html/heritage/kraftb.html)

[98] Available WWW: http://www.candyusa.org. Information obtained from The National Confectioners Association and The Chocolate Manufacturers Association.

[99] Available WWW: http://www.ralston.com.

[100] Information drawn from http://www.kraftfoods.com, and used with permission from Kraft Foods, Inc. (http://www.kraftfoods.com/html/heritage/kraftb.html)

[101] Available WWW: http:// www.peanutbutterlovers.com.

[102] Available WWW: http://members.home.net/starview.

[103] Available WWW: http://www.duncanhines.com.

[104] Available WWW: http://www.smucker.com. (http://www.smucker.com/home.asp)

[105] Information drawn from http://www.kraftfoods.com, and used with permission from Kraft Foods, Inc. (http://www.kraftfoods.com/html/heritage/kraftb.html)

[106] Ibid.

[107] Available WWW: http://www.nabisco.com.

[108] Available WWW: http://www.housemouse.net/.

[109] Ibid.

[110] Available WWW: http://www.quakeroatmeal.com.

[111] Available WWW: http:///www.nestle.com.

Index

EDUCATION INFO. & RECIPE HOW TO'S